Pageman Publishers

MW01658211

LinkedIn Superboost

The Step-by-Step Guide to Creating a Winning LinkedIn Profile. All you need to know but nobody says on Linkedin

Stuart Madison

Sommario

Preface

"LinkedIn? I don't get it."

"Networking? That's not for me."

"Selling yourself on a social networking site? Isn't that unprofessional?"

"I just think it's a waste of time. I don't see why I should be on LinkedIn to begin with."

"I've been on for a year and haven't gotten any value out of it."

"LinkedIn is just for recruiters and people looking for work, isn't it?"

The confusion about LinkedIn, social networking, and utilizing social media sites like LinkedIn to find a job, a candidate for your company, to sell something, or to expand your professional network is unprecedented. Mass media features stories about LinkedIn on a daily basis; however, many people still see little value in using the site. Nevertheless, everyone seems to want to understand what they *may* be missing by not using LinkedIn. After all, I am writing this in the midst of a severe recession, and the media says that being on LinkedIn will somehow help you find a job. With this in mind, shouldn't someone write a book about understanding how LinkedIn can help them achieve career and professional objectives?

If you could reach your career and professional objectives through creating your own LinkedIn Brand, it follows that any book about LinkedIn should also help its readers brand themselves.

There are other books and online resources related to LinkedIn. I wanted to take the approach of providing a social networking framework to understand LinkedIn from within. Furthermore, I wanted to provide a thorough approach, combined with step-by-step advice, regarding how to use LinkedIn to reach your objectives. I also think, regardless if you are using LinkedIn for personal uses or on behalf of your employer, the idea of developing your own "LinkedIn Brand" goes hand-in-hand with reaching your LinkedIn Objective; it is an exercise that should be an essential part of any LinkedIn-related book. I want everyone to understand the role LinkedIn plays in the bigger picture.

Let's take a look at the initial problem at hand: in my experience, most people do not fully understand what LinkedIn and social media are all about. Part of the problem why social media is sometimes misunderstood: the user interface on some of these social media sites is either too simple (Twitter), too complex (Facebook), or doesn't offer enough hand-holding to help new users better leverage the site (LinkedIn). On the other hand, there are some generations that are *still* intimidated by *any* social networking site.

With that in mind, concentrating on LinkedIn, I wanted to write a book that not only gives strategic tips on navigating LinkedIn, but also helps you achieve specific objectives while utilizing the site. I decided to write this book because people lack an advanced understanding of the full value that LinkedIn, as well as other social networking sites, can provide. I also want to provide a framework for you, the reader, to better understand social networking. LinkedIn is one of many tools designed to help you achieve whatever objective you might have in terms of networking. The personal brand you develop for each site will undoubtedly be slightly different because of the different functionality, demographics and "atmosphere" each site creates.

I can share a fresh perspective on LinkedIn and social networking because I started from scratch. I spent most of my career overseas. When I was ready to look for a job for the first time in my native United States, I realized that the rules of the game had changed. My professional network revolved around Asia or at headquarters of companies that I worked for that aren't located in my native Southern California. My friends were in the Bay Area or scattered across the country. I had no strategy to attack the so-called "hidden job market" which I had only learned about after reading What Color is Your Parachute? No recruiters were calling me because they didn't know I existed.

"Neal, you just have to get your resume out there and let everyone know you exist," one of my brothers advised me.

So what did I do? I registered at every single job site I could find on the Internet. 99% of the "jobs" that came my way were either below my level, irrelevant, or were trying to take me down a career path that I didn't want to follow. My job search was going nowhere, and yet I was spending several hours a day on the computer surfing the Internet "looking" for something that just didn't exist. I knew that I had to "network" but beyond contacting some ex-colleagues, I had no clue how to go about it. I was intimidated by networking events where I did not know anyone. What could I do?

At this point in my career, I went back to my roots as a seasoned sales executive. I realized I needed to reinvent my approach to searching for a job into an exercise about selling "me."

In order to do so, I had to better define the following:

- **My Product**—me
- **My Brand**—what differentiates me from everyone else in the market; what are my unique strengths
- **My Market**—target industries, companies and titles
- **My Tools**—resume and web profiles
- **My Marketing Strategy**—how to get the message out and acquire leads

I had to imagine that I was starting a new business development role in a new industry for a new company, only this time the product was me. I did this by first concentrating on utilizing LinkedIn. I reached out to professional networking groups and other individuals that I met through LinkedIn.

This is when I really started becoming a heavy LinkedIn user. I used it to help expand my real and virtual networks. After finding a job and then dealing with the elimination of my position soon thereafter, I found myself ahead of the social networking game. I knew right away I had to be utilizing LinkedIn to attack the "hidden job market."

I began to realize that social networking is really a form of social insurance of which we all can never have enough. Somewhere along the way, I created my own style of networking, which is extremely effective in both understanding and utilizing social media:

Windmill Networking

You can waste a lot of time online on social media sites, so you first have to understand what it means to "network" online in a Web 2.0 context. That is what **Windmill Networking** is all about. With a particular objective in mind (which I will help you create) and a plan to implement your brand via LinkedIn, you can successfully sell yourself or your product.

Although I first defined *Windmill* Networking as a way to help me find a job, I realized that this process, along with other forms of social media, are about much more than career management. These resources encompass a whole range of professional activities.

Before proceeding, I would like to point out a disclaimer of this book. The historical perspective that comes with writing a book is almost irrelevant in today's Web 2.0 world; change is constant due to the speed at which technological advances are implemented through the Internet. LinkedIn began in 2004, took a few years to gain membership in significant numbers, and now has grown its membership to 40 million people. Furthermore, just when you think you have LinkedIn figured out, significant functionalities like Applications or new Group features are introduced (which has forced me to rewrite a few chapters)! LinkedIn sometimes introduces these features without previously informing their free members. With that in mind, please understand that when you implement what I teach, the functionality may have been slightly altered.

In a constantly evolving medium like LinkedIn, where User Generated Content (UGC) is constantly changing the makeup of its user interface, it is difficult to summarize the historical perspective because we are developing it as we speak! I feel it is important to look at LinkedIn and the role it plays in social networking and the development of Web 2.0 technology. Doing so is my best effort to give some historical perspective to the reader and to "future-proof" the content of my book.

For real-time commentary that follows LinkedIn's changes as they happen, please visit my blog at www.WindmillNetworking.com. I created and maintained this blog (which was formerly located at http://linkedinquestions.wordpress.com) to keep readers informed of the latest developments. My blog also provides additional insight into the world of LinkedIn and social media. In addition to my blog, I hope to publish new editions of this book as LinkedIn evolves.

To be honest with you, I never thought I would "cross the chasm" from blogging to end up writing an actual book about LinkedIn. As time progressed and the economy worsened, more people came to me asking for advice not only about using LinkedIn, but also about looking for a job and utilizing LinkedIn for business. One day, my lovely wife mentioned, "E-books are becoming very popular, so why don't you write one?" Seeing that I was in transition at the time, I thought, why not write a *real* book! And so I did!

Through the process of writing this book, I am learning a great deal about LinkedIn, social networking, and myself. I consider myself a humble lifelong learner and am always excited to meet new people and have new experiences. I hope this book embodies this principle. In fact, I hope this book helps you understand how Windmill Networking can work for you. It is my dream that writing this book allows me to reach and potentially network with more people than I could ever reach using any one social networking site.

As you read this book, you will come to understand that I am sometimes critical of LinkedIn and opinionated about its different features. Let me state here there is no bigger fan of LinkedIn than me! Please take this criticism as exactly what it is—my constructive opinion of how LinkedIn can reach its full potential in the world of social networking. I will not paint a rosy picture of all of its features if I do not think the features are worthy of such praise. You, the reader, want to quickly understand how to leverage and maximize your LinkedIn user experience; I will help you do so by offering a guided tour, sprinkled with my colorful analysis, of the pros and cons of each feature through the lens of Windmill Networking. Once again, these are my personal opinions; however, they are based on real experiences of a power user whose only intention is to help you, the reader, quickly achieve your career and professional objectives using LinkedIn.

Finally, where do the windmills fit in, you ask?

I was looking for a way to explain social networking to those who either do not understand it or seldom engage in it. I stumbled across this terminology one day while in the shower, in the midst of writing this book (I know it sounds corny but it's true)! I had subconsciously visualized a picture of a modern wind turbine farm for my LinkedIn blog site, and I knew there was some reason why I thought this was a striking image.

Figure 0.1 Discovering Windmill Networking

The concept of windmills illustrates how we as social creatures can reach our highest potential when plugging ourselves into common grids. Windmill Networking, as you will discover in coming chapters, is not only natural for us to grasp, but is also something the Web 2.0 world provides for us that earlier generations did not have. It should be cherished and used for maximum benefit.

I could not finish this Preface without giving thanks to all of the people who have supported me during this venture, beginning with the one who gave me the idea to begin it—my lovely wife Miwako. Luna and Kyle, my adorable children, were very understanding of daddy doing his "work" late in the evening. I also received tremendous love and support from my Mom & Dad, brothers and sisters Ira, Denise, Mike, Rina, Larry, Christie, Gary & Valerie. Cousins like Dylan Schaffer. Nephews like Jimmy Giokaris (who created the wonderful cover art, logos, illustrations, and formatting of this book—going way beyond my original expectations both in terms of quality as well as time invested!) and his girlfriend Whitney Sones. And Breanne Cooley, my super editor, who not only both surpassed my highest expectations with her excellent editing abilities, but also provided invaluable guidance and advice that greatly improved the way I communicate my message to you. Close behind is my proofreader, Norman Naylor, who blew me away with his deep understanding of the English language and his devotion to spending significant time in helping out a friend. Many close friends gave me their support, including Eric Ho, Eric Tom, James Wang, Larry Liu and Phil Ting. The people that inspired me to take on this task are also the people that I had not even met a year ago—the people who started out as part of my "virtual" LinkedIn network—who quickly became part of my real network. Real people volunteered their time to help me out, always with a "Pay It Forward" attitude. Sometimes, even though our meetings were brief, they often had a lasting impact and thus positively affected the creation of this book. There are way too many to list here, but the people who I am the most thankful for are: my Laguna Niguel Connectors friends Hank Blank and Randy Miller, for teaching me much about networking; Cindy Pickens, for her support and that of her tremendous CafeNet group; Kathy Simmons of Netshare, for giving me the confidence that I could write a great book; my awesome and inspiring Orange County Twitter friends Paul Tran, Ted Nguyen, Rochelle Veturis, and Diana Wei; networking friends like Sven Johnston (We are Orange County!), Raymond Wah, Paul Andrew, and Jeff Gaul; Mr. Pay It Forward himself Check Hester; all of my So Cal Sushi and Izakaya Club friends; Bob Fine from Cool Twitter Conferences; Tim Tyrell-Smith; along with way too many others to list. The above are only a few of the many people that I had the chance to physically meet. There were many, many more who I exchanged emails and sometimes phone calls with (including you, Mr. Gnarly Young Entrepreneur, Bradley Will!); I can only hope that when you read this you realize that it is you that I am also thanking.

PART I:

CREATING YOUR LINKEDIN BRAND

Your LinkedIn strategy and brand can only be properly formulated after understanding LinkedIn and the role it plays in social networking in the 21st century. I introduce the concept of Windmill Networking to help you "cross the chasm" and embrace LinkedIn, social networking, and social media. This section of the book will give you the framework through which you can begin thinking about what you want to achieve on LinkedIn, including examples of popular user scenarios. At the end of this section, assuming you have already registered as a user at www.linkedin.com, we will go through the creation of your user profile and help you begin to develop your own LinkedIn Brand.

Chapter 1

Chapter 1 Introducing Windmill Networking

- A Personal Introduction
- A Social Networking Primer
- Utilizing Windmill Networking to Understand Social Networking and LinkedIn
- Where Does Windmill Networking Fit In?

A Personal Introduction

My LinkedIn Credentials

If you are reading this book, you may be standing where I stood a little more than a year ago—before putting pen to paper. Starting out on LinkedIn, you want to get to the next level, to understand what you might be missing, to make some sense of what you should be doing on LinkedIn. I don't intend this book to be a simple user's manual about LinkedIn. During the last year I have lived the "LinkedIn Life," starting out with a close network, slowly expanding it, and then becoming a LION, or a LinkedIn Open Networker. Along the way I created a filter, Windmill Networking, through which you can look to separate yourself from LinkedIn; using Windmill Networking, you can look at LinkedIn from a completely different, yet invaluable angle. The reader will find this experience, combined with this pre-requisite manual of LinkedIn's features, most valuable. He or she will then be able to reflect upon and implement their own LinkedIn Brand.

According to my own research, I currently now have the more LinkedIn connections than anyone else where I reside in Orange County, California. At my current level of nearly 17,000 connections in early August, I am almost in the top 50 of all LinkedIn users worldwide. But more importantly, while becoming connected to so many people, I have utilized LinkedIn to search for and apply to jobs, to research potential customers, to find sales channels, to learn a great deal about many subjects, and to create my own groups to find like-minded professionals. I have also reestablished contact with old colleagues while helping people in various ways. I have most importantly made acquaintances with many people who are willing to spend a lot of time helping others. It has been a magical adventure I hope you all have a chance to experience on your own. That is really the motivation for me to write this book, to share as others have shared with me, and to give back to the wonderful LinkedIn community. As I will mention in the concluding chapter of this book, the more we connect with each other and become better LinkedIn users and better networkers, the positive effects and increased value will be passed on to everyone within our networks.

Like many of you, I received my first LinkedIn invitation a few years ago from someone whom I cannot remember. I signed up one day in 2004 (turns out that I am member number 235,001, as indicated by the key code in my URL), but I really didn't do anything with the site aside from accepting invitations from people that I knew. I remember having a long email conversation with one person who invited me that I did not know. I remember feeling that somehow my privacy had been violated—a feeling that I have not forgotten.

That all changed in 2008. After building my career in Asia and looking for a job for the first time in the US—without an established network—I took the plunge and decided to use LinkedIn as my primary networking tool. I couldn't attack the "hidden job market," a market where some people say 70% of the jobs are "found" or "created," without becoming a better "networker." Thus, my LinkedIn journey began, and I soon became a heavy user and increased my connections from 100+ to the now 17,000+.

As I started becoming a heavy user, I began connecting to people beyond my immediate group of friends and co-workers while actively reaching out to recruiters. I started to become the "go to" person for LinkedIn in my close physical network of family and friends. Many acquaintances had never heard of or did not understand LinkedIn to the same degree that I did. I could look at the official LinkedIn Q&A sections and begin answering questions about how to use LinkedIn. Finally, as I built out my network to encompass thousands of direct connections, I would offer to help anyone if they had a question about LinkedIn by saying so in an email. Whenever I invited someone to connect or accepted their invitation, I addressed them personally. Many people seemed to find value in what I had to say. I decided to begin a LinkedIn blog to provide a consistent place to publish my knowledge and tips. That blog now resides at www.WindmillNetworking.com.

Through this book, I hope to share all of this information with everyone to pay back the community for what it has given me. When I started my blog, a friend recommended that I write a book. At the time, I scoffed at his suggestion, yet here I am, a year later, putting the final edits to my work.

Am I uniquely qualified to be writing a book on a site that has 40 million users? Hey, I always believed that anyone has enough unique and valuable life experiences to write a good book. Is there information you can gain from me that you can't find on the official LinkedIn site? Most definitely, because any information is based on personal experience. Will reading this book help you become a better networker, find a job or candidate quicker, sell more effectively, and deepen your understanding of LinkedIn? I am confident that it will.

Most importantly, I hope to fill the "information vacuum" that exists around LinkedIn. This really is the missing manual that I couldn't find, and thus decided to create. When I first began my LinkedIn journey, I was surprised at the limited amount of "useful" information there was about LinkedIn on the site itself. It seemed that the people utilizing LinkedIn were either not sharing the "insider" information or didn't know for themselves. At that time there was only one "real" LinkedIn book available. As time progressed, I started receiving many questions; I also began seeing many other questions appear within the official LinkedIn "Answers" section. I realized the timing was right and the audience was there; I was now ready to communicate my approach to using LinkedIn. Since I began writing this book, a few new publications about LinkedIn have appeared. This book, however, provides more than strategic and useful information for the beginner and the expert to use throughout the process: it also creates a framework through which you can better understand and more effectively utilize LinkedIn. For me, the mechanics of LinkedIn are a prerequisite, but you need to look at LinkedIn through the eyes of Windmill Networking and create your own LinkedIn Brand to really fully harness its value.

As a brief introduction to how I've organized this book, I begin with an attempt to help you better understand social networking, Windmill Networking, and what potential value LinkedIn has for you. I also go through potential user scenarios and provide you with a hands-on guide to create your own LinkedIn Brand. I follow this map throughout the "meat" of the book, which details the different sections of interest in LinkedIn. I have decided to focus and delve deeply into those areas that I believe will be of the most value to readers. While the book may not be 100% comprehensive, I have tried my best to provide detailed and unique insight into all of the latest features of LinkedIn that are relevant to you as a user. For instance, I purposefully do not go into length about features that are part of the paid service, nor do I explore utilizing optional toolbars. As the wording implies, these are not features that everyone uses (you may have a free account) or has access to (you may use the unsupported Google Chrome for your Internet browsing and/or use Gmail instead of Outlook for email management).

The final sections of the book offer strategic tips you can use to leverage the power of LinkedIn. I also provide closing commentary that will give you additional food for thought about how to make LinkedIn and social media work for you.

First-time or limited LinkedIn users will get the most out of this book; however, there are enough tips that I recommend any experienced LinkedIn user read this book from cover to cover. I have sprinkled even the basic sections with information I have gleaned from my thousands of hours utilizing LinkedIn. The data I have gathered through my personal experiences will provide insight, even for heavy LinkedIn users. Most importantly, the attitude I want to instill in LinkedIn users through covering the concepts of Windmill Networking will be invaluable to even the most advanced LinkedIn user.

Finally, if you have not connected with me yet, please feel free to send me an invitation through my profile at:

http://www.linkedin.com/in/nealschaffer

Thank you and hope to connect with you soon!

A Social Networking Primer

Human beings are social animals. I don't pretend to be an expert in the field, but it is pretty evident that people like to meet up and communicate with each other. It feels good to connect and help others. Seeing my own little children makes me realize that socializing and social networking begins very early in life. It is apparent that social networking is a basic human function.

How then does social networking evolve as we grow up? How has technology influenced the social networking world? Within this social networking world, where does social media like LinkedIn fit in?

The strongest network that we create in our lives is our own families and caretakers. As children, we rely on our parents, or those who are raising us, for everything. They are the first members of the network that we create, and although we tend to distance ourselves from this network as we enter our teenage years, the extended family often becomes our most valuable network for advice and support throughout our lives.

Going beyond the family network, we go through school creating an extended circle comprising classmates and friends. Through this network, we are able to fulfill our needs for emotional support, entertainment, company, and advice. Some people move during their school years and have to then recreate their network in each neighborhood and school. By the time we graduate from high school, we have already created a group of friends that often become our most valuable networking contacts for life.

For those who go on to a college or to a university, this network continues to grow, adding new classmates and acquaintances. Just as your high school years give you a strong network of friends, the same can be said for your college years.

After graduating, some meet new people in a variety of ways—through work, community or professional associations, new neighborhoods, and introductions through friends. We often befriend parents of our children's classmates as well. Some people end up greatly enlarging their networks, especially if their work environment is a large, socially stimulating environment. If their career requires them to be networkers, within sales, for instance, networks expand even more rapidly.

An interesting thing happens upon entering the work force. Until we begin working, our networks are continually growing as we meet new people in new classes and at social gatherings; however, the trend begins to diminish as we grow older. Some people simply do not invest the time to keep in touch with old friends and colleagues and have lost contact. Others work at smaller companies or have occupations that do not allow them to interact with many people. Growing a family makes some of us more insular. For whatever reason, there are many people whose networks primarily rely on old college and high school friends.

WindMill WISDOM

Regardless of the size of our networks, it is important to realize the following:

- **We all have networks**
- **We are all natural networkers**
- **Social networking is not some difficult thing to comprehend—it is a basic human function**

Every time we ask a friend for advice we are, in essence, networking. Networking should come naturally to all of us once we realize this fact.

Over the past 20 years, as new jobs are created in the centers of population that we know as megacities across the United States, people tend to be more spread out and move to where opportunity lies. This is by no means a new phenomenon. The advent of more convenient transportation alternatives and the lower cost and greater quality of telecommunications services has allowed us to be further spread out across the country—all while keeping in good touch with our networks.

Similarly, with the explosive growth of the Internet over the last 20 years, we can not only stay in better touch with our network, but we can actually create a new "virtual" network with people that we meet online. This is truly the era that has fostered the creation of *Windmill Networking.*

My first experience with virtual networks was in the old chat rooms at AOL. I was blown away by the experience that I could discuss a topic that interested me from my computer, with a complete stranger. Those were the "wild west" days of social networking on the Internet. The potential for "virtual" networking to become mainstream was there, as younger generations became comfortable and adopted the technology.

The MySpace and Facebook phenomenon are built upon this technology, with younger generations creating vast virtual networks based on similar hobbies or common interests in things like gaming or music. As with social networking, most people start out by creating their home page on either site, adding their favorite photos, music, etc. to share with their close friends. These networks tend to grow to include "virtual" members who they have never met personally. This growth helps create virtual communities where people are interacting in ways that are not possible in a physical world. People from different countries who have never met before can play interactive role-playing games, engage in real-time discussions, and share photos at the same time.

Social groups are a lot "looser" and more geographically dispersed than they used to be. The Internet and all of its related technologies, combined with social networking sites like Facebook and MySpace, have given people a chance to connect to others with similar interests, regardless of how well they know them or where they live. It is only a matter of time before this looseness extends to the professional networking world.

We are pioneers at the tip of the iceberg. We are extending the future boundaries of professional social networking by utilizing LinkedIn to execute Windmill Networking. Networking in person is ideal; however, reaching out online through a virtual network is the only way to network across the globe when you cannot physically meet someone. A key to being successful is to refuse to limit yourself geographically nor to a narrow group of people you already know.

For me, networking is a type of social insurance that everyone needs and you can never have enough of it. You never know when someone in your network, someone who may have never helped you out before, can provide invaluable advice or connections during a time of need. The more diverse your network is, the higher the likelihood that someone will give you advice for your particular situation. Although your current physical network of friends/family is also a great source for advice, it is limited in size and may lack the type of real-life experience that applies to your situation.

Going beyond the "Internet Era," MySpace and Facebook have begun the **User-Generated Content (UGC)** revolution that defines our Web 2.0 era. UGC basically means that users are generating content and contributing to the website; essentially, they are the creators of the website. Amazon Recommendations, Wikipedia, and the plethora of blogs that exist are all examples of sites that rely on User-Generated Content. This dependence has generated new types of social networking sites such as LinkedIn and Twitter. **What is the key difference between social media and traditional media? Within traditional media, we are told what to read; within social media, you and other users actually create the content that you read.**

If you think of social networking in terms of having a "real" network and a virtual network, you can see why there are people on LinkedIn (including myself) who have large networks filled with people whom they have never met. Don't get me wrong—your "real" network will usually be the most dependable network; however, you would be surprised how a virtual network can supplement the real network you have built. As you have not met everyone in your virtual network, they may not always be willing to help you. Nevertheless, other Windmill Networkers and I have found there are more than enough good people in this world with a "Pay It Forward" attitude who are willing to help you.

Understanding this virtual networking concept will help you view LinkedIn in a new light. This new perspective will allow you to maximize the benefits of using its professional network. This is what Windmill Networking is really all about. As the MySpace and Facebook generations graduate from college and start working, it is only a matter of time until this type of "loose" or virtual networking begins to dominate the professional networking world. It is no coincidence that LinkedIn recently created a special learning center for graduates, as well as a LinkedIn Group just for "'09 Grads" to help facilitate this transition.

Note that LinkedIn and sites like it are only tools to facilitate networking in person, which is the ideal form of communication. A virtual network serves as an extension of your traditional network, giving you additional opportunities to meet people. When you can't physically meet someone in person, reaching out online is the next best way to network across the globe. This form of online communication is key to becoming successful in 21st century professional networking. By doing so, you are geographically expanding your reach, instead of limiting yourself to a narrow group of people that you know. More specifically, using **LinkedIn** to begin this expansion is essential. If you are an ambitious professional, or hope to become one, there is no better place to be than LinkedIn.

On a final note, as we embark on our LinkedIn journey, never forget about "The Personal Touch." Whatever your LinkedIn Objective is, your chances of being successful are greatly higher if you are real and genuine. Personalize the message you send to each person based on their background, any common interests, and what your objective is in communicating with them. Show that you are interested in them. By displaying each member's profile information in varying degrees of detail, LinkedIn gives you a myriad of opportunities to personally connect and expand your virtual network. LinkedIn fosters Windmill Networking.

Utilizing Windmill Networking to Understand Social Networking & LinkedIn

Below I provide a more detailed definition of what I refer to as ***Windmill Networking:***

Windmill Networking involves understanding the unique value of creating and utilizing a virtual network through Web 2.0 social networking sites such as, but not limited to, LinkedIn. Windmill Networkers build up a sometimes virtual Trusted Network of Advisors to contact for help when necessary, while helping others in their network with a Pay It Forward attitude. It is "Digging Your Well Before You're Thirsty" on a scale that is only possible through social media. Windmill Networking is about being authentic, and never forgetting the importance of "The Personal Touch." It is rooted in the belief that the more you genuinely give, the more you will receive when you really need it. By Plugging Your Windmill into the Grid, YOU determine your networking potential which far exceeds anything that a limited physical network can provide. With a clear objective, supported by time and energy, you will undoubtedly connect with, and help, others while finding those who may be of assistance to you.

As I wrote this book, I searched for an easy way to think about social media, LinkedIn, and how you should utilize it. I wanted a methodology, with a visual, that would allow anyone to understand the value in connecting. On a warm Southern California day, it hit me—**Windmill Networking.**

We, as people, are all stand-alone windmills. Our various blades represent aspects of our life, like family, work, and interests. We spin our windmills around and around each day, constantly generating enough electricity for us to get by. I will label the three blades "Career," "Education" and "Business," as I believe these are the three primary areas in which LinkedIn, as well as any other social networking site, can add value.

Figure 1.1. The Blades of Our Windmills

What happens when we plug ourselves into a grid and connect our windmills? Not only can we share our electricity with others; when we need a boost, we can also obtain fresh energy from new sources to which we connect. There is a natural advantage for us to be connected with others, as we are able to both give and receive.

Figure 1.2. Windmills Plugging into the Windmill Networking Grid

Life is composed of, among other things, health, family, work, friends, community, and religion, which I compare in a broader sense to our windmill blades. In order to allocate the time and energy these activities require, we need to draw energy and expertise from other windmills to keep our blades spinning. Combining this collaborative approach with our natural desire to connect is the strongest form of Windmill Networking, as we then find ourselves plugging into the grid on a daily basis.

Traditionally, once we generate enough electricity for our own windmills, we can only then give energy to windmills that are physically connected to us on a grid—windmills that are close in proximity. More recently, we have developed the ability to travel to each other's windmills via the Internet. Moreover, we have the ability to *hear* each other's windmills on the end of a phone line. Some windmills may have moved to other locations; however, modern communication now affords us the luxury of continuing our relationship with a previously close-by physical connection. Because all of these relationships began from a relationship of physical proximity, these are examples of a traditional "physical" network.

Power plants not only generate electricity for local customers; they also pass electricity along a grid, providing electricity to someone far away—someone who is not even within driving distance of the plant. If our local plants go over capacity or there is a breakdown in the power line, electricity can be moved through the power grid; you can then get your energy from a "virtual," or far-away power source. Once we begin to trust and rely on the grid—those far away sources of energy, or windmills—we can start to understand the power of a virtual network.

All windmills are connected to the power grid in some way. Think of the Internet as a type of power grid, connecting all of us through its network of servers, hubs, and routers. You can see that we are all windmills who are connected to each other, though we may not even realize it. Social media like LinkedIn makes it easy for us to "find" each other on this large grid that we share through its embedded functionality.

While reading this book, I ask you to take a leap of faith. Leap from this old, traditional world of windmills—where connections were only made within a present or one-time local relationship—to the virtual grid of today.

You do not have to have a close physical connection with a windmill to both give and receive its energy.

There obviously needs to be some sort of connection; you have to know how you want to help each other generate electricity. There has to be some synergy, even if it simply means that two parties want to help each other. This is where LinkedIn steps in to help foster this process.

LinkedIn provides users with a growing map of the power grid. This map includes profile information that will guide users to far-away windmills that may share common interests. So how do you connect on the power grid with these far away windmills? LinkedIn gives you the tools to do so.

You must have a purpose or objective when using LinkedIn; without a plan, LinkedIn may not provide much value. In order to devise this plan, you need to understand yourself and what your windmill strategy is. To the many people who ask me "How can I use LinkedIn better?" I *always* answer, "What is your objective?"

As you start reading this book, think of your own windmill and what objective you have when connecting with other windmills. Once you have defined your objective for using LinkedIn, your success with this site will come soon thereafter.

I will go one step further in this book; I will ask you to define your *LinkedIn Brand.* This starts with defining your LinkedIn Objective. I will provide the tools you need to then implement your strategy through a branded approach.

Until the appearance of LinkedIn and other social networking sites, it was almost impossible to Windmill Network with others that lived far away. Meeting someone in person will always bring your relationship to a brand new level; meeting face to face is ideal. Think of Windmill Networking with virtual connections as supplementing your existing physical network.

Most of us are still very new to social networking and LinkedIn, as many of LinkedIn's members joined within the last two years. If you are new to LinkedIn, you may be apprehensive about meeting someone you have become virtually connected with in person. As one of my LinkedIn connections put it, some of you may have a natural defense mechanism that kicks in, telling you to think things over before continuing any conversation with a stranger.

If you have experienced this feeling, the fact that you bought and are reading this book proves that you want to overcome this fear.

I too have experienced this uneasy feeling. I remember feeling afraid to go to any meeting that had the word "networking" attached to it. I just didn't think they were for me. So how did I overcome this fear?

Well, I used to be afraid of flying. I'd get sweaty palms while on the runway. I clearly remember my nerves slowly beginning to take over every time we approached the runway for takeoff. But then I remember coming to an important realization: if it wasn't for the airplane, I would never have the chance to meet so many amazing people—especially my Japanese wife! My father always said he was envious of my generation in that we could easily travel the world at an early age because of modern aviation. I overcame my fear of flying by focusing on the positives that modern aviation has brought into my life. I would have never had the enlightening experiences I have had if it weren't for this amazing technological advance.

To me, meeting people via LinkedIn is a similar type of technological advance. With so many benefits, it is simply counter productive to fear Windmill Networking. There are countless benefits to reap from proactive virtual networking in addition to meeting with people. It is wise to always be Windmill Networking; Dig Your Well Before You're Thirsty! The longer you are plugged in and are developing new relationships, the more the other windmills will spin in your favor.

Where Does Windmill Networking Fit In?

Before delving into specifics regarding LinkedIn, I want to ensure that you firmly grasp the concept of Windmill Networking. In this section, we will review some common social networking concepts; we will then examine what a unique strategy Windmill Networking really is in relation to these approaches.

Windmill Networking is understanding the unique value of creating and utilizing a virtual network through Web 2.0 social networking sites such as, but not limited to, LinkedIn; Windmill Networkers build up a sometimes virtual Trusted Network of Advisors to contact for help when necessary, while helping others in their network with a Pay It Forward attitude.

A **virtual network** is a network through which you are connected not by physical means but by *virtual* means. This connection can be made through the Internet; more specifically, the connection is made through a social networking site such as LinkedIn. Scott Allen and David Teten's book *The Virtual Handshake* takes a revolutionary look at how one can develop and close business deals online. I take this notion of a virtual network to be utilized for anything you would use a personal network for. Your objective for Windmill Networking can be anything you want it to be.

Your **Trusted Network of Advisors** are those people you contact when you need advice, whether it be personal or professional in nature, regarding a specific subject matter in which you do not possess expertise. For example, you could have a friend who is a handyman who always gives you free advice, eliminating the need to hire a costly service provider. Creating a large and diverse virtual network ensures that someone who could potentially become part of your Trusted Network of Advisors is only an email or phone call away. One of the benefits of Windmill Networking is facilitating your creation of your own virtual but truly diverse **Trusted Network of Advisors.**

Pay It Forward is the name of a novel by Catherine Ryan Hyde that describes how a 12-year old, as part of an extra-credit assignment for school, tries to change the world through positive action. Upon doing a good deed for someone, the 12-year old then asks them to "Pay It Forward" by doing good deeds for someone else in return. In terms of social networking, this means first doing something for someone in your network without asking for anything in return. People do not forget when you do something good for them. Windmill Networking will be most successful when you practice it with a Pay It Forward attitude; your own good deeds will extend beyond your own virtual network and will attract even more connections and valuable relationships.

It is "Digging Your Well Before You're Thirsty" on a scale that is only possible through social media. Windmill Networking is about being authentic, and never forgetting the importance of "The Personal Touch." It is rooted in the belief that the more you genuinely give, the more you will receive when you really need it.

Dig Your Well Before You're Thirsty is a classic networking book written by Harvey Mackay. It illustrates how you can build up a network that will always be just one phone call away to help with whatever need you may have. By adding value to others and keeping in touch—by doing something for someone without the promise of personal gain—you take an important step towards creating a future network that will serve as your support system. Creating your Windmill Network is built upon the premise of digging your well before you need it.

The Personal Touch is about being real and genuine. It is about being truthful when writing your online profiles. It is about being genuine in your willingness to help someone. Finally, The Personal Touch involves going the extra mile and showing that you care. The Personal Touch is the key to adding a sense of warmth to online connections that can often seem cold and distant. Being genuine can make potential connections within your virtual network feel they have already met you. This is especially important if your LinkedIn Objective relates to business. People buy from people they like, not from those who send them a random email. The Personal Touch really does differentiate the successful from the failures in social media, because so many are tempted to send you irrelevant communications, which is easy to do through LinkedIn.

By Plugging Your Windmill into the Grid, YOU determine your networking potential, which far exceeds anything that a limited physical network can provide. With a clear objective, supported by time and energy, you will undoubtedly connect with, and help, others while finding those who may be of assistance to you.

You plug your windmill into the grid when you sign up for a social networking site, introduce yourself to the community in a meaningful way, and then establish connections with people that are not part of your physical network. It is this last action that is crucial to fully plugging your windmill into the grid. Without making a personal connection with someone, your Windmill is simply visible on the map. Without action, it will simply remain in the same dormant position. This action should be guided by objective.

When using a social networking site like LinkedIn, it is important to decide what style of Windmill Networking best fits your needs. But without connecting with others and "networking," you may be missing out on fully exploiting all of what Web 2.0 has to offer. It is only in the last several months that the pieces of the social media puzzle are coming together in a way that is beneficial for those that understand them. Reading this book will help you understand the concept of Windmill Networking and how it can be used to gain value from LinkedIn. You will become one of the growing numbers of pioneers who can truly harness the power of social networking in a Web 2.0 world.

Chapter 2

Chapter 2 your LinkedIn Objective & Brand

- An Introduction to LinkedIn
- Why You Need to Be on LinkedIn
- What is Your LinkedIn Objective?
- What is a "Brand?"
- Creating Your LinkedIn Brand
- My Top Five Tips to Write a Great Profile
- Your LinkedIn Home Page

An Introduction to LinkedIn

With 40 million primarily professional members, LinkedIn is by far the biggest social networking site that caters to the professional demographic. There are other social networking sites, such as MySpace and Facebook, that have several times more members; however, their targeted demographic differs from LinkedIn (albeit Facebook is slowly changing).

The concept behind LinkedIn is very simple: Professionals put up their profiles and "connect" with people they know. I will explore this idea later in the book more closely; for now, note that LinkedIn clearly states that they only want you to "connect" with people you know. On the other hand, when you sign on to LinkedIn and open an account, it gives you the chance to import your entire email address book. You can send an invitation to connect with anyone who appears in your Inbox or Sent Items. Google Mail, or Gmail, archives any contact appearing within an email header; without you knowing it, you could be inviting people that you don't really "know," thus violating LinkedIn's policy. Such is the paradox that you will quickly understand LinkedIn to be: A site that suppresses this concept of a virtual network while also encouraging you to connect with people and enlarge your network. With this in mind, please be sure to read the User Agreement at the bottom of the LinkedIn site page before implementing any of my recommendations.

Once you have a profile, you may begin inviting other people to connect with you. You will also start to receive invitations to connect with people you know, as well as with those whom you don't know. This is how you build up your LinkedIn Network with your immediate 1st degree connections. With each additional 1st degree connection, you are able to see that person's 1st degree connections—who then become your 2nd degree connections. You will also have visibility into your 2nd degree connections' 1st degree connections, who now become your 3rd degree connections. Figure 2.1 gives you a view of what your network will begin to look like.

Figure 2.1. Your Windmill Network and LinkedIn Degrees of Connection

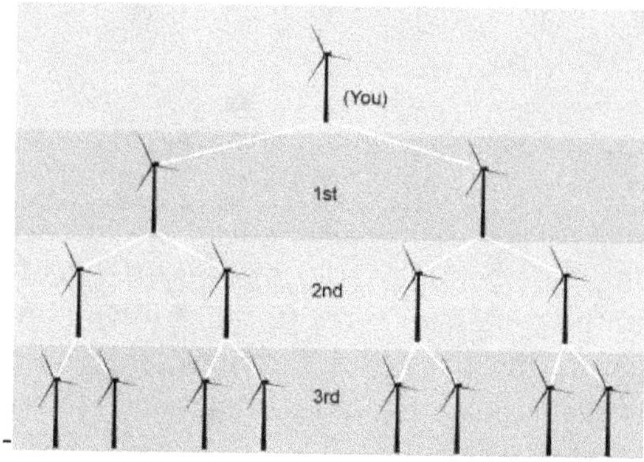

As you can see, the math is always 1st degree connections < 2nd degree connections < 3rd degree connections. As your network grows, you will be able to see these figures and realize the numbers behind the power of your extended network by looking at your "Network Statistics." This information can be found under "Contacts" in the left-hand navigation bar.

So is LinkedIn merely a collection of profiles? Not exactly, but by entering your profile information, you become part of the huge LinkedIn database, which features an excellent search capability as its foundation. You can not only find and contact old colleagues and classmates; you can also see their recent photos and where they have been working. The visibility of this information depends on both parties completely filling out their profiles. You will be pleasantly surprised as to how many people thoroughly do so.

This is the bare minimum that LinkedIn can provide you: An updated contact database, complete with photos and resume summaries, for your "real" or physical network. I have met many people, especially executives, who primarily use LinkedIn in this way—to reconnect. There is so much more to get out of LinkedIn, should you take the time to leverage its capabilities.

The rest of this will book will delve deeper into these sections. LinkedIn has such an incredibly extensive, easy-to-search database. LinkedIn users come from a diverse background of countries and industries and include professionals from almost any company that you can think of. As a result, LinkedIn can be used as your platform for any of the following:

Potential Uses of LinkedIn

- **Finding people** to get back into touch with or to find a specific person to communicate with and potentially add to your virtual network
- **Finding jobs** through the LinkedIn jobs database and associated Simply Hired service
- **Finding new business** through actively seeking new customers and partners; your mere presence on LinkedIn can indirectly attract potential leads
- **Finding answers** to questions other professionals ask about a wide variety of personal and professional topics
- **Finding solutions** to business problems through interaction with other professionals
- **Finding companies** for business development purposes or to create a target list while in transition
- **Finding service providers** recommended by your network
- **Finding groups** of like-minded professionals to connect with
- **Finding events** to attend based on your professional interest
- **Sharing information** like blogs, presentations, or book reviews; to keep in better touch with your network, showcase your expertise, or advertise a service or product

This is not a complete list of what you can do on LinkedIn by any means! It merely scratches the surface of what LinkedIn can do for you.

Just as you are able to search for others, others can also search for you. This leads me to the concept of how you *should* be selling yourself to achieve whatever objective you might have on LinkedIn.

If you bought this book, you are probably curious about what else you can do with LinkedIn. I will show you what capabilities do not appear on the surface but are clearly achievable through your real and virtual network. By utilizing **Windmill Networking**, you will truly take advantage of all that LinkedIn has to offer.

Why You Need to Be on LinkedIn

If you are a professional, there are many reasons why you need to have a presence on LinkedIn. You should utilize the platform as your primary social networking tool.

Some people consider LinkedIn merely a place to find a job. It is true there are a number of recruiters on LinkedIn and it can definitely help you in your job search; however, LinkedIn goes far beyond looking for a job. Personally, I continued to extensively use LinkedIn even after I found my job.

So why should you have a presence on the site?

1) To Get Back in Touch

Are you one of the many members of Classmates.com? Do you use it to keep in touch with people from your school days? You can think of LinkedIn as an extension of that, with the ability to directly connect you to not only former classmates, but also former colleagues. All of this is possible without additional costs to send emails or other restrictions that Classmates.com has. Upon graduating from college, more and more people in your network will be professionals, not classmates; this is the foundation upon which LinkedIn is built. This is the primary reason that most executives have a presence on LinkedIn. No other social networking site focuses on this transition to the professional sector as LinkedIn does.

2) To Be Found

Once you have a presence on LinkedIn, just as you can find your former colleagues, they can also find you. Once you fill out your profile, you are added to the 40 million user database. LinkedIn has excellent search tools that allow people to easily find you. Being found is important if you are in transition or are thinking about new job opportunities. It is even more important for your business!

3) To Acquire Expertise

LinkedIn has many Groups that are open for professionals to join. By joining these Groups, you are not only able to directly contact experts in your industry, you can also engage in Group Discussions and read Group News that is specific to your interests. Most industries are covered, with the largest of these Groups containing anywhere from a few thousand to one hundred thousand members! I know of executives who have landed new jobs in new markets who use these Groups to acquire new expertise. LinkedIn also provides a great Q&A functionality that you can use to ask the network of 40 million professionals any question you like. I have asked questions like "What is the best CRM?" and "What CMS Do You Recommend for First-Time Web Developers?" The Answers section is completely searchable, so you can learn a great deal and feel comfortable knowing that the information is coming from real professionals, not just your standard Internet message board. On these message boards, the majority of these entries are anonymous, displaying usernames that have no profiles attached to them. With LinkedIn, there is an entire profile attached to anything you do on the site.

4) To Further Your Career

If I titled this section "Looking for a Job," you would miss a crucial point: Even if you are not currently looking for a job, a network should be your insurance for your future career growth. Companies are organic entities whose needs change. Few companies can guarantee your job will be there 10 years from now, next year, or even next month. For this reason, you need to be on LinkedIn to expose yourself to potential companies and recruiters. Even if you are happy in your job, there is no harm in having a minimal profile on LinkedIn. You may receive contacts from recruiters in your industry or specialty who may help you out in the future.

LinkedIn is free career insurance! "Buy" into it!

5) For Sales & Marketing

LinkedIn is not a forum to directly sell your product; you will be removed from LinkedIn should you decide to spam people. You will also be banned from Groups should you fill message boards with advertisements; however, there are many companies that *are* finding new business or receiving referrals by adapting to and utilizing the functionality that LinkedIn provides. They combine this adaptation with Windmill Networking. From a personal perspective, I have used LinkedIn for sales & marketing to a) find potential customers, b) map out their organizations, c) request introductions inside the organizations, d) look for potential partners or distributors, and e) look for potential service providers. In fact, I found a lawyer to consult with me while writing this book on LinkedIn! Why start from scratch looking for a service provider when you can utilize your network of real professionals to help you find them?

6) To Extend Your Trusted Network of Advisors

One of my four older brothers is particularly good at helping me map out and execute my professional goals. He once asked me, "Neal, do you have a Trusted Network of Advisors?" In other words, for anything in life, do you have a trusted person who will give you advice? Do you have a financial advisor? A legal advisor? A career coach? A reliable internet marketing consultant? These advisors are essential to not only bounce ideas off of regarding your professional career; they can also advise you about personal affairs. Through Windmill Networking on LinkedIn, I have met and cultivated relationships with people who have become a part of my own Trusted Network of Advisors. I have done so by meeting many through Windmill Networking and following up where possible with face-to-face meetings.

7) To Connect

I recently read a book called *The $100,000 Career* by John Davies. It claimed if you meet 100 people and meet 100 people whom they introduce to you, you will definitely be able to find a job. I have not personally tried this exercise, but the whole idea is that you never know how someone, or someone they know, may be able to help you out when you need it. This is the premise of Windmill Networking. I openly connect with anyone on LinkedIn because you never know how you can help them or vice-versa. Case in point: I recently accepted an invitation from someone who was interested in relocating to Asia and looking for job advice. Six months later when I was looking for advice from him, he was able to guarantee an interview from the lead recruiter of a very large enterprise software company. This could not have happened if a) we never connected and b) I did not offer to help him in the first place.

The real key to all of the above is in building out your virtual network and Windmill Networking with the attitude that, whenever you help people, it will return to you, increasing your bank account of karma. If you do not believe this and start heavily contacting people without offering to help them out, you may not be as successful on your LinkedIn journey. If you are helpful to others even when you don't need to be, believe me, more people will respond to you. You will then be able to ask them for advice when you really need it, and, chances are, they will respond favorably.

I hope I have opened your eyes if you are not currently a LinkedIn user. If you are a LinkedIn user, I hope this information helps you become a more effective user of the platform to meet your own objectives.

What is Your LinkedIn Objective?

You now have some key background information about social networking and what LinkedIn can potentially do for you. It is time to ask yourself what you want to achieve using LinkedIn.

This is by far the most common question that I reply with when someone reaches out to me with any sort of LinkedIn question. If you are still asking yourself why you should be on LinkedIn, I hope the previous chapter answered that question for you. If you are currently a LinkedIn member but don't know where to go from here, I also hope the previous chapter gave you a taste of what is possible. If you are already a LinkedIn user who knows your objective, you are ahead of the game and will be able to quickly implement the strategies I outline in this book.

Many LinkedIn users fall into the following categories. I hope seeing these categories will give you some new ideas for creating your own objective:

- **Am I on LinkedIn? What is My Password Again?**

Many people joined LinkedIn after receiving an invitation, and that's it. They signed up, accepted the one invitation (or maybe a few invitations from friends) and put it aside. If this is you, I hope the preceding chapter has given you more ideas as to what your objective should be and how you can utilize this book.

- **Clueless!**

These are people that have been on LinkedIn, connected with their friends when requested, but haven't done anything else with it. They want to do something on LinkedIn after hearing a lot about it, but really don't know how to utilize it. If you are one of the clueless, no need to despair! There are a lot of people in this category; you will find great value in this book once you decide on your objective and pursue it!

- **Just Checking It Out**

There are a number of social networking sites out there, and it seems that every time one of your connections joins them, you get an invitation to join their network. Every social network wants to naturally extend their reach, so there is often a default "send an invitation to everyone in your address book" option that seems harmless and is often utilized. A lot of people from other social networking sites (Facebook and Twitter come to mind) may sign up for LinkedIn just to check it out. Especially if you are in college or have recently graduated, everyone is saying you need to be on LinkedIn. So, you are checking it out! I believe that people in this category are either early adopters of technology or are already familiar with the concepts of social networking sites. That being said, LinkedIn is unique in its demographic and functionalities (as well as in its limitations), so I hope after you create your LinkedIn Objective (as opposed to an objective which may be different for other social networking sites) that you will be able to fully understand and maximize your presence on the site.

- **Classmates.com Extension**

Many executives I have met see LinkedIn as merely an extension of Classmates.com. To some extent, this is a very valid objective for using LinkedIn—to get back in touch with old colleagues. After all, that first invitation to join LinkedIn should have come from an old friend or colleague, right? As the name "classmates" entails, you can only find old friends with whom you went to school. What if you want to get in touch with ex-colleagues? LinkedIn is definitely the place to make this happen; reconnecting with past co-workers should, without a doubt, be part of your LinkedIn Objective. LinkedIn can offer this in that your basic profile is composed of your work and education history. For each company or college that you enter, you also have the option of to enter which years you worked or studied there. Combining this with the rich database and search functionality that LinkedIn provides allows you to quickly and easily find ex-colleagues. The more information you enter on your profile, the higher the likelihood you will find people. Two words of caution here: 1) you can only find people if they have properly filled out their entire profile (a lot of people don't do this) and 2) although there is a standard drop-down for colleges and universities, this doesn't exist for high school names, so it may be more difficult to find someone pre-college (which is where Classmates.com's strength lies).

- **Recruiter**

With millions of people putting their company names, years worked, past titles, and detailed descriptions at companies they have or are presently working for, you can imagine that, as more people join LinkedIn, it becomes a huge database of talent! Combined with the rich functionality that allows you to pinpoint searches by each of the fields that are entered, you can imagine the goldmine of information that LinkedIn provides to the world's recruiters and headhunters. Rather than cold calling the competitor asking for "the VP of anything," that person more than likely already has a profile on LinkedIn! Through sending an invitation, sending an InMail, requesting an introduction from a common connection, or joining the same Group, that recruiter can now contact anyone they wish without cold calling. You can now see why LinkedIn is the only tool that a recruiter may ever need, and also why there are so many recruiters on LinkedIn. For recruiters their LinkedIn Objective is very clear—to log on and start searching for qualified job candidates!

- **Job Seeker**

It's no wonder how LinkedIn grew with more and more professionals reaching out to ex-colleagues and recruiters, amassing a database of contacts. Just as you can google someone and find information about them, LinkedIn was already being used for finding people without you knowing it. So why use LinkedIn if you are looking for a job? To expose yourself to the incredible number of recruiters who are currently active users! Be found!

- **Sales & Marketing / Small Business Owner**

If you are in sales & marketing, the ability to reach 40 million potential customers is an exciting prospect. But there is more to LinkedIn than just an audience to sell to; this is a professional audience that doesn't necessarily want to be sold to. LinkedIn respects the privacy concerns of its professional members and has publicly stated spamming will not be tolerated; in fact, LinkedIn set up a special email address (abuse@linkedin.com) to report those who are abusing the site. So while you can freely tweet away on Twitter or have a great deal of freedom on Facebook, you need to be aware that LinkedIn is a different beast. That is not to say that LinkedIn cannot be used for sales and marketing; it simply has to be done carefully, following the proper protocol.

- **Professional Networking**

With all of the professionals who are already on LinkedIn, it makes sense that LinkedIn is the perfect platform to find and network with other professionals. If you are looking to build up your Trusted Network of Advisors, look no further than LinkedIn's searchable databases, specialized Groups, and a comprehensive Q&A forum!

- **Windmill Networking**

After becoming more familiar with LinkedIn, many will find that the larger the network they have, the easier it will be to reach their objective. Without knowing how LinkedIn really works, it is difficult to see how this can be done. Even when I received my first invitation from someone I did not know, I felt a little violated; however, as you start to communicate with others on LinkedIn, through Group Discussions or through answering questions, you will undoubtedly find yourself starting to connect with people who you may have never physically met before. There are some who will still stick to their original physical network, saying that quality is more important than quantity. This is a debate in which there are pros and cons for both approaches. If you understand the concept of a virtual network that resides next to or on top of your physical network, you will see the advantages of Windmill Networking. You will find yourself connecting with people you may not have met who can help you reach your personal and career objectives. Remember: Your network is still your network; a virtual connection on LinkedIn simply directly links your two profiles.

Although Windmill Networking implies you are an open networker, there is one thing I would like to point out: this book is not merely about open networking. Open networking is a unique type of LinkedIn activity. LinkedIn specifically warns you against connecting with people you do not know. On the other hand, LinkedIn also encourages you to increase your connections. The official LinkedIn blog by Guy Kawasaki urges you to increase your connections to gain visibility. The jury is out on the subject. I suggest you do what you feel comfortable with, as long as it moves you closer to meeting your pre-established objective. This book will include warnings for certain activities that may draw the attention of LinkedIn, so please read carefully. At the same time, please also know that LinkedIn is constantly changing, so the situation could change, for the better or worse, at any time.

Just remember, if you ever feel lost along your LinkedIn journey, re-visit your original LinkedIn Objective. Make sure your activities are consistent with what you originally planned to achieve. LinkedIn, like the Internet in general, can eat up a lot of your time if you are not careful and focused.

What is a "Brand?"

Before going through the process of creating your LinkedIn Brand, let's first discuss one of the most talked about terms these days: your brand. What exactly is a brand, you ask? In the Preface, I defined my own brand as something which differentiates me from everyone else in the market.

WindMill WISDOM

Your brand is something unique that differentiates you from everyone else. It illustrates your unique skills and experiences and describes, or "brands" these attributes in the appropriate fashion. Ideally, your brand will immediately showcase your unique strengths.

Let us start by thinking about brands of products we see at the supermarket. Produce, for the most part, is not branded. What about cereals? Or soups? Or yogurt? You have many different choices when it comes to buying groceries, but many of us buy based upon a "brand" name. This brand name is formed through the following: TV commercials or other media advertisements, the coloring or imagery of the physical package, and the catchy phrases that are sometimes used in the commercial or on the packaging. There are differences in flavors between each product; however, if we are buying a commodity where something very similar exists, we are buying based upon the branding. If we are buying something more expensive than its competitor, we are putting a premium on that brand.

Another good example is the drug store. You can buy Tylenol or Advil, but now it seems that every drug store has their own comparable "generic" drug on the shelf. If you look at the ingredients of the medicine, they are often exactly the same; however, the price is different. As a result, the feelings we experience when we buy one or the other is very different. We consciously and sub-consciously place value in the name brand or in the inexpensiveness of the generic product. Many people will buy the cheaper alternative, but many others will pay more for the brand name.

If you think of yourself as a brand, your brand value is your salary. If you were competing for the same job as someone with a similar skill set, wouldn't you want to be paid more for your brand? I think your answer is "yes!" That is why branding yourself is so important. Think about it this way: if you are 40 years old, plan to work until you are 60, and are currently making $100,000 a year, your brand is worth a potential $2,000,000 over the lifetime of your career! That is a brand that you want to manage carefully to maximize its value!

WindMill WISDOM

Your brand is your most valuable personal asset. Create it carefully, and utilize social media sites like LinkedIn to develop, broadcast, and even potentially monetize it.

So branding is related to social media, social networking, and LinkedIn? Absolutely! There are 40 million other people on LinkedIn. Don't you want to be thought of as someone unique—someone with a valuable and distinct brand? What happens if you change your headline from "Technology Sales" to "Savvy Technology Sales Executive" or "Global Sales Director" or "Senior Sales Executive" or even "Experienced Sales Executive"? Each one of these headlines will shed a different light upon your skill set; thus, you will be creating a different brand. In some ways, creating your brand is equivalent to carving out your own niche, so you will want to be careful when deciding on one. It is key to utilize LinkedIn to help *create* your brand; you then support this brand throughout your profile to make a strong impression on anyone who may come across it. Your branding will also make it easier for people to remember you and help you should the need arise.

No matter what experience you have had, there is bound to be someone similar to you out there. By defining your brand and carving out your niche, you will increase your perceived value. When you communicate with others, you will be viewed as someone who is aware of his or her capabilities, making you harder to forget. While reading this book, particularly the next chapter about creating your LinkedIn Brand, think about your own niche market brand and how you can differentiate yourself throughout your profile. Think of yourself as your own small business.

When you start tinkering with the "Status Update" text box, you can really affect the way your LinkedIn Brand is perceived. What do you think of people who write "I am currently looking for a job" versus someone writing "Spoke to a class of MBA students on entrepreneurialism today." ***People will feel differently towards your brand based on what you write.*** It really is that simple.

You will be able to Windmill Network more effectively with others once you develop a strong brand. It will make it easier for others to help you, as they will clearly understand your LinkedIn Objective. They will also remember you more easily. The same goes for others whom you are trying to help as well.

I highly recommend reading *Career Distinction: Stand Out By Building Your Brand*, by William Arruda and Kirsten Dixson or Me 2.0 by Dan Schawbel to supplement the branding knowledge I present.

Creating Your LinkedIn Brand

Once you have established your objective for using LinkedIn, and ideally have started thinking about your own unique and differentiating brand, you can begin to create your User Profile. Doing so will help you define and create your own LinkedIn Brand. At this point I assume you are already on LinkedIn, but if not, please visit www.linkedin.com and join.

Your profile is the heart of your personal information that will be exposed to other LinkedIn members. Your profile is, in essence, a resume that you are sharing with the entire world. Although the best way to create a resume is to customize it for each position you are seeking, there is only one universal profile on LinkedIn that everyone will be able to see. **This is the secret to why LinkedIn's database and search capabilities are so awesome: the fields for which everyone enters information are standardized.** For the same reason, it is easier to brand yourself, as everyone else has to complete the same data fields as you. By doing something different you will undoubtedly make yourself more noticeable.

How much information you put in your profile really depends on your LinkedIn Objective. If you want to Windmill Network or are currently in transition, the more information, the better. If you are happily employed and simply want to reconnect with old friends and colleagues, you may not want to go into as much detail. If you want to be successful in achieving your objective, there is a minimum of work history and schools attended that you will need to enter in order to search for and be found by former acquaintances. To develop and strengthen your own LinkedIn Brand, the more data you enter to back it up, the stronger your brand will be.

Don't be shy here. Yes, this will be a publicly accessible resume for you or your product. But if you don't put enough information on your profile, you simply will not be found in competition with 40 million other profiles. I used to think you should not have too much in your profile, as it is best not to reveal more than you need to. The thought process behind this? The more you reveal, the higher the chance that certain aspects of your profile may not be agreeable for whatever reason. I still feel this way to some extent. **But the fact of the matter is, if you don't have enough information in your profile, you might as well not even be on LinkedIn.** If you are not branding yourself enough, you are not taking full advantage of what LinkedIn can offer.

With that in mind, let's examine each part that makes up your User Profile for additional advice on how much you really need to include. If you have already filled out an initial profile, simply go to the "Edit My Profile" tab under the "Profile" section to make any adjustments. You can see how others view your profile by selecting "View My Profile" under the "Profile" selection on the left-hand menu bar.

One last note: LinkedIn conveniently will display your "degree of profile completeness" in terms of a percentage as you add to your profile. If you enter all of the information that I suggest, you should earn a relatively high score. You will probably not reach 100%, as you may be asked to recommend three people. Regardless, do not sweat the details, as you should hit 100% if you heed both my and LinkedIn's advice.

"Basic Information"

This is the information that will first appear with your name. It is the bare minimum necessary to start making connections on LinkedIn.

• **Your Name**

LinkedIn is strict when asking you to include your name, and only your name, where they specify. Do not put a company name or add something to the end of your name to advertise something; there are plenty of other places where you can do this. You will see many people who continue to do this, but here's the scoop: should you need to contact LinkedIn Customer Service for something, they will not help you if you do not show your proper name. You do have the option to show only the first initial of your last name, but unless you have something to hide, you should join the other 99% of members who list their name in its entirety. Finally, if you are a business and plan to put a business name as your name, don't join LinkedIn. LinkedIn is a social network for professionals and people, not companies. You'll have plenty of opportunities to brand your company within your profile!

• **Headline**

You will definitely want to customize your headline to align with your LinkedIn Objective, as this headline appears next to your name within search results. **In fact, your Headline should include your key branding statement.** It is the area, next to your name, that will get the most visibility, so think carefully as to how you want to brand yourself here. You can add more information about your profession and indicate your objective for being on LinkedIn. Enter searchable keywords to increase your visibility. Remember, you are limited to 120 characters, which makes customizing this section very challenging! LinkedIn does include some examples which should give you some specific ideas. Another idea: Search for someone who may have a similar objective or professional background to see what their headline displays to help you brainstorm ideas.

• **Country/Zip Code**

There is no need to deceive anyone here. In order to be correctly found, it is in your best interest to enter your actual country and zip code. Worried about privacy? So is LinkedIn! The actual city name of where you live, based on your zip code, is not displayed—only your closest major metropolitan area appears. So no privacy worries here. The zip code you enter is merely used in searches when trying to locate someone x number of miles away from your address.

• **Industry**

This is a tricky one—you are being asked to compartmentalize yourself into a silo called an "industry." Many of us have worked in multiple industries, or for whatever reason, don't want to be associated with the industry in which we currently work. There are also many companies where the industry is not clear. I looked at several profiles of employees from my previous company; interestingly enough, people's choices regarding the industry they selected varied. Whichever industry you choose, it is very important to pick one that you want to be associated with, as this will be a key field upon which searches will be based. On the other hand, if your objective is to move into a new industry, why not select that industry for your profile? Once again, it all comes down to your objective. Even if your brand is not necessarily tied to a particular industry, pick the one with which you want to be associated.

• **Your Photo**

It is highly recommended that you post a photo to your profile. It will add a personal touch to your profile and will encourage people to reach out to you because you will literally be seen as a "real" entity. There is a debate, since LinkedIn is a site for professionals, about what type of photo you should post. One thing for sure is that you don't want to post a potentially embarrassing Facebook type of photo. I have seen some people post the types of photos you would see on corporate website bios as well as the more personal types of photos that may also include pictures with children. This is really a personal choice; it comes down to how you want to portray yourself to the outside world according to your own LinkedIn Objective. Selecting a photo plays an important role in how people will ultimately visualize your brand.

- **The "What Are You Working On Now?" Bar**

I don't know what the official name of this bar is, but it appears just below your city/industry. I will often refer to this as the "Status Update" text box. If you are familiar with Twitter, it follows the same concept; it broadcasts what you are currently "working on" to the world. You can decide, in the Accounts & Settings section, to who you want to display this information on your profile and whether or not you want to "broadcast" it to the LinkedIn Home Page of your connections. This bar also plays an important role in achieving your objective. Looking for a job? Trying to find a candidate? Looking for help or for particular information? Or do you prefer to just say something to the world? Broadcast it—people are watching! Just make sure you are not broadcasting things that would be more appropriate for your Facebook friends. LinkedIn, after all, is a site for *professionals*. There is a section in Chapter 10 (Customizing Your LinkedIn Experience), which is devoted solely to what you should enter here; at this point, there is no need to enter anything here. LinkedIn is critical real estate upon which you can differentiate yourself and thus strengthen your brand in. Broadcast wisely!

"Profile Synopsis"

This is the resume section of your LinkedIn profile, where the more you contribute, the more likely you will be able to find and be found. The reason being that for each company or school that you enter in your profile, you will enable both present and ex-colleagues and classmates to find you. Keep this in mind when deciding which work experience and schools you want to include in your profile. The details you enter here will be displayed further below in your profile, but the synopsis of titles, companies, and schools will all be collected from the profile information that you input.

• Current (Position)

As you start adding your work experience, your Current Position is the position that will appear at the very top of your work profile. This "Current" position will also appear within the expanded search results, so be sure you put your present or most recent position details here. What you enter here will be the same as what you will input for every other work position that you choose to enter into LinkedIn. LinkedIn will help you narrow down your company name, using an assisted search functionality to draw from the member profiles that contain the same company's name. If it is the first time entering that company name (like for a sole proprietorship) you will have the option to enter the company's URL as well as the industry. You will then need to put in your title, dates worked, as well as a description of the position. Since your description will be seen by potential recruiters, don't be shy when listing your achievements, especially if you are currently unemployed. To effectively brand yourself, you will need to include the details that support the information in your Profile Headline. I recommend including resume-like content, but leave the full details for your resume. **Include enough detail to entice someone to contact you.** If you are employed, you will probably want to be a bit more diplomatic about what you enter in the description so it doesn't appear that you are looking for a job. Note that the most recent position that you enter here will only appear if you check the "I currently work here" option. If you are unemployed and you already updated your most recent position with the final date of employment, this section will have nothing displayed.

• Past (Positions)

LinkedIn gives you the option to add more positions here. I have seen people list more than ten positions, so there may not even be a limit as to how many you can add. I recommend that you list as many positions as you are comfortable with; at minimum, list the same positions included on your resume. Guidelines regarding what to enter here are the same as for the "Current Position" listed above.

• Education

Just as you enter your professional experience as if it were your resume, you can also enter your educational background. Most people stop at their university or masters/PHD program. This is a shame. If LinkedIn is about finding and being found, it makes sense to also list your high school as well as any other foreign institutions you may have attended during your college years. The process for completing your education profile is to enter the country and state (if applicable). A drop down of potential colleges and universities will appear. If your college is not listed here, or you want to enter your high school, you simply choose "Other" and then manually enter the name. There are also fields to enter your degree, field(s) of study, dates attended, activities and societies, and extra notes. I believe for most professionals there may not be a need to enter activities and societies as well as additional notes, but if you are one of the growing numbers of college students utilizing LinkedIn, you will definitely want to use this space to brand yourself with these details.

- **Connections**

This will show an accumulated tally of the total number of connections you have acquired. If you have not yet sent or accepted any invitations, it should display "0 connections." Note that the maximum number of connections that will be displayed is 500 connections, and anything above that will show up as "500+ connections."

- **Websites**

You have the opportunity to list three websites to appear in your profile. They could be your personal website (if you have one), your blog, your company website, or even your profile on other social networking sites such as Facebook or MySpace. It all comes down to what you want to advertise here, which depends on your objective, and on how you want to brand yourself. Note that you can also customize the text label description of each URL site that you enter. You should take advantage of this and use it as part of making your profile more search engine optimized.

- **Public Profile**

This will be the default URL, which is automatically assigned to you, that will lead non-LinkedIn members to your profile. Do yourself a favor: ***edit this and claim your personalized URL now***. If you are the first one to claim your name, your public profile URL will be easy to remember—*www.linkedin.com/in/your name*. You can then include this as part of your email signature or business card (if you are in transition) to drive more traffic to your profile. Since LinkedIn is a site for professionals, I do not recommend that you include a URL name that is different from your real name, i.e. branding your URL. It could sound tacky and take away from your brand.

"Your Summary"

This is your chance to tell the world who you are. It is the most brandable part of your profile, as you are given the largest amount of text area. You could attach your bio from your corporate website if you are an executive, or if you are looking for a job, this could be a synopsis of the highlights of your resume. Your Professional Headline acts as an initial filter when someone views your profile; your Summary is the basis upon which people will form opinions about you and your brand. The content you include here will be intrinsically tied to what you want to accomplish with LinkedIn and your LinkedIn Brand.

Notice that there is also a "Specialties" section that appears at the bottom of the Summary. My advice here is to fill this space with keywords you want associated with your profile. I have personally broken up these keywords into industry-specific and skill-specific paragraphs.

Remember the rule of thumb for data entry here: if there is a keyword that you want to be associated with when it is searched upon, make sure you have included it in your Summary, as this is the most suitable place for it.

Applications

If you have any Applications running, they will appear here below your "Summary" section and above your "Experience" section. Chapter 8 is devoted entirely to all of the Applications that exist on LinkedIn, so if you have not installed any Applications yet, please wait until after we cover these later in this book. So as not to overload you with too much at this point, I'm going to skip over Applications now. Applications are icing on the cake and are not mandatory to brand yourself on LinkedIn, but, depending on your objective, they could be very valuable tools.

Experience

All of the positions you entered under work experience will appear here in descending time order, with your most recent or "current" job listed first. At the bottom of each section, your Recommendations, if you have any, will appear.

Education

Just as all of the work experience details will be listed in the "Experience" section, all of the schools that you attended, together with their details, will be listed here in the "Education" section.

Recommendations

Chapter 5 of this book is solely devoted to Recommendations. If you have received any and decide to display them, they will be shown in full detail, including the name and title of those who recommended you. They will be displayed in the same order that your Experience is shown.

"Additional Information"

There is a host of other information that is displayed at the bottom of your profile. While this section may look dismissible, every inch of space you have in your profile should be utilized to mention anything the standard template does not allow you to communicate. **All of these areas are searchable.** Once you get more familiar with LinkedIn you will find a lot of people put a lot of different things in these sections. There is no golden rule except that you want to make sure that 1) you are found when searched upon and 2) your profile showcases your brand!

- **Websites**

The same three websites that appear in your "Profile Synopsis" will be displayed here as well. Not clear as to what LinkedIn's intent is in having the same information display twice, but this gives your URLs double the marketing power!

- **Interests**

Objectively speaking, you could put your actual interests in this section. If letting everyone know that you enjoy rock climbing will help you achieve your objective, then go for it. Just be careful not to dilute your LinkedIn Brand. But if you are using LinkedIn for a professional objective, why not put interests here that are related to your job? Maybe you can go into some detail as to why you are interested in some aspects of your career. I cannot tell you to put anything under "Interests" that is not objectively related to your interests, but the choice is yours. You will see many profiles where people are putting completely unrelated things here to better advertise themselves and to make sure that search engines pick them up. In my own experience, I have not heard of anyone being notified by LinkedIn that they need to change their wording here to be more aligned with actual interests. What you enter here is at your own risk, but be forewarned that if you go off the topic of actual Interests you may be at risk of violating the LinkedIn User's Agreement. Make sure you check it (the link is on the bottom navigation bar) before doing something that may not be viewed by LinkedIn in a positive light.

- **Groups and Associations**

This section is slightly different than the "Interests" section in that any LinkedIn Group you join will be listed here if you choose to display their logos. When viewing your own profile, all of your Groups will appear on the right-hand side as LinkedIn will understand that those are shared Groups. We will discuss LinkedIn Groups in Chapter 6, but if there is a professional association that you are a member of that does not have a corresponding LinkedIn Group, you absolutely should make sure to include it here.

- **Honors and Awards**

Same as "Interests." I have seen people brag about career achievements and awards here, but I personally think this is the type of material that should really be in the relevant section as part of your "Experience." Include any information that you want at your own risk.

Personal Information

This is a relatively new feature that allows you to input your phone number, address, IM username, birthday, and marital status to your profile. I personally have a problem with this and find it interesting that where LinkedIn is concerned about your privacy, they are asking for some very private information from a professional demographic. I really don't see any advantage to filling out this area at all, unless LinkedIn rolls out some unique feature (other than targeted advertising, which I presume this information is used for) that uses it to your advantage.

Contact Settings

There are two sections here, with the top section being text that you can directly enter, and the bottom section showing what you are "Interested In." This information is culled from what you entered when asked how you would like to use your network. This information can be edited in the "Using Your Network" section in "Account & Settings," located at the top right-hand side of the screen. It is important to check all of the boxes next to the options so you are seen as open to anyone who may want to contact you.

I believe that the "Contact Settings," as opposed to the "Additional Information" section, is the area where you can and should share your LinkedIn Objective and guidelines for being contacted. If you are currently employed but looking for work, you don't want to mention that here. But if you are open to being contacted by certain types of people, or you actively want to create certain types of relationships, why not say so here? If you want to keep your network closed and don't want to receive invitations from virtual networkers, this is the place to say so.

If you believe in Windmill Networking, this is where you should tell the world you are a Windmill Networker and are looking to connect with similar-minded people.

One note is that you will often see email addresses and phone numbers included here as well as in other sections on LinkedIn. It is LinkedIn's policy that these should not be included in your profile; doing so may be violating the LinkedIn User's Agreement. I was afraid of what type of spam might come my way should I enter my own email address. But, since I was in transition, I thought if a recruiter wanted to contact me and another candidate, and the other candidate was easily accessible (had his or her email and or phone details in their profile), the recruiter would probably contact the candidate who supplied his or her contact information. So I listed my email address in potential violation of the User Agreement. They have yet to strictly enforce this, but if they do contact me, I will gladly remove it from my profile.

I was even more hesitant to include my phone number but I have since changed my mind. One day, after I joined a certain LinkedIn Group, I received a call on my cell phone the very next day from someone trying to sell me a service related to that Group. I was shocked that someone who didn't know me had found out my cell number, and when I asked, he simply replied that he had called the company listed as my current employer and asked for me ;-) The point is this: Anyone who wants to contact me will find a way to do so, so why not list my phone number on my profile so people who I may think are important have a way to directly contact me? In reality, since I have listed it, I have received very few calls. But it is out there as a representation that I am always open to talking to anyone, including you, the reader of this book!

My Top Five Tips to Write a Great Profile

I often get asked for tips about how to write a "great" profile. My response is always the same: "What is your LinkedIn Objective?" If you have followed the instructions in the previous chapter, you should be well on your way to developing an excellent profile.

The only additional tips worth offering emphasize the points necessary to successfully **Windmill Network:**

- Your profile is real and honest, from your name and photo to all of the information you have listed. LinkedIn is a network of trusted professionals; if you are not being authentic, people will find out, trust me. You will lose any "social media credibility" that you may have once had.

- Your profile is complete. Don't be shy! You have a lot of real estate to work with, so the more you use, the better you can brand yourself. The better you brand yourself, the easier it will be for people to find you. This includes adding a paragraph and/or at least a few bullet points listing your education and work experience.

- Your profile is heavily branded in every way possible, from the wording in your professional headline to what you write in your contact settings. Don't let LinkedIn tell you what to write; this is your profile page, so utilize it to achieve your objective!

- Your profile is searchable. Make sure the keywords you want to be associated with are found throughout your profile.

- Your profile has Recommendations—the more the merrier! I will cover Recommendations later on in this book; for now, note that the presence of high quality Recommendations adds to your brand and validates that you are a real entity who is who you say you are.

If you have followed my instructions in the previous chapter and have implemented the above tips for writing a great profile, rest assured that you have written a strong profile and move on!

One last word of advice: After you create your stellar profile which embodies your LinkedIn Brand, make sure you revisit it on a regular basis to ensure it still makes sense. You may be working for a new company or develop a new interest; these changes warrant some slight tweaks to your LinkedIn Brand. There are many reasons why it could happen, but always remember to maintain your profile so your LinkedIn Brand is always fresh and up-to-date.

Your LinkedIn Home Page

Now you have entered your profile information. Before you begin to actually navigate LinkedIn, let's take a look at what your "Home" page on LinkedIn will look like. It is the page you will see after going to www.linkedin.com and signing in with your username and password. While navigating LinkedIn, it can also be accessed by selecting "Home" on the left-hand navigation bar.

As a disclaimer, I would like to point out that not everyone's Home Page will look alike. For instance, if you have indicated in your profile that you are currently unemployed, "Company Groups" will not appear in your left-hand navigation bar. I personally cannot see "Groups You Might Like" and have only been able to see the "People You May Know" module on occasion.

That aside, the Home Page is divided into a top section, a left-hand section, the main body (which is in the middle), which contains another right-hand column, and finally the bottom of the page. You have access to all of LinkedIn's features via this screen.

The image on the next page will simplify the LinkedIn Home Page for you, as I have tried to illustrate the most essential items you will be utilizing most.

Figure 2.2. Your LinkedIn Home Page

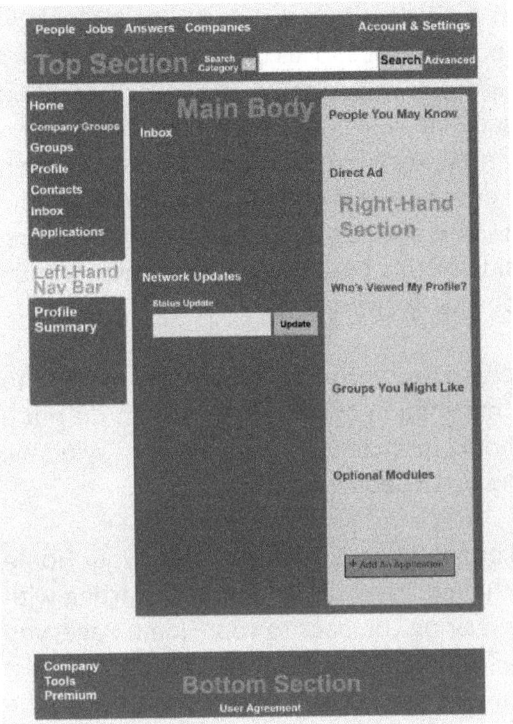

Before tackling the main areas of your Home Page, I want to point out that I find LinkedIn is sometimes repetitive with its user interface; many paths will often lead to the same destination. You will get used to this. For instance, choosing "Advanced People Search" by pressing the downwards arrow to the right of "People" will lead you to the same page that choosing the "Search People" arrow to the left of the Search Bar and then pressing the "Advanced" button does.

In my opinion, LinkedIn is still trying to find the perfect User Interface to show off the tremendous value their site has; in the meantime, I find the user interface somewhat confusing and inefficient at times, which is why I am writing this book—to help guide you. I will not go over *everything* on this page and instead will concentrate only on those things that I think you need to concentrate on.

Let's tackle each section individually. The top section, at the time of this writing, displays "People," "Jobs," "Answers" and "Companies" on the left, while the right side shows "Account & Settings," "Help" and "Sign In/Out" on the top with the Search Bar on the bottom. Let's focus on the Search Bar for a moment. By pressing the downward arrow button to the left of the text window, you will see that you can search a variety of things from this one text box, including People, Jobs, Companies, Answers, Inbox, and Groups. Within some sections, the standard search does not yield enough useable results; the option to do an advanced search on some of these can be selected by choosing the "Advanced" text on the right side of this box. This option appears when you choose to search for People, Jobs, or Answers.

On occasion you may need to access the "Accounts & Settings" button to customize your experience. More information about what you can do there will be spread throughout this book, primarily in Part II: The Windmill Networking Approach to Understanding LinkedIn sections.

The primary area for navigation will be the menu on the left side of your Home Page which I will often refer to as the left-hand navigation bar. Starting with the "Home" button, which will always bring you back to your Home Page, you can navigate to any of the following from here: Company Groups (if they exist for your Company or you are currently employed with a Company listed in the Company Directory), Groups, Profile, Contacts, Inbox, and Applications, should you have any. Furthermore, the "+" symbol next to all of these titles, if pressed, will collapse into submenus which let you choose specifics.

I won't go through every option here, but I will point out the more frequently used features:

- "Home" to get you to back to your Home Page.
- "Groups" to access your Groups, or specific Groups in the submenu should you wish to list them here (this can be customized in "Account & Settings").
- "Edit My Profile" in the "Profile" menu to modify your profile and optimize it even after it has been created. You should get into a monthly habit of looking at your profile to make sure it syncs with your LinkedIn Brand and networking objectives, which may change over time.

- "Connections" in the "Contacts" menu to browse your current connections or add/remove connections.

- The "Inbox." Most messages appearing here can also be sent directly to your registered email address. How often you use this section really depends on which information you decide to access directly through LinkedIn and which information you choose to receive via email notification. I have devoted an entire section to this topic: "Controlling Your Email Notifications" in Chapter 10: Customizing Your LinkedIn Experience.

- "Applications" should you choose to install any and modify their settings.

- The prominent green colored and self-explanatory "Add Connections" button.

The last section on the left-hand side, on the bottom of the long menu, is your current photo, Profile Headline, Status, and display of the number of total connections you have. You have the ability to easily change your Status here, so you can update it without having to jump around.

For the main middle/right section of your Home Page, which looks like a wide middle column and a narrow right column, there is some pretty serious information overload. The middle section is divided between an "Inbox," "Network Updates," and "Company News" (if you are currently employed and your company is in the LinkedIn directory).

On top, the Inbox will simply display your latest five messages, combined with a summary of action items, or messages you have not responded to yet. The bottom Company News will display news from the company you have listed on your profile as being "current." The meat of the information here lies in the Network Updates.

Network Updates begin with a "What are you working on now?" status bar that you can update. I call this the "Status Update Bar" and have devoted an entire section, "The Status Update: "What are You Working on Now?" in

Chapter 10: Customizing Your LinkedIn Experience, to cover this in greater detail.

The information below your Status Update Bar in Network Updates is filled with fascinating content being broadcast to you from your connections. These updates will keep you up-to-date on whatever your Windmill Networking contacts are doing on LinkedIn. From updating their profiles with new job information to posting a new photo, if your connections have agreed to broadcast their activity to their network, it will show up in this area. A lot of LinkedIn users get into a habit of spending the first few minutes of their day screening through this information, as it often supplies insightful information you can utilize to initiate a conversation. The information also helps you keep in close contact with your Windmill Network.

If you click the "See more updates" text next to the "Network Updates" title, you will be led to a screen where you can see a plethora of broadcasted content from your network. Four tabs appear conveniently at the top to help you navigate through "All Updates," "Category View," "Connection View," as well as seeing what you are broadcasting to your network in "My Updates."

It is interesting to note that the following types of information can be found in the "Category View":

- Connection Updates — who connected with whom
- Group Updates — who joined which Group
- Status Updates — who wrote what in their "Status Update" bar
- Events — who has RSVPed or is interested in certain events
- Application Updates — who has updated public information in their application
- Recommendations — who has sent or received Recommendations
- Questions & Answers — who has asked or answered questions
- Photo Updates — who has updated their photo
- Polls — who has created or commented on a Poll
- Job Posts — who has posted a job on LinkedIn Jobs
- Profile Updates — who has updated their profile information

As you can see, Network Updates are unique and are extremely valuable for keeping a pulse on how your network is doing. The fact that everything you do on LinkedIn is recorded and could thus be broadcasted is scary; however, there is a wealth of information you can use here on a daily basis to monitor your network in a timely and relevant fashion.

In fact, by "mimicking" what your network is doing, you can come into contact with valuable people to connect with, events you might be interested in, Groups that may be of value, and questions you might be able to answer. Remember, it is about Paying It Forward. I personally have not yet gotten into the habit of reading this information on a daily basis, but I am going to make it a future priority to do so. I hope you do as well!

Note that you have the power to completely customize what information is broadcast here on your Home Page by selecting "Manage Your Network Update Settings" at the bottom left of the Network Updates section.

Finally, we move on to the right-hand side of this middle section. Like a newspaper, the content here is designed to catch your eye. You have some degree of customization of the modules here, so you will find this section particularly useful.

At the very top, you should see a little module called "People You May Know." This is how LinkedIn suggests you connect with people, similar to the Facebook functionality. I need to be honest in that I have only seen this module pop up for a few days. It should be a regular feature on your Home Page, but if it is not, you are not alone. I wasn't necessarily impressed with the matching of the people that LinkedIn gives me, but depending on the logic of their matching algorithm, you might have better luck.

Once you skim the Direct Ad that appears below this, you should see the "Who's Viewed My Profile?" module. This is an interesting module which tells you how many people have viewed your profile and how many times your name has appeared in a search result in the last day. Below this is a "See more" link, which, if you press it, will give you details about 5 people who have viewed your profile.

Note that in order to see everyone who has viewed your profile, you need to upgrade to a paid account. Furthermore, under "Account & Settings," there is a Privacy Setting for Profile Views. The default setting for this shows your industry and title without giving your name or company. There are options to give your name or to be completely anonymous. Even if you upgrade, you will never really know 100% of the people who viewed your profile because very few people actually show their name. I have devoted a section to this in "Display Your Footprint?" in Chapter 10.

The "Groups You Might Like" module may appear below the "Who's Viewed My Profile?" module. I say "may" because I have never seen it on my Home Page, but other LinkedIn users have told me this module exists. I am assuming this is similar to the "People You May Know" module, so this may prove useful to you.

The remaining modules you display here can all be customized and deleted by pressing the "x" button on the top right hand corner of the module. They can be edited by pressing the "edit" button to the left of the "x" button, and minimized by pressing the downward arrow key on the top left-hand corner of each module. Furthermore, the ability to add modules can be found at the bottom of this right-hand section via the "+ Add an Application" button. This fooled me for the longest time, because in addition to adding an actual Application to your profile (covered in Chapter 8: Applications), you can also add actual modules.

Your choice of non-Application modules here is essentially a category of "Answers" or "Job Search."

Within "Answers" is the opportunity to place several modules on your Home Page, one for each of the tens of categories and sub-categories that exist for Answers. We will discuss this in Chapter 7: Answers, but you may want to play around and browse categories that interest you by selecting "Answers" and then seeing the categories that are on display.

The "Job Search" module, while rudimentary, will allow you to search for a title near a certain location. This may or may not be useful, depending on your title, location and situation.

In my experience, I have been limited to displaying no more than 12 modules, not including the Direct Ad and the "Who's Viewed My Profile?" module.

Finally, we come to the section at the very bottom of the page which contains four rows of selections titled "Company," "Tools," "Premium"; the final row contains your standard User Agreement, Privacy Policy, and Copyright Policy, along with a feedback area just below that. I would call this area the "Reference" section because it contains valuable information and tools that will foster a more efficient and well-informed LinkedIn experience. The sections here that I believe you will find valuable are:

- "Customer Service" is your one-stop support shop for anything to do with LinkedIn.

- "Learning Center" gives you more basic information about the different features LinkedIn offers. User Guides for a few specific professions are available; however, I find the information to be of a basic nature. Yet another reason I am writing this book!

- "Blog" is a real blog with some interesting content about LinkedIn and how people are using it. You should pay attention to the "Categories" title on the left side which lists blog titles in "New Features," "Tips & Tricks," "In The News" and "Success Stories." Recently "Engineering" and "Recent Grads" have been added to the mix. RSS feeds for all of these are available via an email notification subscription to the blog itself.

- "Overview" in the "Tools" section shows off tools that LinkedIn has developed to embed LinkedIn into your PC applications. All of these are accessible on this page. It is a shame their two toolbars are useless to a personal user (i.e. me) who uses neither Outlook (I use Gmail) nor Internet Explorer/Firefox (I use Google Chrome). They have a handy email signature tool, which once again is tied to Outlook/Outlook Express/Thunderbird, which I cannot use. A Google Toolbar Assistant requires a Google Toolbar, which doesn't exist in Google Chrome. Finally, there is a Mac Dashboard Search Module, but I utilize Windows. Needless to say, I have found zero use for any of these tools, so they are not by any means necessary to implement what I teach you in the rest of this book; however, I have heard rave reviews from those who use the Outlook Toolbar, as it could make your time spent on LinkedIn much more efficient. The email signature tool is definitely a helpful feature to have if you are using Outlook. If you are interested, they appear easy to download and install from this section. These tools can make your Windmill Networking more efficient while helping promote your LinkedIn Brand.

- "Upgrade Your Account," should you wish to change from a free to a paid account. We will cover this topic in Chapter 14: Putting it All in Perspective in the "To Pay or Not to Pay?" section.

Now that you understand what is available on your Home Page, it is time to actually start navigating LinkedIn, connecting with others, and building up your LinkedIn network. It is time for you to embark on your journey of Windmill Networking.

PART II:

THE WINDMILL NETWORKING APPROACH TO UNDERSTANDING LINKEDIN

You will be able to register and implement your LinkedIn Brand once you understand the mechanics of LinkedIn. A thorough review of LinkedIn's main features, along with unique, additional insight I have included, will put everything in the context of Windmill Networking. As a result, you will be able to use the strategies and techniques I present to achieve your LinkedIn Objective. The chapters in this section will cover the following topics: invitations, connections, Introductions, Recommendations, Groups, Answers, Applications, jobs, and companies. It will also look closely at settings that can help customize your LinkedIn experience. I will not waste time on things I deem unimportant; instead of being a comprehensive introduction to LinkedIn, this section of chapters will take a thorough and detailed look at the most frequently used functionalities along with their potential restrictions. When finished with this section, you will have started building your network, sending and receiving Recommendations, joining Groups, and answering questions. My goal is to provide you with a roadmap to help you realize the power of Windmill Networking. It will be instrumental in helping you achieve your LinkedIn Objective.

Chapter 3

Chapter 3 Invitations & Connections

- Your First Invitations: How to "Add Connections"
- Connecting with People: The Invitation Mechanism
- Finding People to Connect With Using Advanced Search
- Navigating Through Profiles
- My Top Five Tips to Write a Great Invitation
- Managing Your Invitations
- The Dreaded "IDK"
- I'm Out of Invitations?!?! Help!
- Dealing with Spam? On LinkedIn?
- The Disconnecting Option
- Emailing Your Connections: What You Need to Know
- How Do I Contact 2nd and 3rd Degree Connections?

Your First Invitations: How to "Add Connections"

Since you have come this far, I assume you are ready to roll up your sleeves and begin making connections, starting with those in your immediate physical network. LinkedIn has made this very easy for you by providing the "Add Connections" functionality. You can access this function by clicking on the big green "Add Connections" button, which is near the bottom of the left-hand sidebar. Upon concluding this exercise, based on the size of your physical network, you will already be on your way to building a network of tens and perhaps hundreds of connections!

If you are new to LinkedIn, your profile will display that you have no connections here when you access this screen. The following options appear under four different tabs on this page:

- **Invite Contacts**

If you know the first and last name, as well as email address, of someone you want to add, you can directly input this information here. This is not the most efficient way of adding people as it is extremely time consuming. Imagine if you have a database of several hundred contacts. You would need to input their first name, last name, and email address, all in separate fields, for several hundred contacts! It is also far from error-proof, as email addresses of people you know may have changed. I do not think this option is used very often, unless you wish to invite only a few people at a time.

- **Import Contacts—Check Webmail**

This is the tab you will find the most useful. If you have a webmail account from Microsoft (Hotmail/WindowsLive), Yahoo, Google, AOL or a select group of "other" providers, LinkedIn will log into your account after you enter a valid username and password. LinkedIn will then present you with a list of your contacts in alphabetical order, giving you the option to immediately invite everyone in your address book. This is probably how you got that initial invitation to join LinkedIn!

Before you get excited about finding a few hundred potential connections here, be warned that LinkedIn is looking at your entire address book. If you are a Google Mail user, for instance, this will include pretty much anyone you have ever emailed, regardless if they are a LinkedIn member or not!

You may not want to invite all of these people (or companies that you have contacted in the past) to your LinkedIn network, depending on your LinkedIn Objective. Be extra careful, as LinkedIn will show you current LinkedIn members as well as those who are not yet on LinkedIn. Only those with the blue "in" symbol on the far right are active LinkedIn members. For reasons we will discuss later in this book, if you are tempted to start inviting people, I highly recommend that you start by ***only inviting those in your address book who already have a LinkedIn account***. If you don't have many contacts to go through, I suggest right clicking and visiting the profiles of these people to see how active they are on LinkedIn. If they only have a few connections, they may not be very active on LinkedIn, and thus your invitation may be "wasted" or underutilized. You may want to save the invitations for these people for a later date when they (I hope) get more active on LinkedIn. You will learn later in this book that your invitations are a limited resource, so learn early to use them wisely!

- **Import Contacts—Other Address Book**

If you have your contacts in a database or contact management application such as Outlook, Act!, Palm Desktop, etc., AND if you can export these contacts into a .csv, .txt, or .vcf format, you can easily import your contacts into LinkedIn just as you did with Webmail. The same warning about being somewhat selective with your invitations applies here.

- **Import Contacts—Enter Contacts Manually**

Sends you back to the "Invite Contacts" screen.

- **Colleagues**

For every company you listed in your profile (whether you still work for them or used to work for them) you can now search for your present and former colleagues. LinkedIn displays the first 50 colleagues that are closest to your network, based on the company name as well as the years during which you worked at the company. After using this multiple times, you get to the point where you don't know any of the 50 people recommended to you; by pressing the "I Don't Know Anyone Here" tab, LinkedIn will recommend 50 new people to you. You will also notice if you return to this page in the future, you will have the option to search again from scratch ("View All") or search those who haven't been introduced to you yet ("Find New"). LinkedIn will also list the date you last searched for colleagues. You always have the option to use the "Advanced Search" functionality to manually search for people based on title or where they are current employees (which I will discuss in the "Finding People to Connect With Using Advanced Search" section later in this chapter). In addition, this "Colleagues" section is an excellent place to find potential connections from your past and present workplaces.

- **Classmates**

For every school you listed in the "Education" section of your profile, you will now have the opportunity to search for classmates. Furthermore, with each school you list, you can further narrow down your search by years the students attended. If you are looking for people within your specific graduating class, LinkedIn will also conduct this more specific search for you.

When you explore the tabs I reviewed above, I recommend you send Invitations with a personal note to all of your present and former colleagues, classmates, and friends and family. By doing so, you are well on your way to quickly adding anywhere from tens to a few hundred connections to your LinkedIn profile!

Congratulations! You have completed the first step in utilizing LinkedIn to meet your objective, whatever that may be. Whether your objective is to connect to old friends or to find your next big job, *the first step is undoubtedly making connections; by doing so, you are plugging yourself into the Windmill Networking grid*. Now that you understand the invitation functionality, you will be able to start further expanding your LinkedIn network.

Connecting with People: The Invitation Mechanism

Congratulations on establishing new connections to your LinkedIn profile. The previous chapter detailed the easiest and most efficient way to add connections to your network; however, it is important to understand the mechanism by which you add these contacts: the invitation.

You are now starting to acquire and develop your own network of connections, defined as your immediate or 1st degree connections. These 1st degree connections have made their own connections, who have now become your 2nd degree connections. Furthermore, you can see your connections' own 2nd degree connections, which then become 3rd degree connections to you.

By inviting someone, you are requesting they join your network as a 1st degree connection; thus your 2nd degree connections become their 3rd degree connections and vice-versa, as illustrated in Figures 3.1 and 3.2.

The images on the following page may look confusing at first, but after using LinkedIn for some time, the degrees of connection will become easily recognizable. The invitation mechanism works the same regardless of which degree the person you want to invite is. Although we will cover it later in the book, the degree of separation will affect the following things you do on LinkedIn:

- Requesting an Introduction from a 1st degree connection will be easier if they are directly connected to the person you want to invite; in other words, a 2nd degree connection will be easiest to be introduced to.

- Search results can be sorted by "relationship," or degree of connection.

Figure 3.1. Disconnected Networks Before Connecting

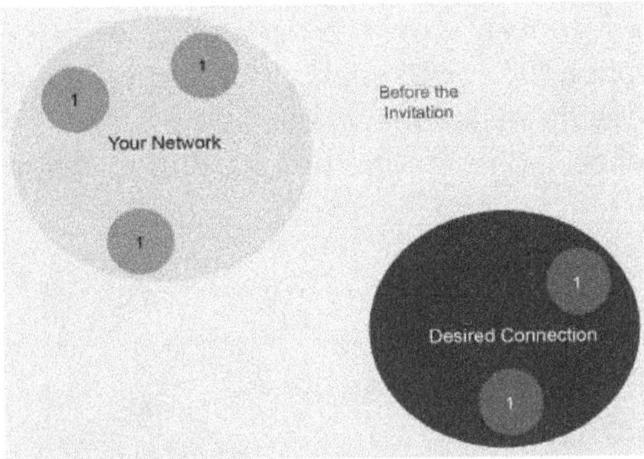

Figure 3.2. Connected Networks After Accepting the Invite

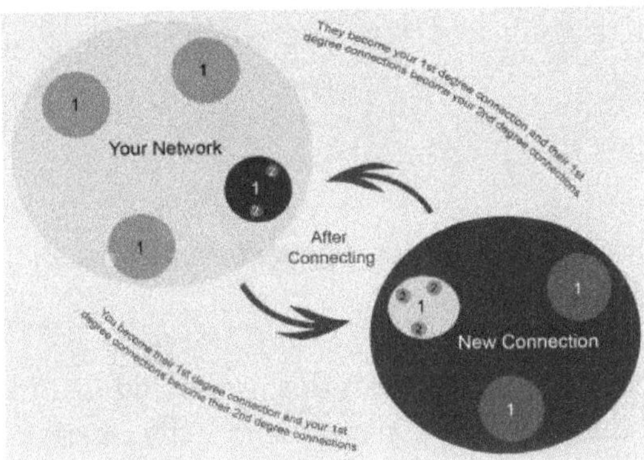

As mentioned before, inviting people is easiest when utilizing the "Add Connections" feature; however, after reading this book and becoming an experienced user, you will find yourself inviting people via the Advanced Search results page (to be discussed in the next section of this chapter) or by directly looking at their profile.

For the purpose of explanation, please enter a sample keyword in the People Search Bar and perform a search. When looking at this search result, there are two different ways to invite new people into your network. If you want to learn more about that person before inviting them, you can click on the person's name to see their profile; then press the "Add (Name) to network" link that appears in the top right-hand corner of their profile. On the other hand, if you are already confident that you want to invite this person to your network, when you put your cursor anywhere within a single result box in the search result screen, a link will appear in the top right hand corner of that box; this link will give you the option to "Add to network." Selecting either of these options will bring you to the same invitation screen. You are now given the following options to identify your relationship with the individual to whom you wish to connect:

- Colleague
- Classmate
- We've done business together
- Friend
- Groups & Associations
- Other
- I don't know (name)

I highly recommend that you are truthful and accurate when checking a particular box.

WindMill WISDOM

After all, this is what Windmill Networking is all about: Being real and genuine. This process starts with your first LinkedIn interaction.

Right above the "Send Invitation" tab you will see a notice reminding you to only invite people who you know, along with an explanation of why LinkedIn states this. You will then be led to another window with a warning. We will cover invitation restrictions in following chapters; however, at this point, I will assume you are only inviting people you know or with whom you have had some sort of relationship.

Let's take a closer look at the options you have when describing your relationship with the person you want to invite:

- **Colleague**—Choose this option if you worked at the same company as the person with whom you are trying to connect. This is based upon only those companies you entered in your profile.

- **Classmate**—Choose this option if you attended the same school as this person. Again, this is based upon the schools you listed in your profile.

- **We've done business together**—Choose this option if you knew this person when you worked at a company—but this person did not necessarily work at the same company as you. This is the perfect choice for inviting partners, vendors, subcontractors, etc. to your network. You will get the same company choices as you had in the Colleague pull-down menu.

- **Friend**—If you choose this option you will be asked to enter their email address. If this is your friend, you know this, right?

- **Groups & Associations**—Choose this option only if you are members of the same LinkedIn Group. A pull-down menu indicating all of the Groups that you are a member of will conveniently appear for your selection. Associations you may be a member of, but are outside the sphere of LinkedIn, will not appear here.

- **Other**—A valid entry for a "none of the above" selection; however, you will once again be required to input an email address.

- **I don't know (Name)**—I have never selected this option, and I recommend you do not either. Why? If you use this option, you can attempt to send an invitation without knowing the other person's email address; however, take note of the warning that appears below the personal note box:

Important: only invite people you know well and who know you.

It is safe to say you know this person if one of the following applies:

- You have worked or gone to school together

- You are members of the same LinkedIn Group

- You are an acquaintance and know their email address

Inviting someone you say you "don't know" means you are going against my understanding of LinkedIn's official policy, which in its User Agreement states: "DON'T...invite people with whom you have no prior relationship to join your network." I hope you never use this as a selection in your invitation, as it is wise to follow the site's guidelines. They are there for a reason!

"What's the big deal?" you ask. In my opinion, LinkedIn strives to provide a network based on trusted relationships. **Inviting someone into your network that you "don't know" opens the door for a potential weakening of the entire network.** Remember, LinkedIn is not a Facebook or a MySpace.

I sense that LinkedIn's unspoken mission seems to be to provide a professional network where CEOs and other Executives can interface with others and build "trusting" relationships in a comfortable environment—without the fear of being spammed.

Once the spamming begins, people will turn away from LinkedIn. The fear is that people who are inviting other people they don't know are doing so solely for the purpose of building email lists and spamming. Regardless of how you decide to implement Windmill Networking throughout this book, always keep this important point in mind.

Now that you have specified the relationship you have with this individual, let's discuss the box you are given to enter a personal note. It is ironic for a professional social networking site that LinkedIn has labeled a personal message to include with your invitation as "optional" in parentheses.

I highly recommend you create a standard paragraph which you can cut-and-paste into the "Personal Note" section, customizing the note for each person. This paragraph should briefly describe who you are, what your LinkedIn Objective is, why you would like to connect, and why they should connect with you.

This text will become very important as you develop your Windmill Network, so be honest and genuine. Remember, this paragraph becomes part of your

LinkedIn Brand, so choose your words carefully. When writing this note, ask yourself the following questions:

WindMill WISDOM

- **How do I want to be perceived? (brand yourself)**
- **What am I trying to achieve? (your objective)**
- **What value does this person receive in accepting my invitation? (How can you offer Pay It Forward help?)**

This is all you need to know when sending an invitation. By this time you may have already started receiving a few "Invitation to Connect on LinkedIn" emails; YOU have entered the "being found" phase when people are conducting searches! Following the link to one of these invitations will show you exactly what someone will see when they receive your invitation.

As a recipient of an invitation, you will have the following options:

1) Accept - Once you press this button you are instantly connected. Feel free to accept if you feel comfortable allowing this person to be part of your network.

2) I don't know this user - If you press this, not only will you be rejecting the invitation, but the sender of the invitation will no longer be able to connect with you. Within the LinkedIn community this is referred to as an "IDK" for "I Don't Know"; pressing this button has serious implications for the sender. Detailed information will follow in later chapters, but, for now, I recommend that you NEVER press this button. Press the "Archive" button instead. Should you press this "IDK" button, be forewarned that the sender can find out that you did so.

3) Archive - By archiving the invitation, you are merely giving yourself time to connect with this person later, should you wish to do so. As your LinkedIn Objective changes, someone you may not want to connect to today may be seen in a different light down the road. Once you archive an invitation, you can always access it at a later date by selecting "Archived" under "Inbox" in the left-hand navigation bar and then choosing "Invitations" from the list that appears after pressing the arrow to the right of "Archived." It will be harmless for both you and the sender should you archive an invitation.

4) Reply - If you want to confirm this person's identity and learn more about their interest in connecting with you, feel free to ask them before connecting. This is an acceptable practice; I did this myself the first time I received an invitation from someone I did not know.

5) Flag as Spam - I have never pressed this button (and I hope no one has selected this for any of my invitations); however, if you feel you are being spammed by someone (I am not sure how an invitation would constitute that...) this is how you can easily report it to LinkedIn. Similar to the "IDK" response, unless you feel strongly that you are being spammed, it is probably not a good idea to respond with this choice. I define "spam" in the context of LinkedIn as being sent an email advertising something you did not ask for, and this mail was sent simply because you were connected with that person.

Being connected with someone does not give you the right to add them to a mailing list or send them an advertisement in which they might not be interested.

We will cover IDKs, invitation restrictions, and advice on how to manage invitations, in addition to some commentary on spam in future chapters, but this should give you a good understanding of how the invitation mechanism works. Now let's see who else on LinkedIn we may want to invite using the Advanced Search functionality.

Finding People to Connect With Using Advanced Search

You've created your LinkedIn Brand—who you are and how you want to be perceived. You have thought about your LinkedIn Objective—what you want to use LinkedIn to achieve.

You've developed your LinkedIn profile. You've sent out invitations to people you already know from your physical network. You may have received a few invitations as well by now, and you understand how the invitation mechanism works. Now what?

First, I recommend learning more about the LinkedIn search functionality, as this will be one of the key applications you will use to find additional people to whom you can connect. Furthermore, there may have been people you wanted to invite who may not have appeared in your address book as part of the "Add Connections" exercise. Similar to the classmates.com example, one of your objectives is to connect with people who you may have been out of contact with for a while.

If you are scoping this section in hopes that you will find a definitive manual of who you should connect to, you aren't going to find it here. Why? Because, like everything else in this book, who you should connect with depends on your objective and your LinkedIn Brand. No one can decide who to connect with except you.

That being said, let's look at how you can go about finding people on LinkedIn using the "People Advanced Search" functional. It is especially helpful to use this feature after some of your invitations generate connections. You will be notified that a connection has been made when your invitation has been accepted. These notifications can be turned off. We will cover this later in the "Controlling Your Email Notifications" section of Chapter 10: Customizing Your LinkedIn Experience.

With some connections under your belt, you will see how you are generating overlapping Windmill Networking grids of 2nd and 3rd degree connections.

These grids expand with every new connection! Below is an example of how four 1st degree connections could potentially become part of a 38-person network to which you have access!

Figure 3.3. Your Network of Overlapping Windmills

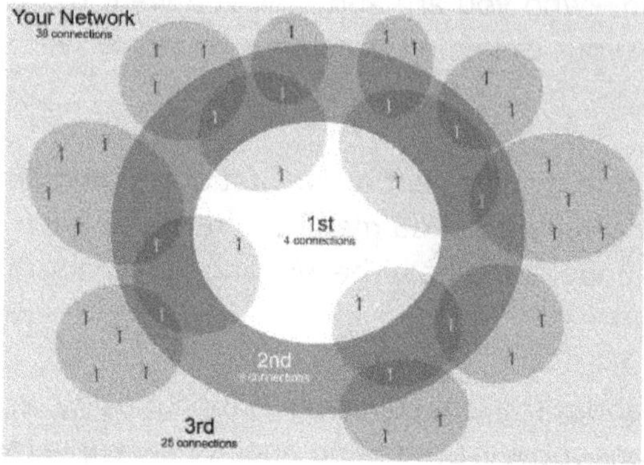

The "Advanced Search" functionality is the central functionality that makes LinkedIn's database usable. Not only does LinkedIn use the information you input in creating your personal profile to create a neatly organized database; the "Advanced Search" functionality allows you to search for people using various combinations of keywords and filters. LinkedIn also gives you options to sort and view your search results. Once you start using the search mechanism, you will begin to feel the awesome power that LinkedIn holds. Trust me, you will want to learn how to leverage it!

Figure 3.4. Utilizing Advanced Search to Find Other Windmills with Various Search Criteria

Various Search Criteria for Finding Other Windmills

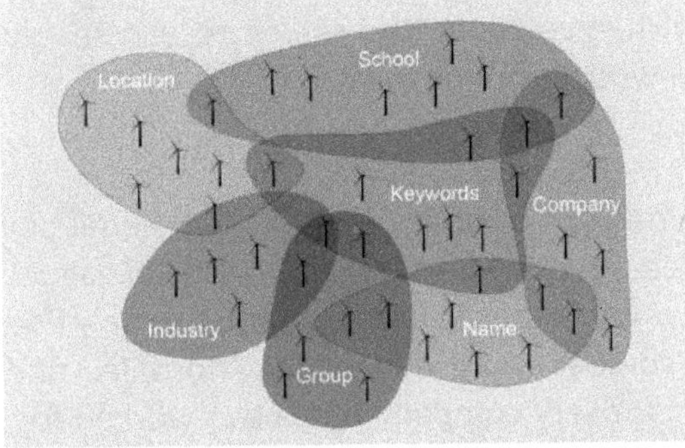

LinkedIn gives you the ability to search for an individual using any combination of the following criteria:

- **Keywords**

Just as you conduct a keyword search on Google when you are looking for someone, you can do the same on LinkedIn! This is especially useful if you are looking for someone with a common hobby or expertise, as the Search function will scour entire profiles looking for information. There are endless ways to find people, depending on your choice of keywords.

- **Location**

LinkedIn allows you to specify a location to find people by country or by postal code. Note that the postal code function does not work with every country, but it definitely works like a charm if you are searching for someone within the United States. Upon entering a valid postal code, you will see a new drop-down bar called "Within," which asks you to specify the number of miles outside the zip code from which you want to search for people. If you do not know a particular zip code of a city in which you want to search people, the United States Postal Service (USPS) website has a great search application (*http://zip4.usps.com*). More details on searching locally will be covered in the "One Virtual Networking Strategy: Going Local" section of Chapter 12: Growing Your Network.

- **Name**

If you know someone's name it will be easy to find them by entering their first and last name directly. You can also input their name as a keyword; however, you often get too many results to digest. I recommend entering their name in this area to conduct a more precise search. LinkedIn will often conveniently recommend alternative spellings of names above the search results should you misspell the name of the person you are trying to find.

- **Company & Title**

Under normal circumstances we enter our company name when we fill out our profile; as a result, we can easily view present and past colleagues associated with these companies. It is important to note that you can only find people by company if they put their company information in their profile. I find a lot of people have not done this for every company they have worked for; instead, they concentrate on filling out their profile for their most current jobs only. LinkedIn even gives you additional filters of "Current," "Past," and "Current & Past" to help you further pinpoint company & title information.

- **School**

This is the same concept as the "Company" search: assuming you entered this information in the Education section of our profile, you can now find people who attended the same institution as you. Once again, this functionality works best for those schools that are included in the drop-down list that appeared when filling out your Education profile. For schools that aren't included in that list, like foreign universities, it still works well. Sometimes putting the school name in the "Keyword" section is more productive. For example, I have yielded better results by putting my high school name in the "Keyword" section rather than in the "School" section. I suppose since LinkedIn is for professionals, people only go as far back in their profiles as they would on their resumes, which typically starts with college.

- **Industry**

Industry is defined as the field in which your current occupation lies. Popular industries on LinkedIn include "Staffing and Recruiting," "Information Technology and Services," and "Computer Software." At first glance, being able to find someone in the same industry as your own doesn't look like it may be helpful. After all, if you know their name, company name, or school name, why do such a broad search for people working in the same industry? **If you are trying to narrow down results and can pinpoint a probable industry in which you want to Windmill Network you will be putting this field to good use.**

- **Groups**

When you join LinkedIn, you have zero connections and do not belong to any Groups. There is a whole section of this book devoted to Groups, as they play an important role in implementing your LinkedIn Brand. Groups also help you engage in Windmill Networking. These are groups specific to LinkedIn, so regardless of what professional group you may be a member of, you will have to apply separately for its LinkedIn Group, if one exists. We will cover Groups in Chapter 6.

- **Interested In**

LinkedIn tries to make it easier for you to find certain demographics by splitting users into different groups such as "Industry Experts" or "Deal-Making Contacts." I believe this information comes from your "Using Your Network" preferences you entered when filling out your profile, which can be reviewed in "Account & Settings." I recommend you keep your results to "All Users" at all times and then find these demographics on your own based on your own search criteria. This way you can ensure your search results are not filtered.

- **Joined**

If you search on a regular basis using the same search criteria, it makes sense to have an option to only search for new LinkedIn members or those who have joined LinkedIn within the last three months. Unless you are doing so, I suggest you keep the default set at "At any time" for unfiltered results.

- **Network**

Why limit the results of your search to just your own network? The purpose of LinkedIn is to find people, right? Leave this box unchecked so you don't limit your search results.

- **Language**

Unless you speak multiple languages, or are targeting another language-speaking region, I would also keep this at the default with everything unchecked. I believe most profiles on LinkedIn are in English; however, LinkedIn recently introduced versions in French, German, and Spanish, and is working on gaining traction in other foreign markets. This could be an interesting feature for global marketers in the future.

There are two additional options remaining at the bottom left-hand side of the page: "Sort By" and "View."

"Sort By" determines how your results will be sorted. For free users of LinkedIn, your results will be limited to 100 people (used to be 500 people but I will stop complaining). The results will usually display 10 per page, so how the information is sorted may not seem important to you. But if you plan to utilize LinkedIn on a daily basis, how the information is sorted can make your day that much more efficient.

Let's take a closer look at the sort options:

- **Relevance**—I am not clear on which methodology is used here to determine "relevance"; therefore, I stay away from this.

- **Relationship**—Your 1st degree connections will show first, followed by your 2nd and 3rd degree connections. Next, people will appear who may not be connected to you, but belong to the same Group. This is noted by a "Group" message in the same bubble in which you usually see a "1," "2" or a "3." This is a good sort method to use; however, I prefer the following sort method:

- **Relationship + Recommendations**—This is the same as the Relationship sort method; however, the degrees of connection are displayed in descending order based on how many Recommendations they have received. A general rule I have: The more Recommendations that someone has received on LinkedIn, the heavier of a LinkedIn user they are. The more they used LinkedIn, the greater the chance they are already Windmill Networking. You can see why this is my preferred sorting method.

- **Keyword**—The assumption here is that you are looking for someone based on a certain keyword. It would make sense to use this sort method to list those results containing this keyword appearing the most at top.

If you are confused by these sort options, I recommend you simply stick to "Relationship + Recommendations," which is what I do 99% of the time.

Beyond choosing, filtering, and sorting the results, LinkedIn gives you a few options regarding how you would like to view these results:

- **Basic**—Shows you the Name, Degree of Connection, Profile Headline, Location, Industry, and Number of Shared Connections & Groups. The Basic format also includes "Actions," which are options that will appear when your cursor is positioned over a profile box. If you are connected to someone, you can directly recommend them or send them a message from here. If you are not directly connected yet you can send an InMail (which requires a paid account) or a message (if you are in the same Group and that person has opted to receive email from Group members), get introduced through a common connection, or directly send an invitation to connect. For most people this is sufficient.

- **Expanded**—Includes all of the above (including the Actions) as well as the Current and Past Title at a company they are currently working for or have in the past. You will want to use this view if you are interested in this information.

- **My Customized View**—You can choose what to include or not to include in this view. In addition to turning off any of the above, you can also show the number of Recommendations they have, names of Groups they are members of, and the number of connections they possess. You can easily get information overload here, so you may not want to use a customized setting until you are familiar with using LinkedIn.

- **Create a new view**—Used to create your customized view.

I believe that, for the most part, the Basic view will give you enough information, without giving you too much. You should also realize that the ability to customize this view, as well as the ability to display additional information, exists, should you find it necessary.

Furthermore, although I have never used it, LinkedIn gives you the ability to save the variables you entered in your search query for future use. Three search alerts are provided to each user. If you are constantly searching for the same type of person on a frequent basis, this functionality may be valuable to you.

I hope this gives you a good taste of how to find people and how to perform various actions straight from the search results. The Advanced Search received a major upgrade in late 2008, adding the "Actions" functionality as well as some other new features. It seems to me that LinkedIn understands the value in this Search application; I look forward to future modifications that will further increase this value to users.

Navigating Through Profiles

Now that you have created your own profile, and know how to search for other profiles, I want to advise you on what to look for in profiles you find via the "Advanced People Search."

When looking at someone's profile, the top, left-hand, and bottom navigation bars of your screen will remain the same. You will notice the center and right-hand portions of the screen will be filled with personal information about this contact. *You will be most interested in the right-hand side of the profile; this is where all of the actions, as well as relationship information, will be displayed.*

Let's start with the actions.

If you are already connected to this person, in the top right corner you have the following options:

1) "Send a message" - directly send a message through LinkedIn
2) "Recommend this person"
3) "Forward this profile to a connection"

If you are *not* connected, these options will change to:

1) "Send "InMail" (or "Send a message" if you are the member of the same Group and they have agreed to accept messages from other Group members)
2) "Get introduced through a connection" (note this may not appear if you are able to send a message)
3) "Add (name) to your network"
4) "Forward this profile to a connection"

There are also symbols that allow you to easily print, save in PDF, or (if you are connected) download the Vcard information for the person. Interestingly, although you cannot flag a profile, there is an option to flag the profile photo (if one exists) and inform LinkedIn if you think it is inappropriate.

Below this, what you see will be different depending on whether or not you are connected to that person. If you are directly connected and the person has chosen to display their network activities (in accordance with their "Member Feed Visibility" option that can be found in "Account & Settings"), under the Direct Ad you will notice a relatively new feature, which I call the "Activity Tab." Included here are all of the activities that would be broadcasted by this person to the "Network Updates" section of your Home Page. This includes information about their new connections, their status updates, Groups joined, Events that they have RSVPed to, and Recommendations they have received. If you are interested in a person's profile for a particular reason, this could be a potential treasure trove of information for you. For instance, this person may live near you and RSVPed for an Event or joined a Group that may also interest you.

Below the "Activity" tab, and once again assuming you are directly connected with this person, there is a "Private Information" module that appears, listing the personal email address of the contact. This area also provides a place to enter "notes" about that person. This means you could potentially use LinkedIn as a type of online Personal Information Management (PIM) application, although I believe you can't do much with the information in terms of printing and sorting.

I do know some Windmill Networkers who use the "notes" to write down more information about how they know their contacts, their contact history, and even notes about how they can help this person. This may make sense to do if you don't already have your own system of doing so. There is a way to export the notes information together with your connections' contact details. Using the "Export Connections" functionality by selecting "Contacts" from the left-hand navigation bar can do this.

Also, if you are connected to the user AND the user has opened up their connections list (see later chapter for more on this), both shared and non-shared connections will appear below this module. If you are an acquaintance of this person through school or work, navigating the connections may help you find other people to whom you should connect. If there are a high number of shared connections, you probably have a lot in common with this person; it *might* be safe to connect with this person should you wish to do so. This is a potential goldmine of contact information to utilize to expand your network. Sending a note that says, for example, "I notice that you were connected to

John. We went to school together." gives you common ground upon which to base a potential connection.

If you are *not* officially connected to the user, a box will display the degrees of separation between you. If you are interested in making an Introduction, you can start reviewing your options to see if your connection is strong enough to ask to be introduced. Regardless of whether or not you are connected, you will see further information such as:

- Groups to which you both belong
- That person's questions and answers (should they decide to include them on their profile)
- The latest Recommendations they have written
- Which profiles viewers of this profile also viewed

At the minimum, this will show how involved this person is with LinkedIn—if they are members of many Groups or if they are recommending a lot of people. The information about similar profiles viewed could be an interesting source of information for recruiters to find "similar" candidates, but the information listed isn't always on target, especially for users with a lot of connections.

The middle column of the profile lists all of the information about this person, just as you would have filled out yourself, so I won't go into further details here. That being said, the "Additional Information" section near the bottom will display websites this person lists as well as the Groups they are members of; this may give you additional information not only about them, but also about potential LinkedIn Groups you may want to join. In fact, before the LinkedIn Group Search was available, this was the only way to glean information regarding which Groups existed.

If you are thinking of connecting and Windmill Networking with someone, please make sure they indicate somewhere in their profile that they are an open networker/LION (usually found in their name or headline summary), a Windmill Networker, or that they explicitly indicate they are open to new

connections or being contacted in their Contact Settings. Being a member of certain open networking Groups also implies they will accept your invitation, though there is never any guarantee.

For more tips on growing your network in this fashion, please refer to Chapter 12: Growing Your Network. Unless you feel comfortable doing otherwise, I recommend you hold off on sending invitations to people you do not know until you have read through that chapter.

In addition to serving as your potential Personal Information Manager, LinkedIn can help you to gain targeted insight into any person who has a profile on LinkedIn. By looking for the information I have outlined, you will gain valuable insight that will help you Windmill Network with countless people and discover Groups you probably never knew existed.

My Top Five Tips to Write a Great Invitation

By following the exercises outlined in previous chapters, you will have already begun the initial stages of Windmill Networking by reaching out to potential connections. So how do you draft an invitation to someone that you have never met? You may want to hold off on sending an invitation to strangers until you really have time to read this book in its entirety and absorb all of the advice; however, once you are ready, take a deep breath, and use my tips for guidance:

- **State Why You Want to Connect at the Beginning.** Be direct at the beginning and state why you want to connect with this person. Did you used to work at the same company? Are you in the same industry? Do you live in the same area? Do you have the same hobbies? You can have many reasons to connect, but by far the best reason you can use to connect is that you are a Windmill Networker; if the other person is as well, both parties will understand this. This is also true for Open Networkers and members of other Groups that I discuss in further detail in Chapter 12: Growing Your Network. Regardless, state why you want to connect early on so the other party understands that you chose to invite them to your network for a particular reason. This will help them realize you are not just randomly inviting them.

- **Introduce Yourself.** Be genuine and let this person know you are real: The Personal Touch. Give your elevator pitch—just a few sentences will do. Letting this potential new connection know what your LinkedIn Objective is early on is important, as it gives them an idea of who you are and why you want to connect with them. Once again, if you are communicating with other Windmill Networkers, let them know you too are a Windmill Networker as part of your self-introduction.

- **Provide Value to Your New Connection.** If you have a blog or a Group that may provide value to this new connection, go ahead and introduce this information together with the appropriate URLs. If you are a true Windmill Networker, do as I have and offer to help your new connection should they ever need it. *Even if there is nothing to "Pay Forward," offering this in advance is the centerpiece of Windmill Networking.*

- **Always Brand Yourself.** Your invitation should reflect your brand. As with everything else you do on LinkedIn, make sure you are portraying yourself in the way you want to be seen.

- **Be Real.** Enough said. Never lie or try to stretch things. Be yourself, and your integrity will shrine through. This will give you credibility. I have included a real example of an invitation that I might send. Everyone's invitation will be different, but I hope you will see how this invitation supports my own LinkedIn Brand, as well as how it helps me achieve my own LinkedIn Objectives—all in a real and honest way:

Hello,

I am a fellow Windmill Networking Group member looking to connect with other open networking professionals, so I hope you'll accept my invitation to add you to my LinkedIn network for our mutual benefit.

I believe in Pay It Forward networking, so if there is anything I can do to help you out networking-wise, please do not hesitate to contact me. I am also a heavy user of both LinkedIn and Twitter andwish to contribute to your social networking success, so please feel free to review my blog (http://WindmillNetworking.com) or follow my tweets on Twitter (www.twitter.com/nealschaffer).

As for myself, I am looking for opportunities to educate companies and organizations on Wind mill Networking and utilizing social media for business. Should you know of any speaking engagements or consulting opportunities, please do not hesitate to contact me,

Thanks and make it a great day!

Managing Your Invitations

You are now on your way to searching for people to add to your network. You are sending invitations and replying to those invitations you have received. Invitations are a wonderful thing and are the key to actively growing your network.

Invitations become more valuable when you realize ***you are limited to 3,000 invitations***. That's right, invitations are not limitless, and if my memory is not mistaken, after you send your 2,000th invitation you will be reminded of how many invitations you have left. Until then you have no way of knowing. Don't get me wrong: 3,000 invitations is a lot to work with, but, because they are limited, they should be considered a precious resource. Tactics on dealing with the situation when you run out of invitations will be covered later in this chapter in "I'm Out of Invitations?!?! Help!"

Managing Your Invitations

With potentially hundreds or even thousands of invitations being sent out, it is wise to implement a system for managing these invitations as early as possible. I developed a system that you may find too tedious to emulate, but I hope you will review it to get a feel for some important concepts when it comes to keeping track of your invitations.

What happens if you don't keep track of your invitations? These are the potential situations you could encounter:

- **Double Invitation**—Let's say you used your address book file to send out a batch of invitations using the "Add Connections" feature. If you, for whatever reason, have the same name in another file that is used to "Add Connections," an invitation will be resent to that person and the old one will be replaced if that person has not yet accepted your previous invitation. In other words, you will have wasted one of your invitations. I estimate that I receive a double invitation for every 15 invitations sent to me on average.

- **Lack of Clarification on Certain Profiles**—There are certain profiles where the user has requested an email address be input before anyone can send them an invitation. If you have already sent someone an invitation and try to send them another one after accessing their profile, the same prompt screen requesting an email address will be shown. Have you sent this user an invitation before or is the user requesting that you enter their email address? You cannot know for sure unless you keep a record as to whether or not you sent this user an invitation in the first place!

I hope it is apparent to you that without a proper invitation management system, you could potentially waste a lot of invitations. As I said before, invitations are a precious resource and should not be wasted!

How do you keep track of your invitations? This is very easy. Create a Word, text, or Google document. Every time you send out an invitation, simply insert the name in alphabetical order into the document! If you get used to doing this you will find it becomes automatic and won't take too much of your time. If you do decide to pursue this route, I recommend you list the names in alphabetical order according to the ***first*** name. When you receive notification that your invitation was accepted, the first name will appear first; doing so will save you time when organizing. To complete the cycle, after they accept your invitation, simply delete that name off the list and consider sending a thank you message to your new connection. Remind them you are a Pay It Forward Windmill Networker and that you may be able to provide them with useful information. Furthermore, communicate any requests you have for them to help achieve your LinkedIn Objective.

The default invitation management system that LinkedIn provides, in comparison to what I recommend, can be found by navigating to the "Contacts" or "Connections" page on the left-hand navigation bar. You should see a "Showing x of x connections" line on the top left and "x outstanding sent invitations" [note: this is an important number to monitor in the future, especially if you run out of invitations] on the top right. Select the "x outstanding sent invitations" link, which can be done by pressing the area where it displays "sent invitations" (the link is indicated by these two words being underlined). The next screen will show you all of the invitations you have sent.

The problem is LinkedIn does not allow you to delete things; instead, you can only archive them, creating a growing mass of data that becomes harder and harder to manage. Moreover, within the sent invitations page, you cannot archive your sent invitations; you can only mark them as "read" or "unread." You can only see about 25 items per page, so it will take you a long time to confirm whether or not you sent someone an invitation. You will have to navigate through page after page looking for that name after sorting. There is a "Search Inbox" function, but for some reason, it only seemed to work for invitations received: A sample person to whom I sent an invitation did not appear in the search results. There is also the dreaded "We're sorry. The inbox is temporarily unavailable," message, which I have been seeing more frequently as of late.

The important information that LinkedIn ***does*** provide us here is the "Status" column, where you can see (in order when you press the "Status" wording to sort) invitations that were greeted with the following responses:

- Accepted
- Doesn't Know
- Sent
- Withdrawn

Those invitations that are marked as "Sent" are still pending; you could use this information to create a separate database. Most importantly, you can now see who responded to your invitations with an "I Don't Know." I will explain the importance of the "I Don't Know" response in the following section of this chapter.

As for managing your sent invitations, if you open up each one, LinkedIn provides you with a way to either withdraw or resend the invitation. It may make sense to withdraw or to resend an invitation that has been pending for a long time. Furthermore, in the past, the resend option did not exist; upon sending an invitation for a second time, it would count against your 3,000-invitation quota. I just resent an invitation: After I entered the email address, LinkedIn allowed me to resend an invitation, despite the fact that I am out of invitations. Perhaps this is a concession that LinkedIn has made: As long as you know the email address of the invitee, resending an invitation will not count against your invitation quota.

As for the withdraw option, one rule of thumb to remember: If they haven't responded to your invitation within 30 days, resend it—assuming you know their email address. If they don't respond 30 days after, I advise you to push the "withdraw" button. I believe that LinkedIn Customer Service recognizes that if you diligently withdraw invitations, your success rate in terms of who accepts your invitations will increase. I say this because I contacted LinkedIn during the summer of 2008, asking if I could get sent but unanswered invitations back. Their response was "No." However, I was told, by withdrawing these invitations, the chance of others replying to my invitation with an "IDK" would decrease.

At this point it is critical you understand what it means if you get a few "IDKs" and why you need to be careful to whom you send your invitations.

The Dreaded "IDK"

As noted before, when you invite someone or receive an invitation, the recipient has a choice to do the following:

- **Accept the invitation**
- **Say they don't know the person who invited them ("IDK")**
- **Report the invitation as spam**
- **Reply to the sender**
- **Archive the invitation without performing any direct action**

If the invitation is accepted, the two of you become immediately connected. If the invitation is archived, you can always accept the invitation at a later date. If you report as spam, I would venture to say the invitee would not be permitted to use LinkedIn for long.

The "I Don't Know" response (hereafter referred to as "IDK" for short) *seems* to be an innocent way of letting the invitee know you only want to accept known people in your network. However, LinkedIn does not look favorably upon these responses. According to the LinkedIn User Agreement:

"The purpose of LinkedIn is to provide a service to facilitate professional networking among Users throughout the world. It is intended that Users only connect to other Users who they currently know and seek to further develop a professional relationship with those Users."

In other words, LinkedIn was originally created to connect people who already know each other, not for Windmill Networking.

In my opinion, it appears LinkedIn has accepted the type of open networking that is inherent to Windmill Networking, so long as it does not involve spamming others. This is evident in that it allows tens of thousands of people like us, and open networking Groups, to interactively use the site to connect with each other.

You should be forewarned that, although LinkedIn has apparently not officially implemented this policy of only allowing people to connect with people they personally know, its User Agreement does clearly state:

"Any other use of LinkedIn (such as seeking to connect to someone a User does not know or to use LinkedIn as a means of generating revenue through the sale of contacts or information to others) is strictly prohibited and is a violation of this Agreement."

On the other hand, LinkedIn states:

"LinkedIn encourages all users to connect to their trusted professional contacts, and to welcome other connections with new contacts."

I interpret Windmill Networking to be one such form of welcoming "other connections with new contacts."

Returning to the IDK topic: If you receive five cumulative IDKs, you will need to enter an email address for every invitation you send thereafter. This means if you find an old colleague on LinkedIn and want to connect—but don't know their most recent email address—you will be unable to connect.

I personally have never responded with an IDK, and I *recommend* that you don't either. I have received my share of them, even from self-professed LinkedIn Open Networkers ("LIONs," details to be covered in Chapter 11) and members of Groups for open networkers. I believe it is an unwritten but understood rule that LIONs should never respond with an IDK, but should instead merely archive any invitation with whom they do not want to connect. You never know when you may want to connect with that contact if you move to a new place or a new industry, so why not just archive it and keep the potential for connecting open?

When you reach out to people who are not open networkers, you really are inviting them at your own risk. Some people make a point of sending an email beforehand requesting to connect. Although this is a realistic approach, it is very difficult to execute if you want to build a large virtual network quickly.

On the other hand, if you do not want to receive invitations, I highly recommend you state so in your profile and/or contact details. Without this precaution, you can assume you will receive invitations. If you receive them, please do not punish the sender; merely archive them if you do not want to connect.

You will know when you start receiving a few "IDKs" when you try to invite someone new. A text box will appear at the top of the invitation screen telling you:

"Several recipients of your invitations indicated they don't know you. If enough recipients indicate they don't know you, then you will be required to enter an email address on this page in the future."

Once you receive the 5th IDK, the invitation mechanism is locked and you must either enter the email address of each recipient or contact Customer Service, letting them know you understand the policy they have implemented. To put it in LinkedIn's words: "*This safeguard is in place to protect users from receiving invitations from people they don't know.*"

I have contacted Customer Service on multiple occasions concerning this; each time they have lifted the restriction for me. Contacting Customer Service is easy. Simply press the "Contact Customer Service" link at the bottom navigation bar from your Home Page, press the "Ask Customer Service" tab, and enter the relevant information. Each time I have indicated I am sorry for what I did, repeating that I understand the policy, and telling them I will strive to abide by this, which I have. The important thing is to:

1) Follow the instructions that Customer Service indicates

2) Treat Customer Service with respect

3) Genuinely make an effort to do your best to be more careful in the future when sending out invitations

I always try to contact the people who sent me the IDK in an attempt to resolve the situation diplomatically and help them understand the consequences of their actions. Often they were cooperative and invited me to their network. In my opinion, this potentially nulls the IDK in the eyes of Customer Service, although there is obviously no guarantee. I recommend you follow up with these people at the very least to prevent them from sending IDKs to other people. It is your responsibility to do so as a Windmill Networker.

One final thing I would like to point out regarding the IDK: According to a correspondence that I had with LinkedIn while proofreading this book, the IDK is a choice that LinkedIn provides to its members to make their own personal choice regarding the receipt of an invitation to connect. With that in mind, I cannot tell you *not* to respond with an IDK if you choose to do so—it is your personal freedom and I would be going against the LinkedIn User Agreement if I instructed your otherwise. As an advocate for LinkedIn it is important that I mention this. However, as a LinkedIn user, it is equally important that you understand the significance of the IDK and the potential consequences it has should you be on the sending or receiving end of one.

I'm Out of Invitations?!?! Help!

LinkedIn presently offers you 3,000 invitations to build your network. That is a lot of people to invite! You may not end up using more than 100, or you may burn through 3,000 quickly, depending on the LinkedIn Objective you create. But, like other restrictions on LinkedIn I have encountered, it always feels like you are never given advance notice until it is too late. So there it is—3,000 invitations is the limit!

I know this from experience: After I sent out invitation number 2,000, I received this odd message at the top of the screen every time I wanted to invite someone. The message said I only had 1,000 invitations left! What? Are you kidding me?

WindMill WISDOM

Knowing your invitation limit early in your LinkedIn life will help you understand that invitations are precious assets, not endless resources.

I burned through my remaining invitations, sticking to my objective of building out a targeted virtual network—suddenly I was out of invitations! If this happens to you, the following message box from LinkedIn will appear:

"LinkedIn initially allows all users to send up to 3,000 invitations. This limit is an automatic method to prevent accidental abuse and protect both senders and recipients. The limit is in place only to prevent abuse, not to block invitations sent by careful inviters. LinkedIn encourages all users to connect to their trusted professional contacts, and to welcome other connections with new contacts. Users who limit their invitations to these two groups have high invitation acceptance rates and LinkedIn will usually raise the limit for such inviters. If you have encountered the limit, you can contact Customer Service to find out more about how the limit works, and how it can be raised."

I did exactly what the dialogue box told me to do: I contacted LinkedIn Customer Service. There was no reason to be shy about it as I was out of invitations; in order to get more invitations, I needed to speak to them. In my previous dealings with LinkedIn Customer Service, I found them to be polite, professional, and quick in responding to me. They had been fair to me when dealing with the 5 IDK situations, so why not expect the same for invitations, right? When I communicate with them, I go out of my way to be polite and treat them with respect. Well, I was told, that every 30 days they monitor the invitation situation; if a great number of my invitations turned out to be accepted by the other person ("high invitation acceptance rate"), they would consider granting me more invitations.

So I marked my calendar 30 days out and played the waiting game. 30 days passed, so I sent a reminder email. I believe within 48 hours of that email they granted me 500 invitations, further explaining that every 30 days they would evaluate my invitation status and grant additional invitations as they see fit.

What did I take away from this? After you reach a certain point—i.e. you have sent out 3,000 invitations—you need to be even more careful and do additional research before sending out new invitations. I do so and estimate that my acceptance rate for sent invitations is about 80%. If enough people don't accept your invitations, LinkedIn may be inclined to never grant you additional invitations. I have been able to receive additional invitations several times, but there is nothing stopping LinkedIn from continuing to give them to me.

LinkedIn does not guarantee they will grant you new invitations, so make sure that you get enough mileage out of your first 3,000 to safely achieve your objective. If you are granted additional invitations, be thankful and continue to exercise caution when sending out new invitations.

Dealing with Spam? On LinkedIn?

Does spam exist on LinkedIn if you are building out a large virtual network? Well, yes and no. LinkedIn is extremely sensitive about controlling spam. The goal is to make LinkedIn a comfortable place for professionals and executives to operate; I am estimating that anyone who appears to inhibit this mission is not permitted to use the site.

LinkedIn gives you the ability to report spam, either through its abuse@linkedin.com email or, in the case of receiving an InMail, you will see the option on the bottom right after opening the email. But the spam that happens on LinkedIn often occurs *outside* the network.

People obtain your email address through LinkedIn when you connect with them. In the past, Group Managers could also obtain your email address when you joined their Group, but LinkedIn has recently put an end to this. On the other hand, Group Managers can "spam" you by directly sending out an Announcement to all Group members.

If you define spam to be "unsolicited" mail, you will definitely receive some spam on LinkedIn. Spam seems to be on the rise as more and more marketers target the lucrative LinkedIn demographic. The more connections you have, the more spam you will most likely receive.

Remember, this is social networking in a Web 2.0 world where the communications are "looser." Over time, many people with whom you may have never physically met could become members of your network and attempt to spam you.

Some of this unsolicited mail may interest you, like an invitation to a LinkedIn Group that aligns with your objective; however, there will be other mail you will want to delete right off the bat. How do you deal with this?

In the "Accounts & Settings" section, you have the option to control which emails you want to receive within the LinkedIn environment. I have devoted the "Controlling Your Email Notifications" section in Chapter 10: Customizing Your LinkedIn Experience to this subject, as your Inbox could soon start getting flooded with all sorts of mail.

If I am subscribed to a newsletter without my permission (you may find yourself in this situation down the road) I immediately unsubscribe from it. Even those people who want to utilize your contact to sell you something are usually using "Constant Contact" or another enterprise email account program that makes it easy to unsubscribe with one push of the button, no questions asked ("Safe Unsubscribe"). If you are angered by this and feel the email was completely irrelevant to you, there is a mechanism where you can report spam after you unsubscribe. Go ahead and report that the mailing was spam if it makes you feel better. The sender *will* be penalized.

In closing, please remember the people who "spam" you make up only a small portion of the entire LinkedIn population; don't let them ruin it for you or for all of the other great networkers on LinkedIn! I believe that LinkedIn, as shown by its recent limitation of providing email addresses to Group Managers, is also seriously addressing this spam issue. You can help LinkedIn by reporting potential abuse to abuse@linkedin.com.

The Disconnecting Option

On the subject of spam, it is important to point out you do have the right to disconnect from anyone should you see fit at anytime. A lot of people forget about this fact; knowing this should give you some sense of security when tapping into the virtual grid.

Disconnecting is as easy as going to the "Connections" screen, pressing "Remove Connections" at the top right-hand side, and then choosing and confirming with whom you want to disconnect.

The beauty of disconnecting:

- Your connection will *not* be informed that you disconnected with them.
- Should your disconnected connection wish to invite you again, they will get an error message saying something to the effect that "This user cannot be invited at this time."
- If they contact you directly about this, be prepared to explain why you disconnected with them. I have been in the same situation in the past so you will have to explain in your own words.
- You can re-invite the person you disconnected with, in which case the connection will be fully restored.

The ability to disconnect should give you the confidence that for whatever reason, if you want to disconnect with someone, the option is available and easy to use.

On a final note, I engaged in a Twitter chat with someone who wanted to stop someone from repeatedly sending him invitations. If you accept the invitation and then immediately disconnect from that user, they will be blocked from inviting you in the future. Although this sounds unprofessional, it is a realistic workaround until LinkedIn institutes a "Block This User" type of functionality upon receiving an invitation.

Emailing Your Connections: What You Need to Know

LinkedIn, in addition to allowing you to connect to people, gives you the ability to communicate with your connections through the LinkedIn Inbox email message system. Before you invest too much time into making this the centerpiece of your communication strategy, you should understand your options, along with the pros and cons of each.

You can email a connection within LinkedIn at the very top right-hand corner of each profile page where it says "Send a Message," or follow the same shortcut from search results to directly send them a message from your Inbox. One thing you should note is, if that recipient does not receive an email copy of that message, they may not read this until the next time they log on to LinkedIn. In other words, LinkedIn Inbox messages are not necessarily being received in real-time. This is a potential problem when communicating this way. With this in mind, you should first of all make sure that *you* are receiving these messages. To do so, go to your Account & Settings > Email Notifications > Receiving Messages and ensure that you check "Individual Email" for every type of message that you want forwarded to your personal email account. As long as you do this, any LinkedIn Inbox message sent to you will appear as an email in your personal email address account in addition to your LinkedIn Inbox, where you can archive it.

In general, within LinkedIn, you have no choice but to utilize this system to communicate with your fellow connections. There is no chat functionality like you have on Facebook. Remember that every social networking site has its own unique atmosphere and functionalities.

One benefit of the LinkedIn Inbox message system is that after creating a message, you can add up to 50 connections to the same message by typing in their names. LinkedIn will automatically populate the rest of the name, giving you a selection of connections to whom you can decide to send the same letter. It is similar to the auto-fill functionality you may have in your Internet browser when you type in a URL that auto-completes it from your history.

There is an easy way to circumvent the LinkedIn message system all together, which you may want to consider when developing your LinkedIn communication habits. You should notice that once you are connected to someone, their email address will be populated in the "Your Private Info About" module, which appears on the right-hand side of their profile page under the DirectAd advertisement. You can simply copy and paste that and send that connection an email from your own personal account.

Better yet, go to your "Connections" page, located in the left-hand navigation bar under "Contacts;" then go to the bottom of the page where it says "Export Connections." Press that, create a file, and then import it into your favorite contact management software such as Outlook or Goldmine. Then you can email all of your LinkedIn connections with the flexibility you are accustomed to when using your own personal email client or web service.

You will realize the benefit of communicating through your own personal email client when you start receiving the various LinkedIn Inbox messages. Every time you receive a message in your Inbox and want to reply to it, you will not be able to do so directly from your personal email account. You will need to press "Reply to this message" and then be forwarded to the Inbox page in LinkedIn. There is always a few second pause here. After you send your email you will notice an additional few second pause. As you ramp up your Windmill Networking and you want to make your communications more efficient, you will feel a time lag every time you have to access the LinkedIn system in order to send a simple email to your LinkedIn connection.

My Windmill Networking advice: connect on LinkedIn, but communicate OFF of the LinkedIn platform. It is tedious searching through your Inbox; it will be a nightmare searching for sent messages when compared to the robust search functionality available in email programs such as Gmail. Do yourself a favor by recognizing this early. Create your own system to communicate with your LinkedIn connections via your own personal email account.

How Do I Contact 2nd and 3rd Degree Connections?

At this point you should have a good feel for inviting connections and then communicating with them. But what if you do a search and you want to contact someone without necessarily connecting with them? Or you want to send an email to a 2nd or 3rd degree connection?

If you have something you want to tell everyone, or something you want to sell, it makes sense for you to go beyond your first level connections to the millions of people that are in your 2nd and 3rd degree connections. For example, with 17,000+ direct connections, the number of connections within my third degree network is 19+ million; you can check your own at "Network Statistics" located under "Contacts" on the left-hand navigation bar. But how do you contact them directly all at once in an efficient manner?

Unfortunately, this cannot be done. I believe that LinkedIn intended it to be that way to limit what they see as potential spamming.

As I mentioned in the previous chapter, you can download the contact information for your 1st degree connections in the "Connections" window and then contact all of them at once.

If you happen to be a Group Manager, you can send out an "Announcement" to contact all Group members at once, assuming they elected to receive such notifications when they joined the Group. This communication cannot be done with your email program and can only be done through the LinkedIn Inbox infrastructure.

Other than that, the only way to contact 2nd and 3rd degree connections is in the following situations:

1) You can send an InMail. You need a paid account to do this, although I have found that sometimes it is possible to send an email for free if they are a paying member and "OpenLink" enabled. I have also heard it may be possible to send an InMail for the cost of an Introduction, but I have yet to confirm this.

2) If you are in one of the same Group as they are AND they have allowed Group members to message them, you will be able to send them a message.

This will be a critical strategy in Windmill Networking. If you want to contact someone and are not connected, join a Group they are a member of and try to send them a message.

3) You can find their email address if they have listed it on their profile.

Unfortunately, each of these methods must be done on a one-by-one email basis. Although sending messages to other Group members utilizes the same Inbox functionality, when you try to add more people to the same message, only your 1st degree connections will be auto-populated.

The only other way to advertise what you are doing without this ability to send a mass email is:

- **Putting it on your profile**
- **Using an Application to embed in your profile**
- **Asking questions about it in the Q&A**
- **Conducting a Poll on it**
- **Starting a Group**
- **Placing messages on Group Discussion Boards**

I realize there are no quick fix solutions here, but part of the challenge (and fun!) of working within the LinkedIn Platform is to find creative ways around the barriers. Remember—LinkedIn is the leading social network for professionals. As a result, I am guessing additional measures will be taken to prevent potentially "unnecessary" communication in the future.

Chapter 4

Chapter 4 Introductions

- The Importance of Introductions
- Advice on Utilizing Introductions
- Warning: Your Precious Introductions May Be Stuck
- Before Sending the Introduction, Forward the Profile!

The Importance of Introductions

It is appropriate that we begin this chapter after discussing how to contact 2nd and 3rd degree connections in the previous chapter.

Introductions give you the ability to directly communicate with someone you are not connected with and who does not belong to any of the same Groups as you. Because LinkedIn is a network for professionals, LinkedIn created a system of allowing you to utilize your trusted 1st degree connections to introduce you to 2nd or even 3rd degree connections.

This is the ultimate networking ability: Asking another windmill that you are connected with to refer you to a third windmill that they are connected with for a particular purpose.

In the old days, you would ask someone, "Do you know a good [insert your profession here] with a specialty in [insert your specialty here] to whom you could introduce?" Now, through using Advanced People Search, you can pinpoint the person that you would like to contact AND see how you are connected to that person so that you can tell your contact who you would like them to connect you with. Networking doesn't get any easier than this!

LinkedIn also realizes the Introduction is a precious asset and thus only provides free users 5 Introductions at a time to use. Should you become a paid member, this number increases depending on your level. With only 5 Introductions to use at a time, you need to be careful with how you use them. Be sure to only use them as a last resort to connect with someone that is extremely helpful in achieving your objective. In other words, don't waste this precious resource.

Both the concept, as well as the execution of Introductions is simple. First, find someone outside of your network with whom you would like to communicate. Remember, we are not discussing "connecting" with someone here but merely opening a direct line of communication with them. From there, you both can decide if you really want to connect with each other or not.

Think of an Introduction as a way to temporarily use your Windmill Networking grid to reach someone.

Usually you will find this person through an advanced search. If this is the case, you can request an Introduction directly from the search results screen when you navigate to the person and see the "Get introduced" text on the top right hand of the search result box. If you have already navigated to your contact's Profile Page, you will see the "Get introduced through a connection" text on the top right-hand side of the profile. Either selection will lead you to the same page.

As shown in the image on the next page, there are three different methods to request an Introduction. If you are only commonly connected through one person, that person will be your intermediary. If you have more than one common connection with this person, you will be able to choose which person you wish to make the introduction. Unfortunately, if you are requesting to connect with someone who is a 3rd degree connection, you cannot choose which of their 2nd degree connections they request.

Figure 4.1. Comparing the Scenarios for Introductions

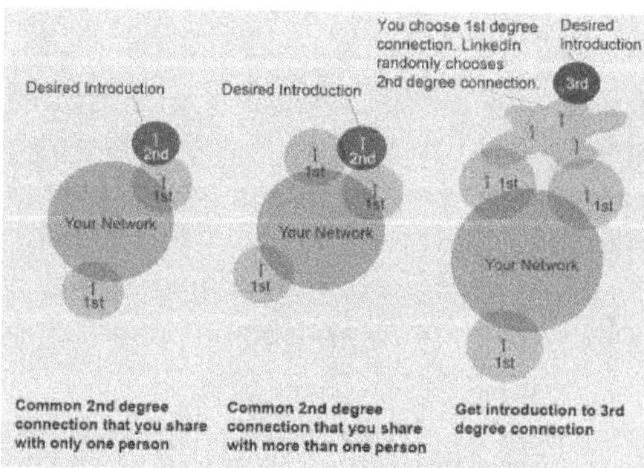

The differences between these three methods of asking for Introductions is significant enough that I will provide some helpful advice in upcoming parts of this chapter.

Once you have chosen your method of being introduced, you will go to the main screen where you will try to write a convincing reason why you want to do the following:

1. **Why you want to be introduced to that person.**

2. **Why you want your connection to make the Introduction for you.**

There is a distinct difference between the two messages: The top part of this screen is intended for the final recipient, and the section at the bottom provides a brief note for the common connection from whom you are requesting to make the Introduction.

The only other preference to set here is whether or not you want to include your contact information, which I highly recommend. The final recipient will probably at least read your introduction, assuming they are able to receive it (I will cover how to confirm this later on this chapter). The selection of a Category is probably not that important, but you should map the Category to match any particular categories from which they are interested in receiving contacts. This information is conveniently pulled from the Contact Settings of the person you want to communicate with and is displayed in the "Person is interested in" section just to the right of the text box where you will be typing your message. For example, if the person you want to be introduced to indicates in their Contact Settings that they are interested in "new ventures" or "career opportunities," it is safe to choose the corresponding category in the drop-down list for "Category."

Advice on Utilizing Introductions

You can see how Introductions allow you to easily cut through various degrees of LinkedIn connections and directly communicate with a desired person. This person should have strategic value because you are only granted 5 Introductions to play with at a time.

With this in mind, you need to be careful from whom you request Introductions. Are they someone who would openly accept an Introduction from a trusted colleague (i.e. your connection)? Sometimes just by looking at their profile you can tell. Clues that the recipient may not be open to Introductions:

- Few categories for which they are interested in receiving contacts in their "Contact Settings"
- Incomplete profile
- Few LinkedIn Group memberships

In such cases, you may want to spare yourself the pain of potentially wasting an Introduction request. These are clues that the recipient may not be on the same wavelength with you in terms of realizing the value of the Introduction. Note there are some people who openly refuse to accept Introductions; this will be noted in their Contact Settings. **Remember, not everyone on LinkedIn has the same attitude as a Pay It Forward Windmill Networker!**

The next thing to be careful of is how you word your Introduction request to both the final recipient and to your connection. I already mentioned mapping the Category of the Introduction with the "Interested In" section of the final recipient's Contact Settings. The next thing is the Subject. Think of yourself as someone who receives hundreds of emails a day and deletes a majority of them. Create a Subject title that is both genuine in what you want to achieve through the Introduction and *offers mutual value to the recipient*. You want the subject to be something catchy enough to ensure they don't delete your message without reading it. **One thing I recommend is including the person's name who is introducing you in the Subject.** This adds a certain degree of familiarity and credibility to your request. If an email you received had someone's name in it that you recognized, chances are you would be more hesitant to delete it without reading it.

Your message to the final recipient should be clear. People don't have time to try to figure out what you are saying, so make sure your writing is concise and to the point. Be sure your message to them is both relevant to who they are and presents some sort of potential benefit to them. As part of this strategy, you want to include why you are contacting them. You also must communicate a reason they should reply. Perhaps you can identify an area of expertise or an experience that may be interesting to them. This isn't always necessary; however, the more well thought out your Introduction request is, the higher probability it will be met with a kind response.

What about your note to your connection who is making the Introduction? Although most people place no importance on this, it is just as important as your message to the person with whom you want to get in touch! Why? Because that person holds the fate of your Introduction in their hands. Should they not wish to pass on the Introduction, it will be stuck (see next chapter for details on dealing with this). If the person introducing you is a good friend or close contact, there shouldn't be any problems. However, as your virtual network grows, you may begin to feel some of your connections are more trustworthy than others. Therefore, always take time to go with the most reliable connection you have—go with the person who you are confident will forward the Introduction response on your behalf. At the same time, give your connection a good reason to do so! **Remember, your connection is putting their reputation on the line when they send out an Introduction request, so give them enough information to prove why it is worth their time. Ask yourself, "what's in it for them?"—then tell them!**

The last thing you need to consider is whether you even request an Introduction to a 3rd degree connection. The simple reason for this: When requesting an Introduction to a 3rd degree connection, your chances of being connected decrease from 3-to-1 to 4-to-1. Not only should you make sure your messages to the final recipient and to your connection are crisp, but you also have to hope your connection will be thoughtful in how they pass on this

Introduction request to their connection. You definitely lose control here, but sometimes if the 3rd degree connection is that strategic for you, it can be worth the risk.

Getting introduced via a reputable connection is always going to be the best and most trusted method of communicating with someone new—whether it be on LinkedIn or in any other social networking situation.

A way of getting around Introductions altogether, in the case of a 3rd degree connection (or even a 2nd degree connection), is to try to join a similar Group to which the desired connection belongs. It does no harm to see whether or not this person is accepting mail directly from Group members.

If you are lucky, the contact you want to get in touch with lists his or her private email address and/or phone number in the contact settings section of their User Profile. Unfortunately, listing this personal contact information is rare and goes against the LinkedIn User Agreement (despite the fact that many people do display this information by simply entering it somewhere in their profile). This proves the inherent value of Introductions and why it is in your best interest to use them strategically. It is equally important to remember to monitor how you use them.

Warning: Your Precious Introductions May Be Stuck

Since Introductions are so precious, it makes sense to monitor both how many you have left as well as the current status of pending Introductions. You can see how many Introductions you have left by selecting “Account & Settings”; the number will then prominently appear in the top portion of the screen. The rule for free members is you can have only five outstanding or pending Introductions at any time. So what happens if these Introductions do not get forwarded? Have you checked on the status of your Introductions lately?

LinkedIn provides a tool to check on the status of your Introductions; however, it is not easy to use. Since you sent an Introduction to begin the process, you can access these sent invitations by selecting “Sent” under “Inbox.” The problem is that Introductions you have sent will be displayed here, along with Introductions you have forwarded on behalf of others. This section also displays Introductions for which you were the final intended recipient. Basically, there is no way to see only your outstanding or pending Introductions; they are mixed in with the various kinds available on LinkedIn.

The only way to sort through this is to utilize the “Status” sort. You must then look for those Introductions marked “In Progress.” Any Introductions I sent or was the final recipient of will have the subject start with a “RE:” while those that were forwarded will start with a “FW:” Opening up each of those “In Progress” status Introductions with a Subject beginning with “RE:” will show you your pending Introductions and who is potentially delaying them.

In my case, there seems to be a bug preventing this functionality from working: the numbers on my Introductions don’t add up. Furthermore, for some Introductions that say “In Progress,” there is no green dot showing who is holding up the Introduction. There are also some Introductions where, even though the Status shows “In Progress,” I can view the original Introduction—and these show they were Accepted! I have heard of others who have had to contact Customer Service to have this cleared up, so if the information displayed in this section looks fishy, I recommend you do the same. In fact, one person mentioned to me that emails she had sent to Group members who she was not connected to, were actually counted by LinkedIn as Introductions, despite the fact that she thought she was innocently sending them a free message! Confusing indeed, so it is best to actively monitor and intervene when necessary to make sure you are getting the full benefit of this limited resource.

LinkedIn users have the ability to withdraw an Introduction if it is "In Progress." This button should show up when viewing the original Introduction you sent. You may want to use it if your Introduction has gone AWOL and is still "In Progress" after a week or two: If someone is not looking at their LinkedIn mail within that timeframe, chances are the fate of your Introduction is not going to be a good one.

Before Sending the Introduction, Forward the Profile!

Because of the lack of user control over delivery, and other inherent limitations and inherent risks, you may want to rethink your approach for utilizing Introductions. The Introductions functionality is a formalized way of asking someone for an Introduction. You can bypass the entire limitation of five Introductions by merely doing the following *if the person you want to be introduced to is a 2nd degree connection*:

1. When you find the profile of someone you want to be introduced to, select "Forward this profile" in the top right-hand corner of that person's profile. You can forward a profile whether you are connected to that person or not.

2. Send a message (which will automatically be launched) to the person that connects the two of you. Ask for an Introduction to that person via email, and copy yourself on the request.

3. In order to increase the chances of that person accepting your Introduction, and to make it easy for your connection to make the Introduction soon, communicate how you would like to be introduced. Be sure to answer the following questions: What is the purpose? What is the value in that person accepting your Introduction?

The same logic can be applied to requesting an Introduction to a 3rd degree connection, but you will have to trust your 1st degree connection's judgment as to whom they should use to forward the request.

Note that regardless if you use the LinkedIn Introduction functionality or bypass it completely, your chances of success are the same. I only recommend this as a workaround should your Introductions be stuck in Neverland.

Chapter 5

Chapter 5 Recommendations

- The Importance of Recommendations
- How to Write a LinkedIn Recommendation
- Asking for a Recommendation & Other Recommendations Etiquette
- Are LinkedIn Recommendations Legit?

The Importance of Recommendations

LinkedIn is unique in the world of social networking because it caters to the professional demographic. Just as you ask for recommendations from professionals in the working world or references for your resume, there is a "Recommendation" feature that will add value to your profile, making you stand out as someone who is "real."

Recommendations on LinkedIn are written references from former colleagues, service providers, business partners, or classmates who recommend you.

Regardless of your LinkedIn Brand or Objective, it is in your best interest to get the most Recommendations from the highest value people in order to strengthen your social credibility.

One danger social media presents is the potential existence of fake profiles. Recommendations are your chance to show that you are for real and are valued by others. **The reason why you are valuable, as indicated in each Recommendation, adds value to your brand.**

If you are new to LinkedIn or don't have many Recommendations, one way to ask for a Recommendation from someone is to write one for them. You may feel awkward writing a Recommendation for a former boss or a business partner, but if they are serious about building their brand on LinkedIn, they will be overjoyed upon hearing this gesture! Every Recommendation strengthens the image they want to convey online. Don't worry if you're unsure as to how they will take your Recommendation; be real and genuine. They always have the option of getting back to you if they want you to change your wording or angle for whatever reason.

Recommendations are not just for the value of the person receiving the Recommendation. Those who write Recommendations can always display

those Recommendations on their profile. If they are written well, it will add to YOUR credibility, thus strengthening your LinkedIn Brand.

Just as you ask for references from employers before leaving them or ask former bosses to speak with a potential new employer, ask these same people to write you a LinkedIn Recommendation as well. **As with references, it is always easiest to ask for this *before* your last day, while your memory (and achievements!) are fresh in your colleagues' minds.** This Recommendation will then be a permanent part of your record. You can actually tell recruiters to look at the Recommendations in your LinkedIn Profile as an indication of the caliber of your work. Recommendations are that important! Recruiters and others will look at your Recommendations, so make sure the wording matches and supports your LinkedIn Brand and professional experience.

You have full control over displaying both given and received Recommendations on your profile. This functionality is conveniently accessible through the "Recommendations" text in the left-hand navigation bar under the "Profile" section. Here you will find links to all of the Recommendations you receive at the bottom of each of your work profiles, and the entire text of the Recommendations will show up immediately after your "Education" section. Essentially, Recommendations you receive will be prominently featured in your profile. Even the Recommendations that you give, should you wish to display them, will appear on the right-hand navigation section of your profile.

I hope I have given you enough reason to realize the importance of Recommendations. There are more fundamental reasons that you need to concentrate on building up this part of your profile. Specifically, as I mentioned in the Advanced Search functionality for People, there are four different sorting methods to display the results when searching for people:

1. Relevance

2. Relationship

3. Relationship + Recommendations

4. Keyword

As previously mentioned, I personally prefer and recommend searching by "Relationship + Recommendation," as this will display those with higher numbers of Recommendations before those with lower numbers. What does this mean for you?

WindMill WISDOM

The more Recommendations you have, the higher you will appear on Search results when someone uses this sort method, which is a four to one chance. Receiving lots of Recommendations will make it easier for you to be found on LinkedIn.

I believe LinkedIn does this in order to transform itself from a network for professionals to a network of *trusted* professionals.

So there you have it: Recommendations will make you appear more credible, add value to your branding, be viewed by potential employers or business partners, and will help you become more visible by placing you higher in search results. So what are you waiting for? Let's get the ball rolling by writing some Recommendations!

How to Write a LinkedIn Recommendation

Writing a LinkedIn Recommendation is both easy and complex. The easy part is LinkedIn walks you through the entire process of writing the Recommendation, but the hard part is writing the actual content. Let's take a deep breath and take this one step at a time.

I hope you have realized through my explanation of Windmill Networking—conveyed through terms like "Pay It Forward"—that it is better to give than to receive. When you engage in Windmill Networking, take the leap of faith that what you give always returns to you, many times in a more meaningful way.

If you agree with this philosophy, instead of asking for Recommendations, start by *writing* Recommendations for those people you would like to write Recommendations for you. Search for them on LinkedIn. The one catch is that you need to be connected with them to write them a Recommendation, so it is in your best interest to connect with anyone you might consider valuable in writing you a Recommendation.

If you feel awkward about writing a Recommendation for someone for any reason, LinkedIn does provide functionality that allows you to request one in a professional way. Some people write Recommendations that appear to be done just to thank someone for writing one for them. I am not going to tell you that you need to do it one way or another, as you need to do what makes you feel comfortable. You should know there are these two schools of thought on the subject. Perhaps a mix of the two is the best approach. I will cover asking for a Recommendation and other etiquette in the following section. Either way, I have found that if you ask for a Recommendation from someone, chances are they are going to ask you to write one for them in return.

When you are ready to write a Recommendation for someone, you can recommend them either directly from the "People Search" results screen in the top right-hand corner of the text block where it says "Recommend" or by directly accessing their profile in the top right-hand corner where it says "Recommend this person." LinkedIn (like any other Web 2.0 social networking site) seems to be in a constant state of flux: as I write this, each of the above two methods will navigate you to a different screen with the same result. You will start by being asked to qualify your relationship with the person (i.e., did you work together in the same company, hire them for a service they provided to you, were a business partner, or went to school together). Interestingly enough, depending on your choice of relationship, your variables for data entry in your Recommendation changes. Let's look at each option, as this should give you plenty of ideas for who you can ask for a Recommendation.

- If you choose "Colleague" or "Business Partner" as the basis of your relationship, you will need to enter your exact relationship to said person within the company, your title at the time, and said person's title at the time. You need to make sure your profile indicates the company that you worked for at the time. Even if the person you want to recommend hasn't included that company in their profile, there is an option to choose a position not yet listed in their profile.

- If you choose "Service Provider" you once again enter their title and company name, but this will be followed by a category of what type of service they provide to you. You will then need to enter what year you first hired them as well as if you hired them more than once. Finally, before you write your Recommendation, you will be asked to provide three attributes of what you liked about that provider from a list of choices like "Personable" and "High Integrity." This information will feed into the Service Provider directory that we will cover later in this book. **If everyone started recommending their Service Providers, LinkedIn would turn into a true source of pinpointing professionals to add to your Trusted Network of Advisors at every possible level.**

- If you choose to recommend your contact as a "Student," the information you enter will be similar to the "Colleague" or "Business Partner" category. You will need to indicate whether you taught, advised, or studied together with your connection, and you will also need to choose their place of education from their Profile.

Once you have filled out the required sections for each type of Recommendation, what remains is the body of text where you will write your actual Recommendation. It goes without saying that you want to write a positive Recommendation, but other than that, there really are no guidelines. You can browse through some profiles to view some examples, but I have seen great Recommendations that have been both short, as in a few lines, or long, as in a few paragraphs. The only guidelines I would lay down are to be real and genuine with what you write, and to help your contact brag about themselves.

Highlight good attributes or experiences you had with them that they may be too shy to write about themselves or may have even forgotten. Look at their profile and what they write as some of their great achievements and echo those to add to their branding. Make them happy, in an authentic way, by capturing what they have done. If you do this, I am confident you will have created an excellent Recommendation that will make your connection very happy.

- There is an option to edit the message that is sent together with the Recommendation. You should always add to the text to ask if there is anything inappropriate or something they want you to highlight that you may have forgotten. If there is, ask them to let you know so you can edit it.

- If you'd like, go ahead and ask them for a Recommendation for you when they have the time.

- If there is something that *you* want included in *your* Recommendation, this is the place to let them know.

Never write a Recommendation just to receive one. Such messages lack conviction, and will reflect poorly on the integrity of your brand.

Remember, this should be an exercise in Paying It Forward; should they give you a Recommendation, you should express gratitude appropriately.

Asking for a Recommendation and Other Recommendations Etiquette

Recommendations are professional references. They should not be taken lightly, just as the way you ask for them, along with their source, should not be taken lightly.

As mentioned earlier, you can access anything and everything about Recommendations by clicking "Recommendations" under "Profile" in the left-hand navigation bar. There is a special tab labeled "Request Recommendations" which will help you navigate through the entire process.

You need to choose which company or school for which you want to be recommended. There is a drop down menu populated from your LinkedIn Profile which makes it easy to decide. After that you basically choose which connections to send the request to as well as the actual text of the email. If it looks incredibly easy, it's because it is. But before we send off the same sample text to 200 connections, let's really put some thought into this process so we get the best Recommendations possible:

- First of all, only ask for Recommendations from people that you actually know. It may surprise you, but every now and then I get a request for a Recommendation from someone I don't know! Yes, it surprised me as well, and even if they may be a mutual Windmill Networker it makes me want to disconnect from them. Remember, this is a professional networking site, so please be cognizant of that—be sensitive to asking strangers to recommend you. This stands to look like spam.

- Your best chance of getting a good Recommendation is to customize your message for each recipient. So, although the option exists to send out one request to 200 people simultaneously, take the old-fashioned approach of sending out one at a time if at all possible. **Taking those few extra minutes to add The Personal Touch will go a long way.**

- You also don't want to use the standard text here, especially if you are contacting someone that you haven't spoken to in awhile. Start with a greeting showing your interest in how *they* are doing and how you can help *them* out. **Remember, in Pay It Forward Windmill Networking your investment will likely reap rewards.** The people you are asking to write you a Recommendation from may be very busy, so thank them in advance for their time.

- Give them an update of where you are at and why you are asking them for a Recommendation. Let them know how much it will mean to you. It is always best to, as a reminder, list the major achievements you are proud of that your connection can validate.

- Once you get a Recommendation, it is OK to ask them to edit it if there is something incorrect in the wording. For the most part, the Recommendation you get should work and show each person's individual color in the way they describe you. If all of your Recommendations sound alike because you asked them to use certain wording, it will show—and it will not be to your benefit!

- After receiving a Recommendation, always send a follow-up thank you note and offer to do the same for them should they ever need or want one. **This is just pure Windmill Networking common sense.**

As a reference, on the following page I have included sample wording of a Recommendation that I have used. I am not saying this is ideal or needs to be emulated, but I hope it will inspire you to write a great Recommendation request.

Hi There,

How go things at X Company? It has been awhile since we last chatted, but I assume that you have been doing well. Do let me know what you've been up to and if I can do anything to help you out networking-wise!

As for myself, I am in the job market (again) and could really use your help! I'm sending this to ask you for a brief recommendation of my work that I can include in my LinkedIn profile. Even if our careers only intersected for a short period of time or during a single project, anything you can write in a sentence or two to prove that I was "real," hard-working, results achieving, intelligent...you know, a good guy that anyone would be crazy not to hire;-) etc. would be extremely helpful. If you have any questions or need help remembering what I actually did at Y Company (hey, we're not getting any younger...), let me know.

Some of my achievements that year in Z Location were:
- Coordinated launch and was (Director of AAA Sales Office
- Acquired first design wins for strategic targets in BBB and CCC industries
- Achieved $ Billions quota

You can also take a look at some of the recommendations in my profile for ideas. Thanks in advance for helping me out. If you would like me to write you a recommendation in return please do not hesitate to ask. Also, to repeat myself, if there is anything I can do to help you out networking-wise please let me know! If you hadn't realized it I have become a heavy LinkedIn user, so I would be more than happy to provide advice on using it to meet your objective, whatever that might be.

Keep in touch and have a most fruitful 2009!

Cheers,
Neal
(My) phone-number

Are LinkedIn Recommendations Legit?

Many wonder what the real value in LinkedIn Recommendations are when there are a lot of "if you scratch my back, I'll scratch yours," Recommendations on LinkedIn. Be aware they could potentially limit the credibility of said Recommendations.

Another way of looking at LinkedIn Recommendations is what my old boss once told me, *"You know when someone is looking for a new job when they start receiving lots of Recommendations from ex-colleagues."*

To be honest with you, there is a bit of truth to both of the above arguments. But let me play the devil's advocate by pretending that LinkedIn did *not* offer Recommendations.

Wouldn't you like a way to confirm how "real" this person is, to back up the claims that are in his or her profile from a third-party and ideally objective perspective? Well, that's what Recommendations are for, and I believe that they serve this purpose well.

The danger in an Internet World is that people can hide behind their anonymity and do bad things. On LinkedIn, this could potentially mean someone could set up a fake profile to spam (or otherwise harass) LinkedIn users. To combat this potential problem, LinkedIn rightfully implemented this Recommendations feature. When you ask a friend or someone in your network for a referral, aren't you asking them to recommend you to their contact? I believe this was the original spirit of LinkedIn Recommendations.

The problem, then, is not a function of LinkedIn Recommendations, but the potential way in which they can be used or abused. **Hey, this is Web 2.0, my friends. We're talking User Generated Content here.** No one can control this, not even the mighty hand of LinkedIn or even Google for that matter. That being said, as viewers of this content, we reserve the right to judge the content as we wish.

With that in mind, I would like to offer my three-point advice as to what filters I would use in judging the value of a particular LinkedIn Recommendation:

1. Who wrote the Recommendation? If it was a colleague it is one thing, but what if it was coming from a CxO position within the company or from a customer or partner? Look at the people writing the Recommendation and you will see there are a lot of professional people who are putting their reputations on the line; they are not writing a Recommendation for everyone out there. In other words, first judge a Recommendation by who wrote it.

2. What was the relationship of the person that made the Recommendation? As LinkedIn is a professional site, a Recommendation from someone who used to work or do business with that person should always have greater value than a Recommendation from an old friend or networking acquaintance. This is not to say that Recommendations from networking acquaintances are not of value. They can indicate you are a "real" person and can sometimes best describe your attributes in a candid fashion. **Personally, I believe those involved in a business relationship with this person are in a better position to write the most objective and professional Recommendation.** I recommend you also judge what you read by the relationship of the person writing it.

3. What objective qualities are described in the Recommendation? No two Recommendations are alike, but there are some great Recommendations that highlight qualities that go above-and-beyond what the person has written in their own profile. On the other hand, there are Recommendations that really mention nothing about the particular qualities of that person. One thing I watch for: Recommendations that contradict what the person has written in their own profile. This is a big red flag. Recommendations should highlight specific qualities that are consistent with the rest of the profile.

In an ideal world, LinkedIn Recommendations make someone look more "real" and are a welcome addition to a person's profile.

I always suggest you get as many Recommendations as you can whenever you have a chance. Dig Your Well *Before* You're Thirsty and don't wait until you change jobs to ask for a Recommendation! Consider it part of implementing your LinkedIn Brand.

From the viewing side, so long as you read LinkedIn Recommendations with my suggested filters, you should be able to sort out the “real” from the “if you scratch my back, I’ll scratch yours” Recommendations.

Chapter 6

Chapter 6 Groups

- What are LinkedIn Groups?
- Which Groups Should I Join?
- Joining a Group and Understanding Your Options
- My Suggestions for LinkedIn Group Etiquette
- My Top Five Tips to Get the Most Out of LinkedIn Groups
- Optimizing Group Membership
- Create Your Own LinkedIn Group
- Managing Your LinkedIn Group
- How Do I Promote My LinkedIn Group?
- Providing Value to Your Group Members

What are LinkedIn Groups?

I have recently heard that every second a new member is joining LinkedIn. This is an incredible testament to the growing popularity of LinkedIn. But if there are 40+ million registered users, why is it that the largest Group at the time of my writing only has about 170,000 members? Why aren't LinkedIn Groups more popular? After all, if LinkedIn is a site for social networking, and Groups are, in essence, communities, why aren't more people becoming Group members?

Maybe some of you are intimidated like I was. When I first joined LinkedIn, I was a little intimidated by the profiles of people that showed they were a member of all sorts of groups and associations. How did these people have the time to attend all of the Group meetings? How could they be qualified to join so many diverse Groups?

Which leads to a bigger question...what exactly ARE LinkedIn Groups? And do they have tangible and physical Group meetings?

Until recently, there was no limitation as to how many Groups you could join on LinkedIn, and there was no search functionality available for LinkedIn Groups. The only way you could find out about Groups was by looking at the logos on other people's profiles. And, even then, you never knew how many members were actually in each Group unless you joined and did a search within the Group (and, of course, the search results for free members were limited to 500, so you never knew the exact membership number for any Group with a membership larger than 500). I never felt that I had the qualifications to join any LinkedIn Group and was quite intimidated by all of them.

The first LinkedIn Group I joined was one that I saw on a particular colleague's profile. At the time I was working in the IPTV (Internet Protocol TeleVision) industry, so it was a pleasant surprise to find a colleague who had joined a Group called "iptv." Yes! Finally, a Group that I was qualified to join! I applied to join the "iptv" Group, and after seeing the display saying I could contact the

Group Manager, I immediately sent him a long message explaining how I was qualified to join his Group. After gaining acceptance to his Group, I slowly started joining more Groups that looked interesting and pertinent to implementing my LinkedIn Brand whenever I saw the logos appear on other profiles. *Now that I am a Group Manager I realize it is not necessary to contact the Group Manager when you request to join their Group because they will receive notification of your request separately.*

Fast forward to when LinkedIn announced several months ago they were limiting the number of Groups to 50; at that time I was a member of 90+ Groups! As I manually removed myself from enough Groups to get below 50, I began to realize the value that LinkedIn Groups could offer. I hope I have been clear up until now; do not be intimidated about joining LinkedIn Groups! LinkedIn Groups are collections of people with a common interest who belong to a joint community. They are opening themselves up to potentially be contacted by other members, or at least virtually meeting them on Group Discussions Boards.

If you plan on Windmill Networking (outside of directly inviting people to build up your virtual network), joining Groups is an excellent strategy. You can build relationships by finding people through searching or communicating through the discussion boards. The important thing is to join Groups aligned with your LinkedIn Objective!

Which (and how many) Groups you join really depends on your LinkedIn Objective. **I have found that, 99% of the time, I have been accepted into any LinkedIn Group I have attempted to join.** If a Group will reject your membership, the reason why is usually written in their Group Profile beforehand. Some Groups *are* exclusive to a particular demographic or qualification, so **you need to make sure you check the details of each Group Profile before you request to join.**

One more note: Please do not join alumni Groups if you never went to that school (or worked at that company). This can communicate the wrong message and your brand might be damaged. Because LinkedIn is for professionals, you WILL be noticed and potentially reported by someone to LinkedIn Customer Service.

In case you are still confused about LinkedIn Groups, consider them as virtual groups built around people with similar backgrounds and interests. That "background" might be physical proximity, or it might not. The important thing is that these Groups give members more opportunities to interact and network with like-minded people.

That being said, my two oldest LinkedIn Groups (So Cal Sushi and The Izakaya Club) are what I would call "virtual-to-physical" groups. They are aligned with my LinkedIn policy of creating a vast virtual network and slowly bringing these connections into my physical world through Windmill Networking. **My Groups are among the few on LinkedIn that actually physically meet in person!**

Joining a Group is simple: Do a Group Search, look at the Group Profile, and select the choice to join the Group. You will then have a chance to change your profile settings for each Group, choosing whether or not to display said logo on your profile. By default, the logo for each Group you join will appear on your profile. If it does not (or if you want to turn it off), you can access all of your Groups through your "User Groups" selection on the left-hand panel; then choose the "Settings" selection for each Group to access this feature.

On some profiles, logos for Groups and Associations are not displayed. Instead, you will see what appear to be links—these are really not links at all, but are a very useful tool. If a Group or association you belong to does not have a corresponding LinkedIn Group and if you, for some unfathomable reason do not wish to start one (can you tell I think this would be a mistake?), you can use this feature to be found during a keyword search. This is done by entering text into your Groups and Associations portion of your profile through choosing to "Edit My Profile"; these will then display on your profile as if they were links.

There is further value in joining LinkedIn Groups other than just being connected and being able to communicate with others. There are Discussions Boards, News Boards, as well as Jobs postings that are specific to each Group; these can provide valuable information to you depending on what your LinkedIn Objective is. With the recent addition of Subgroup functionality, the value in joining Groups increases exponentially.

If you are a business owner or are in sales, LinkedIn Groups provide even more benefit because they can bring you more business. Because LinkedIn Groups are:

1) full of professionals,
2) often concentrated on a niche industry or a niche location, or a combination of the two, and
3) are a community where people regularly visit the Discussions Boards—or at least receive the daily/weekly digest of activities.

This makes LinkedIn Groups an ideal target audience for professionals who may be looking for business or a business partner.

There have been many success stories of companies finding additional business on LinkedIn Groups. I have personally posted messages on Discussions Boards on behalf of several networking friends looking for business partners, distributors, or even suppliers for certain products. The people who look at the Discussions Boards of these specific Groups will be one step ahead of the businesses who are not. I have even used the Discussions Boards of some Groups to look for help to create this book. You can see how there is potential business, however small, to be found.

If your LinkedIn Objective is business-related, LinkedIn Groups should be an important part of your strategy. But you need to be in the right Groups and be aware of Group etiquette.

Which Groups Should I Join?

LinkedIn Groups allow you to be virtually connected to a number of people that share a common interest with you. One of the largest LinkedIn Groups, *Executive Suite*, has more than 150,000 members as of August 2009. According to TopLinked.com, that is almost *triple* the number of connections that the most connected LinkedIn user, Ron Bates, has!

If you join Executive Suite, which is run by the career management site ExecuNet, you will be able to directly send a message as well as invite, without knowing the email address of, anyone in this group.

One thing to note: You will be able to directly send a message to a Group member who is not directly connected to you, *assuming the person has chosen to receive messages from Group members* (which is the default setting).

Whether or not you use Groups as part of your invitation strategy is another story, but the ability to see and be seen, especially in your core areas of expertise or interest, is a reason why you should join the maximum of 50 Groups allowed.

My strategy, and one I would suggest to you, is to join the following types of LinkedIn Groups. Once again, it all depends on your objective; however, if you are on LinkedIn to find or be found, you should have a vested interest in joining at least one of the following types of Groups:

1) Regional Groups

Regional Groups are those based on people living, working, or wanting to connect with people in a certain region. Since I live in Southern California but often travel to Japan for business, I have created two Groups, one for Southern California ("So Cal Sushi") and another for Japan ("The Izakaya Club"). Maybe you want to join a regional Group based on your hometown, or maybe you plan to travel somewhere and you'd like to find people that you can network with while you visit. This is the ultimate form of Windmill Networking. By becoming part of a virtual networking group, you then bring these members into your physical network through meeting them. Regional Groups will also give you the opportunity to be informed of potential face-to-face networking events in that locale. Beware that there are some local Groups that cover so much territory that it may not make much sense to join them. *The choice is yours.*

2) Industry Groups

If you presently work or in the past have worked in a particular industry, wouldn't it make sense to join industry-related Groups? There are many Groups dedicated to various industries on LinkedIn, and, within each Group, you not only get access to members who specialize in your industry, you also gain access to Discussions Boards and News posts that provide extra value to your professional networking.

3) Occupational Groups

Whether you are in Sales, Marketing, Human Resources, or Project Management, there is bound to be a Group that specializes in creating a community for you. Just as with the Industry Groups, you get access to similar-minded professionals in your field as well as Discussions Boards, News Posts, and Jobs posts targeting your profession.

4) Large Groups

One day I noticed that, when I didn't enter any text in the Group Search Bar, it returned, in descending order, the LinkedIn Groups with the most members. Since joining a LinkedIn Group allows you to be visible within that Group and also gives you the opportunity to send a direct message to other members, joining large Groups makes sense. Of course, if you are not qualified to join the Group, you may not get accepted. If you are happily employed and yet join large Groups that help you find jobs, it may not send a good message to your employer. So, if you are going to join some of these Groups, make sure it is in a related field or aligned with your LinkedIn Brand.

5) Networking Groups

There are Groups that exist solely for the purpose of open networking or fostering mutual increases of LinkedIn connections. Once again, your objective will inform you whether or not these Groups are the right choice for you. They do exist, and I will cover them in more depth in Chapter 12: Growing Your Network.

6) Alumni Groups

There are many Groups that specialize in creating LinkedIn communities for alumni of colleges and companies. In addition to directly connecting to former colleagues, you can always join this type of Group to find alumni with whom you don't want to directly connect. It also facilitates more efficient networking with your alumni if you are in the same Group.

7) Special Interest Groups

There are tons of other Groups that exist on LinkedIn. It all comes down to what your LinkedIn Objective is and what Groups you want to be associated with your LinkedIn Brand. One rule of thumb: If there is a keyword you want to be associated with, do a keyword search on Groups and look at the top 10 or 20 results. You are bound to find a Group that sparks your interest AND helps you achieve your LinkedIn Objective.

If one of your objectives is to be seen as a Subject Matter Expert on a particular topic like Wine, using Twitter, etc., joining and becoming active in the associated LinkedIn Groups could help you publicize your expertise.

8) Windmill Networking Groups

If you are a fan of this book and would like to become more involved in Windmill Networking to virtually meet other like-minded professionals, consider joining the Groups that I will create for you, the reader, to utilize. You will also be able to access my latest blog posts on the news boards. I hope it will become a forum for all of you to share YOUR Windmill Networking success stories and experiences. And yes.... I will accept your request to join my Groups!

Joining a Group and Understanding Your Options

OK. You've joined a LinkedIn Group. Now what do you do? Let's go through the options of how you can utilize your LinkedIn Group membership for whatever your purpose may be.

1) Inviting a Fellow Group Member to Connect

You've joined the same Group. You see someone in the Group that you'd like to connect with, so you leverage the fact that you don't need their email address in order to send them an invitation. After all, we're members of the same Group, right? They'd accept my invitation, right? WRONG!!! This is the usual mistake that LinkedIn beginners make that gets them 5 IDKs and a slap on the wrist from LinkedIn Customer Service.

Unless an unknown person somewhere in his profile (usually in the Contact Settings at the bottom) states they are open to receiving invitations, OR you are both part of the same open networking Group (covered in Chapter 12), do not invite him to connect because you might receive an IDK. If you absolutely want to invite him, send him a message, and clearly explain why you want to connect and the mutual value in your connecting.

2) Sending a Message

Assuming the other Group member has allowed you to send them a message, go ahead—communicate! But make sure that contacting them is somehow related to the Group that binds you two together; otherwise, you may not get a response. Remember, some people are passive Group members and don't want to communicate. A personalized, well written, and to-the-point message is your best chance for success.

3) Joining Discussions & Reading News Posts

The Discussions and News posts on each Group's page are the wildcard. If a Group manager is dedicated enough and the members are passionate about what the Group is about, you can theoretically find great value here. Unfortunately, within the Groups I am a member of, the news posts are few and the "discussions" are filled with advertisements and requests for people to connect. This may be because the Discussions and News post options are still fairly new. The Group Manager does have the right to delete these posts, but, unfortunately, he or she cannot moderate the posts in real-time. Instead, the Group Manager must wait until after the fact to review the posts. I subscribe to weekly digests of many of the Groups I am a member of, and every week I do post some news of value. I recommend you do the same, though these weekly digests can inundate your Inbox. *Stick with receiving these digests on a weekly basis and stop subscribing to those digests that you think offer little value.* One great feature LinkedIn provides when joining discussions is the ability to follow them: This means that, if someone comments on a discussion after you, you are immediately notified. Another great feature that LinkedIn recently implemented is the "Action Bar" that appears at the top of each News Post. This allows you to easily "share" a news article with someone else in your network you think might find it of interest. This form of information sharing can contribute to the implementation of your LinkedIn Brand. In fact, if you are the first to recommend a news article that you post, it will indicate your name in the Action Bar as the person recommending the post. Another great branding opportunity!

4) Job Postings

Until recently the "Discussions" boards, in addition to being filled with advertisements and requests to connect, were also filled with job postings. This is natural since there are a lot of recruiters on LinkedIn: The Group Discussions Board provides a forum for free advertising. Recently, LinkedIn created a separate "Job postings" tab to separate these from the Discussions Board. This is a win-win for all involved; the recruiters get a special page for their job offerings, and the Group members who are not looking for work do not need to skip over job openings on the Discussions Boards. Needless to say, if you are in transition, you may find jobs here that do not appear on Internet job boards or even within LinkedIn Jobs. Why? Because advertising in Groups is free!

5) Search for Members

An often overlooked benefit of being a member of a LinkedIn Group is the ability to do a search limited to the Group to which you belong. If you were looking for someone from L.A. to help you meet a particular objective, wouldn't it make sense to search within Groups you joined that were specific to L.A.? Since your LinkedIn search results are limited to 100, you can first do a search within your network for someone living within a certain distance from a representative zip code. If you can't see all of the results, try searching again; however, this time, limit your search to within Groups. You should be able to get a different subset of results that provides more leads. Trying this for several different Groups will yield more results than the 100 that LinkedIn limits to free members. This can be performed by choosing the Group filter directly from the "People Advanced Search" or directly from the "Members" tab in each Group.

6) Joining a Subgroup

Subgroups are LinkedIn's newest feature as I write this book. Since not too many Groups have created them, it is hard to say what value they might possess. **Nonetheless, the potential for joining Subgroups within larger LinkedIn Groups, for more targeted Windmill Networking, is tremendous.** Apparently, from what information I gleaned from various LinkedIn Group Discussions Boards, you can join up to 50 Subgroups, in addition to your 50 LinkedIn Groups. It makes sense, should you find Subgroups that interest you, to join the maximum number of them as well. Being a member of 50 LinkedIn Groups, as well as 50 Subgroups, could potentially make it impossible to keep up on all of the varying Group activity on a daily or even a weekly basis. I predict the Subgroups will end up being more focused and will provide greater value to you; however, the LinkedIn Groups will always have larger numbers of members, providing maximum visibility. A healthy balance of joining both Groups, and some of their respective Subgroups, would probably be the best approach. Note that you can only join a Subgroup if you are a member of that same LinkedIn Group.

My Suggestions for LinkedIn Group Etiquette

You've joined some Groups and now understand your options. But before you start aggressively posting messages on the Discussions Boards, it is important to follow the proper etiquette. As someone who is a member of fifty Groups and also owns his own Groups, I can see things from a dual perspective. I would like to offer my thoughts as to what the proper etiquette should be after joining a LinkedIn Group.

It is important to note we are sailing uncharted waters when we talk about social networking. There really are no rules written in stone. We are generating the content on the fly; as a result, LinkedIn is slowly evolving into something new with each day. LinkedIn Groups are miniature networks, subsets of the entire database of LinkedIn users, that people join based on common interest. LinkedIn gives each Group the ability to display member information, conduct member searches, post and respond to discussions and news, and even post and look for targeted jobs. A crucial question we must ask: Within each of these Groups, what are the rules by which we should abide by in our communication?

1) **The heart of each LinkedIn Group community**, assuming it does not have an external networking site associated with it such as a Yahoo Group or a Ning.com site, **is really in the Discussions Board**. This is where members of the Group congregate the most, engage in conversations, connect with each other, and provide value to the larger Group community. As the centerpiece of the community, the Discussions Board is also where Group etiquette will be the most important.

2) **Group etiquette starts with each Group manager. It is up to the Group manager to set the tone for his or her Group by posting a distinct mission for the Group along with its policies.** The Group's mission and policies should not only appear in the introduction to the Group (included in its profile); they should also be featured as a discussion when necessary. If you join a Group, the Featured Discussion at the top of the Discussions Board is the first place to look to understand what is and is not "proper" behavior in that Group. Most importantly, Discussions Board posting guidelines should be displayed here.

3) **In general, posting etiquette should dictate that a discussion: a) is aligned with the Group mission and policies and b) adds value to the Group.** There is a significant increase in the number of people and companies looking to Discussions Boards as a new marketing channel. I suggest that, if what these companies and individuals are saying both aligns with the Group mission and adds value to the Group, there is nothing wrong with posting messages that may have a link to an external site. Nonetheless, be prepared to respond intelligently to a Group manager who may have a different opinion. If you are unsure if it is appropriate to post a questionable discussion in a particular Group, your safest bet is to first ask the Group manager for his or her permission.

4) **I recently posted a new policy on my Group asking members to limit their new discussions to a maximum of one per week.** LinkedIn recently told Group managers we can only send out only one general announcement to all members per week, which I think is a positive guideline. The potential problem with Groups is that someone could be posting many Discussions posts—essentially "over-advertising" something directly or indirectly. This is why I think frequency of Discussions postings is an important part of Group etiquette. This does not include *commenting* on another member's posting, but rather *initiating* your own new posting. If you find yourself creating more than one discussion a week, you need to ask yourself why you haven't created your own Group. Alternatively, you should consider asking the Group manager for a larger role in managing the Group if you feel you are providing a lot of value.

5) **My last rule I will call "KY."** "KY" is an abbreviation for "Kuuki o Yomu," one of my favorite Japanese terms, **which literally means to "read the atmosphere."** There are many Groups where no policies exist to govern the discussions. If this is the case, after joining, spend some time to "KY"; see what other people post on the Discussions Board as well as those discussions that seem to attract people's comments. KY allows you to gauge the proper etiquette for the content of your Discussions posts. Furthermore, KY ensures you are providing value to that Group when you do post.

My Top Five Tips to Get the Most Out of LinkedIn Groups

"OK, Neal. I joined a LinkedIn Group. Now what do I do?"

That is a very good question. The previous sections described the options you have to interact within each Group, as well as some recommended etiquette. But how can you ensure you are getting the most out of your Group experience?

In order to be both successful AND efficient in your **Windmill Networking,** follow these tips:

1) **Join 50 Groups.** Windmill Networking is about going out and exploiting social media to make new connections with people who aren't already part of your virtual network. Why would you not want to maximize the number of communities you can interface with and, thus, the number of potential new Trusted Advisors that you can interact with? If out of the more than 300,000 Groups you can't find 50 that interest you—then create your own!

2) **Filter Group Information.** If you join 50 Groups like I recommend, you will start getting 50 weekly digests and will have to look at Group Discussions Boards all day long just to keep up. This is crazy, and you can avoid this efficiently by filtering your Group information intelligently. I don't care which LinkedIn Group you are a member of, the Discussions Boards can quickly get filled with spam and other messages that might have no meaning to you. Yes, there are some diamonds in the rough with some Groups providing valuable information in the Discussions Boards; however, I would recommend to first subscribing to the weekly digest. If you come to find it offers no value to you, you can and should unsubscribe to it. On the other hand, when you find valuable weekly digests, follow them! **You will be able to follow all of the discussions from the comfort of your personal email account, without having to log into LinkedIn all day, and then only jump directly to those selected discussions that interest you**. It is easy to get information overload from LinkedIn (or social media in general), so I hope this will help you avoid this problem.

3) **Ignore the News.** The news on the LinkedIn Groups is only going to be as good as those who post it. I have yet to see a Group that does the news better than doing a Twitter search. If you are not on Twitter, subscribe to some keywords in the excellent Company Buzz application, which I will cover in Chapter 8: Applications. You will find the news you want a lot faster than searching through LinkedIn Groups. If you do find a Group that provides just the news you are looking for, great! Follow it religiously, just as you do with discussions.

4) **Make New Connections.** Windmill Networking is about making new connections—about building out your virtual network. Try to make a personal connection with people whom you don't know in the same Group. Now you're networking—**Windmill Networking!** This is what social media is all about—use it!

5) **Use the Discussions Boards.** There are many opportunities here to further brand yourself as well as implement your LinkedIn Objective. Offer some Pay It Forward help when others seek it. Network and connect. Again—you're **Windmill Networking!**

Optimizing Group Membership

I won't answer the rhetorical question, "Should we be limited to only joining 50 Groups?", as that is the restriction LinkedIn has enacted. As for which 50 Groups to join, we can use the "Group Search" capability, combined with the total number of membership information, to create a sound strategy.

For instance, I have a variety of areas of expertise and a multitude of interests, including networking, sales, Japan, Southern California, telecommunications, etc. I simply enter these types of keywords into the Group Search Bar and LinkedIn will tell me which are the most popular Groups in terms of membership in descending order. It cannot get any easier than this to find an appropriate Group to join.

If you start thinking about your objectives in Windmill Networking and what type of people you want to connect with, you should be able to create your own keyword strategy and start joining appropriate Groups. Using this keyword approach to identify Regional Groups, Occupational Groups, Large Groups, Networking Groups, Alumni Groups, and Special Interest Groups can yield even more optimal results.

Note that Group membership numbers vary from month to month. I do a monthly check, performing the same searches to make sure that my memberships still align with my LinkedIn Objective. For instance, I recently received an invitation for a new local Group I wanted to join, so I went back in and looked at membership numbers; I realized I didn't need to be in as many networking Groups as before. By realigning your Group memberships with your current objectives and membership numbers, your Group membership will always be optimal. I find that every month I am tweaking my membership in 2 or 3 Groups as new Groups evolve and old Groups don't serve their purpose anymore. As your network gets larger, you will start receiving many Group invitations that will seem enticing to join, so you need a method to sort out the madness to help you prioritize.

In order to manage my Group memberships, I create a very simple Microsoft Excel spreadsheet with columns for Group name, objective type (i.e. regional, industry, etc.), number of members, and situation (which usually doesn't change unless I recently applied or dropped it). I sort all Groups by membership and then all of those Groups that I dropped or are on my "watch list" I place two columns over so it is clear I am not currently a member of them—but could join them in the future. In addition to providing a snapshot of what types of LinkedIn Groups you are in and how much visibility they provide you, it is fascinating to see membership changes over time. Give it a try if you really want to take full control over your Group memberships.

As a final note on optimizing your Group membership, you should understand that as you start receiving more and more invitations to join various LinkedIn Groups, it will become clear that LinkedIn Groups are competing for your membership.

Almost every LinkedIn Group Manager would like to build a large community, and there are many reasons why your membership is valuable to them.

Let's look at one example. If you are the Vice President of Human Relations for a company, you may want to be able to contact engineers that have a special skill you often seek. You may do a keyword search and find many individuals you would like to have access to, but without being directly connected, you can't achieve this. Well, if you create a LinkedIn Group—which we will go through in the next chapter—and your target members join, you can send them Messages, plus you can send all of your members an Announcement once a week. You can fill the Discussions Boards with messages that are relevant to your industry, post job openings from your company, and link up your corporate blog of news releases with the News board. You do not need to spend any invitations in order to do any of this; these members merely need to join your Group.

Creating your own Group is like creating your own custom LinkedIn world within LinkedIn—a world that is geared towards propagating and advancing whatever objective you might have.

On the other hand, as some of the bigger LinkedIn Groups approach membership in the tens of thousands, it is no surprise that some are starting to think about monetizing the number of eyeballs that may be peeled to their Group messages. These Groups may start to see your membership as less of a community-building affair and more of a marketing effort.

Compounding this is the fact that users are limited to only 50 Groups. I know, it sounds like a great number, but you don't know how many times I have tried to promote my own Group to new members only to receive a "Sorry, I'd love to join your Group, but I'm maxed out at 50 Groups now" response. After all, with more than 300,000 Groups on LinkedIn, it is no surprise that the competition for your membership is only going to get worse. It's pure supply and demand.

Then again, many Group Managers, upon realizing this trend, are trying to maintain their own strategies in order to increase Group membership, retain your loyalty, or increase the value they provide to their members. I believe this background of increasing competition will create better and more valuable LinkedIn Groups for you to join.

On a final note, Groups do change. If you no longer feel comfortable in the Group or if you resent new monetization efforts, simply leave the Group. I have seen very little of this up until now, but it wouldn't surprise me if we start seeing more of this in the near future. Be forewarned.

Create Your Own LinkedIn Group

With all of those LinkedIn Groups out there, you are bound to find one that appeals to you, regardless of what your interests are. But what happens if that ideal LinkedIn Group does not exist? Or what if you absolutely want to create one as part of achieving your LinkedIn Objective? Go ahead! The reason so many LinkedIn Groups exist is because they are incredibly easy to create.

Just as everyone has a good book they could write, everyone has a good LinkedIn Group they can create.

I am a believer that everyone has a niche of special expertise; thus, you can argue that everyone should have their own LinkedIn Group. Whatever your reason for being on LinkedIn, if you are looking to connect with similar minded people, there is no better way to do this than to **start your own LinkedIn Group**. Live in a region where there is no LinkedIn Group? Start one. Work for a company that doesn't have a LinkedIn Group? Start one. Do you like 1980's Southern California Punk Rock music and can't find a Group with whom to share that interest? Start a Group (and let me know after you do so that I can join!) Be creative and take the initiative! I think you get the picture.

There are many reasons why you may want to create a LinkedIn Group:

- If you are a business owner, creating a Group around your line of business may help you build a new customer base.

- If you are in sales/marketing, creating a Group around your industry can help you win influential mindshare, as well as yield you influence.

- If you want to promote your Subject Matter Expertise as part of your LinkedIn Brand, a Group is the perfect way to do so.

- If you already have a blog, it makes sense to create a LinkedIn Group as an extension of that blog to foster more followers and improve communication.

The above are just a few examples, but if you are really interested in Windmill Networking, creating a LinkedIn Group will increase your communication; you will expand your virtual network to people you may not have interfaced with before. Of course, creating the Group is the easy part; the challenge will be in both promoting your LinkedIn Group as well as adding value to it. We will cover both topics later in this chapter.

I was once asked how a LinkedIn Group works, is managed, and how much time is taken up by creating one. It really is up to you and what your objective is. Creating the LinkedIn Group itself, assuming you can easily create a logo (see below for more information), only takes a few minutes. If you choose to automatically allow applicants to become a member of your Group, and if you have an RSS feed from your blog or company website you can integrate into the News board, you can literally manage your Group on auto-pilot without taking up any time. That's right: zero time.

But if you want as many people as possible to join your Group in the spirit of **Windmill Networking**, it is wise to spend a little time advertising and promoting your Group. Of course, there is creating and managing the many discussions that will come up, but that is the fun part. Definitely the most concentrated time you will invest in the Group comes in the early stages of promotion.

Beyond that, it depends on the quality and type of community you want to foster. I mention this because there are Discussions Boards, Jobs boards, News postings, and your once-a-week Announcement that allows you to interact with your Group. I think if you get into a daily habit of spending a few minutes posting appropriate news, starting discussions, responding to other people's discussions, et al., it shouldn't eat up too much of your time.

Now, on to the **mechanics of creating a Group**. First of all, when you see your User Group page, there is already a tab that exists to create a Group. All you need to do is fill out everything on the form, and, presto! your Group is submitted to LinkedIn. You then receive confirmation that your LinkedIn Group has been created. For the first Group that I created, it took a few hours to receive this confirmation. For the second Group I received immediate confirmation. I have never heard of any Groups that have been rejected, but just remember that LinkedIn does reserve the right to reject you.

Rather than go through the entire step-by-step process of how to create your group, which is pretty easy to understand just by looking at this page, I wanted to point out those areas that you will probably want to pay close attention to:

- **Creating Logos**

Believe it or not, this is the part that will probably require the most time. Just like the thumbnail cover of this book competed for your attention on the Amazon web page, the thumbnail of your logo will be competing with all of the other LinkedIn Groups when someone does a Group search utilizing a particular keyword. Make sure the wording and image stands out when compared to others. If you want to make it look really good, I recommend hiring a professional designer to create the logo for you. You could use a service like VistaPrint (www.vistaprint.com) in order to do this, or you can ask a family or relative who has the right skills to do this on your behalf. A relative donated his time to create my So Cal Sushi logo, but I actually designed The Izakaya Club logo myself. I am not a graphic designer, but I went on to CNET (www.cnet.com) and found a free software program that allowed me to create a logo image and to customize the settings to save it in the two formats that LinkedIn requires. It is not difficult to do, but before you submit it, compare it to other logos and optimize appropriately. On the other hand, if you are not confident in your IT skills, why not ask someone in your network for help, and then give them credit after they help you? **This is what Windmill Networking is all about!**

- **Group Name**

As part of the branding of your Group to both differentiate it from other Groups and to attract people to your brand, you need to think critically about an appropriate and catchy Group name. Compare it to the others you are competing with and make sure you create something both unique and more appropriate for the target demographic. Also, as in your Summary, make sure you have the keywords in your Group Name with which you want to be associated. In other words, when someone does a Group Search, what keywords do you want to find your Group? The branding of your Group Name is important: You do have a lot of real estate to work with here—maximize it.

• **Group Type**
I have always just used the "Networking" category here. Although there is no "Advanced" option for Group Search like there are for other searches, if you do search for a Group, the search results will be displayed along with a way to narrow down those search results by Category or Language. I doubt this is utilized very often, but if your Group does align with one of these categories it makes sense to use that one for your Category.

• **Summary**
Obviously, the Summary is here to obviously spark the interest of anyone who finds you on the Group Search and wants to learn more about your Group. It also needs to go into your Group Mission in some detail. Once again, the SEO (Search Engine Optimization) of your Summary is important, as the Group Search will also pick this up. Any keywords that you could not fit into your Group Name should be listed as part of your Summary.

• **Full Description**
While this text does not get searched for keywords during a Group Search, it will show up on the Group Home Page for your members. If you want to go into more depth, go ahead and do so. Otherwise, repeating what you said in your Summary is sufficient.

• **Website**
You don't necessarily need to have a special Website for the Group. If you have a blog site or are a small business owner, you can simply create a page introducing your Group on your blog as I did. At the minimum you can go into more detail about your LinkedIn Group on your website. It may also serve the dual purpose of leading them to a website where you can introduce Group members to your products and/or services as well as your blog posts.

• **Group Visibility**
Unless you want to create a private Group on LinkedIn, which goes against what Windmill Networking is all about, make sure you stick with the default. This makes your Group searchable and ensures your logo is visible on Group members' profiles who agree to display it.

• **Group Access**

If you have a completely open Group, you can allow anyone who applies to join your Group. If you don't check this, you will either have to check on the status of your User Group to see new applicants or wait for an email from LinkedIn telling you there are applications awaiting your approval. This usually happens within 24 hours after an application is submitted. Even though I have open networking Groups, I still like to have an idea of who is joining my Group; as a result, I have chosen to manually accept applications. That being said, most recently I chose to automate this to optimize my Windmill Networking activities. The choice is really a personal one, but if you don't plan to reject anyone, why not automate this process and spend your precious time elsewhere?

- **Location**

I have never checked this box, which would inform LinkedIn that your Group is based on a single geographic location. This may limit the visibility of your Group to members from a certain geography. I don't think you ever want to do this, simply because there may be new or old members who presently live in other regions who may want to still keep in touch with your Group. **Once again, limiting your geography goes against the essence of Windmill Networking.** Case in point: I had someone from Northern California join my So Cal Sushi Group and show up at an event here in Southern California!

- **Language**

Enter whatever language you are targeting here. English is obviously the default, but if you have a Spanish-only Group and you don't want English speakers, you definitely want to make sure you choose Spanish.

At the very end of creating a Group, you are forced to agree to LinkedIn's Term of Service. It is appropriate to mention here that LinkedIn owns all of its member-created LinkedIn Groups. You are governed by their rules so read carefully. As I write this book, there is a real-life example of a Group that I believe may have been forcibly removed by LinkedIn, according to what I have read. And, although the Group Manager may have known this was coming, LinkedIn never notified the actual members of the Group. The Group merely "disappeared."

One final note (that you should be aware of here): The Groups you create will count towards your 50 Group limit.

Managing Your LinkedIn Group

LinkedIn has added various features in 2009 that allow you to manage the many aspects of your LinkedIn Group. Before you start promoting your Group to others, let's look at the functionality LinkedIn provides and consider what you may want to implement right away.

You can find all of the Group management tools under the "Manage" tab, the last tab on the right. A new window displaying all of the members on the left, with the management tools on the right, is shown. Let's go through each of these one at a time and consider their value.

Create a Subgroup

Subgroup is a new functionality that LinkedIn recently added just as I came to the final editing stages of this book. Subgroups have the potential to revolutionize LinkedIn Groups. You can now create micro-groups within your own LinkedIn Group that can be searchable in the Groups directory. It is potentially like owning several Groups in one.

As the screen that appears after selecting "Create a Subgroup" suggests, "A subgroup is a space within your group where members can collaborate based on a function, project, topic, location or anything you wish." Once the Subgroup is created, a lot of the functionality that applies to your Group also applies separately to your Subgroup. For instance, there is an "Announcement" you can send out to all of your Group members once a week. In addition to this Announcement, you can send out a separate Announcement once a week to each Subgroup that you own.

If you create too many Subgroups, your LinkedIn Group can easily become fragmented. One obvious idea for Subgroups is to divide your Group into Subgroups by location. If your Group is a regional one to begin with, this may further dilute the identity of your Group. It will be interesting to see how Subgroups evolve. I am sure there will be much more to write about Subgroups in the next edition of this book!

Once you have selected "Create a subgroup," you will see that the process for establishing a Subgroup is just like creating a normal LinkedIn Group. So, if you want to start your own dynasty of LinkedIn Groups, be creative and have fun with Subgroups!

Send an Announcement

The only way for you to directly send an email to all of your Group members (assuming they have chosen to receive them) is through the "Announcement" functionality. You are limited to sending out one per week. You can also choose to make the Announcement a "Featured Discussion" to appear at the top of your Discussions Board. This ensures that those who are not receiving Announcements still have a chance to read the information. Be careful about the frequency of sending these Announcements, as people in your LinkedIn Group probably only want to receive very relevant information.

Send Invitations

If you want to use the Inbox functionality to send out invitations to join your Group, tediously choosing contacts and adding them one at a time, LinkedIn provides this functionality. LinkedIn has added the ability to upload an address book (in a .csv format) of email contacts. LinkedIn will then send out the email on your behalf. While I do not know if there are any restrictions on the number of people you can invite at once, it seems this would be the best way to let your LinkedIn connections, as well as people that aren't on LinkedIn, know about your Group. Just as with any other communication on LinkedIn, make sure you personalize your wording so it reflects your LinkedIn Brand and gives others incentive to join. Also note, regardless of your "Group Access" setting, anyone who accepts the Invitation you send will automatically become a member of your Group.

Pre-approve People

If you chose not to allow people to automatically join your Group (refer to the previous chapter in the "Group Access" section) you may want to pre-approve some or all of your LinkedIn connections. Just as in "Send Invitations," you can choose contacts individually or update a file to have your contacts pre-approved for Group membership.

Members

This simply leads you to the default screen, showing your Members that were displayed when you first came to this "Manage" page.

Managers

You can promote up to 10 managers to help you run your Group. Managers will be able to perform all of the functions you can with the settings that LinkedIn provides. If your LinkedIn Group grows to become a very large one, it will take time to manage the Discussions Boards, Jobs postings, Subgroups, etc. Consider adding a Manager from your Trusted Network of Advisors.

Requests to Join

If you elect to manually approve members in "Group Access," this is where you approve all of the requests to join. In my experience, I have usually received an email from LinkedIn when there is a new request to join. This is because I choose to receive daily digests for each of the Groups I created, and the timing of receiving these requests to join could be related to this. If you have a request to join, it will also appear highlighted under the respective Group when you select "Groups" from the left-hand navigation bar.

Invited

All of the people who you invited using the "Send Invitations" functionality will appear here. This will be an important reference to ensure you don't spam your Windmill Network contacts by sending the same invitation out multiple times to the same person.

Pre-Approved

Lists all of those that were pre-approved in the "Pre-Approve People" menu.

Blocked

Shows a list of members that you blocked from joining the Group. Note that you can only block a member after they have joined. To do so, choose the "Remove and Block" option from the "Members" page.

Manage Subgroups

Here is where the manage options from your Group will be made available to provide specific functionality for each of your Subgroups.

Manage News Feeds

LinkedIn gives you the ability to add a News Feed utilizing RSS technology. News items will appear automatically in the News tab of your Group. You cannot filter this RSS feed by keyword or decide on frequency, so be sure the News Feed you choose is really appropriate or relevant to your Group.

Manage Templates

LinkedIn gives you the ability to send an automated message you create under one of the following conditions: Someone requests to join your Group (and you have chosen to manually approve them), someone joins your Group (a welcome message), declining someone membership in your Group, and declining as well as blocking someone from joining your Group again. At a minimum, I suggest you create a Welcome Message to welcome new members and give them the lay of the land.

Edit Group Information

Should you wish to modify any of the original information you used to set up your LinkedIn Group, this is the place to do so. Options include changing your logo, Group Name (which, interestingly, you can only do 5 times), Group Type, Group Summary, Description, and Website URL.

Edit Group Settings

Edit Group Settings allows you to edit some of the original settings you decided on when you created the Group. It also offers some new features. Specifically, the Discussions, News, Jobs and Subgroups features can all be disabled from this screen. I believe disabling these functions defeats the purpose of why you created a LinkedIn Group in the first place; however, the option is there if you need it. You can also change the “Group Access” feature, your email address, and the language and location of your Group.

Change Owner

Group management takes time; it is not entirely unlikely, should you have other priorities in the future, that you might want pass on ownership of your Group to someone else. This is where you can easily do so.

Delete Group

Just in case you ever want to delete your Group, the option is available.

In summary, LinkedIn gives you a powerful set of management tools that allow you to tweak many aspects of your Group. It is time to inform your Windmill Networking friends and attract new Group members!

How Do I Promote My LinkedIn Group?

Now that you have created your own Group and the profile shows that it only has 1 member (you), how do you promote it to get as many LinkedIn members to join as possible?

Promotion starts with your own network of connections. If you are really interested in creating a large Group, then you should be Windmill Networking. Why? How can you hope to have a lot of people join your Group if you don't have anyone to invite? Do you plan to spam people you don't know?

Windmill Networking provides a base (a database, to be specific) where you can search and pinpoint who might be interested in your group. When you contact someone saying that you are a fellow Windmill Networker and are already connected on LinkedIn, you immediately have some credibility with this person.

This brings me to the topic of communications and your LinkedIn Brand. Every time you write something on a Group Discussions Board, send out an invitation, or, in this case, invite someone to your LinkedIn Group, what you say will be seen as part of your LinkedIn Brand. I am a firm believer that, if you created a Group of interest to a specific demographic, and you contact them using the right language, your message will absolutely contribute to your LinkedIn Brand as well as win over new Group members. **Your LinkedIn Group is an extension of you! Consider how best to introduce it to your connections!**

Make sure you only send Group invitations to those you think might be interested in joining the Group. For instance, if you want to target a particular industry or geography, you can isolate those who fit your target through the Advanced Search functionality and then only send the relevant information to them. I think a lot of people are annoyed when they receive Group invitations for Groups that are totally irrelevant to them, and this is where people may think of disconnecting from you because they see this as spam.

In your introduction, be sure to include details regarding the Group that will resonate with your targeted demographic. You should definitely think about your Group "brand." It is important to differentiate yourself from the hundreds, if not thousands, of LinkedIn Groups that already exist. Finally, there should be a good reason for those reading the email you send them to join. What is the benefit to them for joining?

So if you think about your....

1) **Target Audience**
2) **Branding/Differentiation**
3) **Benefits of Joining**

.....you are bound to create an email sent to the right people; I anticipate that a good percentage of people you contact will actually join. My two Groups, So Cal Sushi and The Izakaya Club are very much niche Groups, but already have several hundred members each through employing the techniques I have described.

Also, think critically about your Group name, especially if you run a business and want to name it after your company. If you name it, for example, after your wine company, it may be seen as too narrow, and people may think you just want to sell to them. But if you name it something like "California Wine Fans" or "Wine & Food" to attract more people, you will be more successful at getting people to join your Group, while enjoying the opportunity to potentially *indirectly* sell them your wine.

If your Group focuses on a particular demographic or industry, you want to make sure you are connected with the power connectors in that demographic (those with at least 500+ connections), letting them know about your Group. If they join, others that look at their profile may find you and join as well.

Another tip for promotion is to go on the Discussions Boards on similar Groups that you are a member of and post a message introducing your new Group. This happens quite a lot so I wouldn't worry about etiquette, so long as:

1) **You are differentiating your Group as complementary to the Discussions Board of the Group about which you are writing.**

2) **You are not posting a message everyday. Post it once and move on.** Make sure you are searchable when someone does a search under LinkedIn Groups for whatever keyword or keywords you want associated with your Group. *You can do this by planting these keywords in your Group name or description.*

It will take time, but relax, your Group will slowly and organically grow. Concentrate now on providing unique value to your Group members.

Providing Value to Your Group Members

If you create and promote a Group as I recommended, you will create a new community of tens or even hundreds of professionals who share the same objective in joining together. In essence, **you will create a virtual Windmill Networking farm**. Some of these initial Group members will probably be previously connected within in your network; however, there are bound to be new members in your network who are connected solely through being a member of your Group. The below image illustrates what this will look like.

Figure 6.1. Connecting Random Windmills Through Your Groups

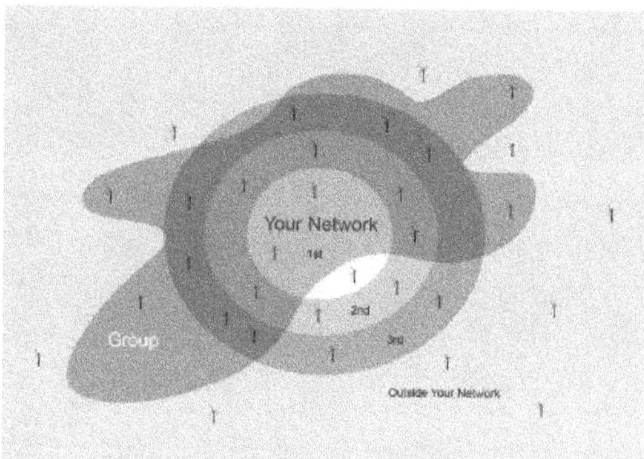

But what to do next? Obviously, every person's objective for creating a Group will be different, but the common thread among all Groups is that you must communicate well with your Group Members and provide them value. There are always new Groups appearing that will compete with your Group for membership. This is because of the dreaded 50 Group limit that we cannot change.

Now I write this at a very sensitive time when LinkedIn has made it very difficult for Group Managers to communicate with their members. Until March of 2009, you could export a list of your Group members in an Excel-readable format called ".csv," just as you can with your direct connections, and then pick and choose how you utilize the email addresses to contact different members for different reasons. This functionality is no longer supported. You can't even see the email address of each Group Member unless you are directly connected with them OR you spot it when they apply for membership to your Group. This is a very unfortunate event that a lot of people (including myself) have already complained to LinkedIn about, so I will not use up valuable space here to add to the complaints.

Your options for communicating and providing value to your Group to make it a "sticky one" are as follows. I believe this is a comprehensive list, but I am always fascinated by the organic growth of certain Groups and how they find creative ways to add new value.

Doing the things I list below should give you a good idea of what is possible to keep your Group Members happy:

Send out a valuable Announcement. This is the only way to communicate with all of your Group Members at once. If your Group has a website, you can include a URL in this message to guide them somewhere else where you can provide them more information, but you don't want to over use this feature and potentially be seen as a spammer. You are also limited to only one Announcement per week.

Add an RSS feed. There is an ability to add an RSS feed from a website or blog to automatically populate the News tab with data. I don't see the value in this unless the RSS feed is clearly aligned with the objective of your Group. If it is not, this may be seen as RSS Spam and people won't look at your News tab. This raises a larger question as to whether people are going to your LinkedIn Group looking for news. If you have a website that fits perfectly with your Group, then great. But, if not, it's probably better to let people organically contribute news articles that they find interesting. You can do the same by creating a Google Alert around a keyword and contributing content when you see a suitable article.

Generate Discussions. As previously mentioned, Discussions is probably the most interactive section of your LinkedIn Group and will generate the most activity. If you have an interesting topic to discuss, you should actively start discussions. Because Group Members may receive weekly digests of Group activity, it is important to do this at least once a week, if possible. Make it interesting, provide value, and try to generate lively discussions. Don't forget to comment on everyone else's discussions to encourage them to contribute more.

Monitor Discussions. Another note about Discussions is the importance of monitoring them to make sure others are not diluting the value of the Group. I create a policy of things that can and can't be posted on the Discussions Board and list it within the "Featured Discussion." Although I do believe in freedom of speech, there may be posts that are irrelevant to the rest of the Group. These are things that should be discussed on a one-to-one basis, as the Discussions Board should not be seen as an Advertisement Board. You can do what you want, but if you see a lot of "spam," I would step in and take action. **You have the freedom to delete any post that you don't think is aligned with the objective of your Group. This is why it is important to create a Discussions Board Policy.**

Manage the Jobs board. It is no secret there are tons of recruiters on LinkedIn. The Discussions Board used to be filled with their job openings. LinkedIn finally stepped in and created a separate Jobs board, as well as the ability to move any discussion to the Jobs board. Two things you can do to increase value here are:

1) *Make sure that Jobs in Discussions are moved to their proper place, as there are some members who don't want to see them and view them as obnoxious.*

2) *If you have a lot of Group members in transition, try contacting recruiters that are members of your Group to get them to contribute more jobs to the Jobs board.*

LinkedIn recently added a "Message Template" functionality, enabling users to automatically send a message to anyone who joins your Group. This is a valuable application to help you efficiently disseminate information automatically to new members.

Until now I have discussed various things you can do within the LinkedIn framework, but there are many things that you can do *outside* of the LinkedIn framework that provide tremendous value to your Group. Many people forget about this. **Windmill Networking is not and should not be limited just to LinkedIn!**

Here are some examples of things I have seen done (without naming names) that have provided value to LinkedIn Groups—while operating *outside* of its framework:

1) Having physical meetings can provide tremendous value to your Group.

Physical meetings bring Windmill Neworking to a new level and can help you quickly and deeply develop relationships.

If your Group is based on a certain geography, this is something you can easily organize. Even if you are spread out, there are creative ways to accomplish this. If you are an industry-specific Group, you could hold meetings at industry exhibitions and conventions. You can do Group Chats or Webinars. **The only restriction here is your imagination.**

2) If you want more of the features that Facebook has for your Group, try starting a complementary group on Ning.com. It is very easy to create such a group, and many of the advanced Web 2.0 features you don't find on LinkedIn are already there. There are quite a few LinkedIn Groups that are already doing this, some better than others. Beware: Asking someone to invest their time in registering on a new group on a new site is asking a lot of them. Make sure you provide enough value and incentive to get them to sign up.

3) Having a weekly or monthly newsletter is another thing you can do to add value. You can feature regular articles you write yourself, as well as encourage people in your group to contribute. Make it a truly collaborative effort. **Once again, your creativity is the only restriction here.**

4) If you have a Group dedicated to Open Networking, or if everyone in your Group buys into Windmill Networking, you could provide a service that allows people to sign up to have their email address put into a .csv file, which is then distributed to its members. The .csv file can then be uploaded on any social network site, including LinkedIn, to find new and trusted people with whom to connect. I would like to point out that I have never offered this to any of my

LinkedIn Groups, but there are LinkedIn Groups who do provide this. In my opinion, I do not think that LinkedIn is very happy about this, as they are very serious about protecting user's privacy and providing a truly "professional" environment. However, if everyone agrees to "opt-in" to this service, and its members are not spamming each other, this could be something of great value to provide to the members should they want it.

I hope this gives you some great ideas. Just remember that LinkedIn Groups should be seen and treated as the communities they are or should become. As with anything else you do in Windmill Networking, your building and fostering a high value community will reap benefits for you.

Chapter 7

<u>Chapter 7 Answers</u>

- LinkedIn Answers: An Introduction
- LinkedIn Answers and Your Trusted Network of Advisors
- Finding Information
- Asking a Question
- Answering a Question
- Becoming an Answers Expert
- A Note on LinkedIn Answers Etiquette
- What Happened to My Question?
- Is There Business to be Found in Answers?

LinkedIn Answers: An Introduction

Many websites on the Internet have been created in an attempt to encourage people to ask and answer questions relating to just about everything. Over the years, the popularity of these sites has waned to the point that Google no longer operates Google Answers. Yahoo Answers and Answers.com still do exist, but it's hard to say what real traffic they attract. With that in mind, what value does LinkedIn Answers provide? How does its Q&A functionality relate to Windmill Networking?

LinkedIn Answers, as with any Web 2.0 application of User Generated Content, is only as good as the people who use it and create quality content for it. Because the demographic is professional, and you can't ask an anonymous question because your Profile Headline is always displayed together with your question, the potential that highly qualified professionals are both asking and answering questions is there. Indeed, I have found LinkedIn Answers to be of tremendous value. I believe you will as well.

Did you know that LinkedIn Answers already posts more than *two million* answers to various questions?[1] This should be enough to warrant your interest!

So when would I use it? Well, my domain of expertise is in social media as well as international sales & business development. What if I want to gain expertise in another field? For instance, I am not an IT person, yet, being a blogger and someone who wants to build a better website, I may want to get people's opinions regarding the best website platform that is available. You can ask your close physical network for their feedback, but just as with social networking in general, your answer is always going to be limited by the experiences and diversity of those around you. That is why I Windmill Network—and why you should too. What if you could ask that same question of 40 million professionals, many of whom have much more expertise in certain areas than you do? That is the idea behind LinkedIn Answers, and I have found many experts in their fields answering questions here with solid advice.

Let's take another example: If you are in business, have you ever been faced with a problem upon which you wanted third-party advice or a second opinion on? LinkedIn Answers is there for you. Furthermore, by scanning the Answers boards, it *is* possible to find business. I have given my own business to people who have provided me advice via LinkedIn Answers. As more and more people discover the value in LinkedIn Answers, I believe there will be more business out there to gain. **You can see how Pay It Forward and Windmill Networking go hand-in-hand with both asking and answering questions on Answers.**

That is the real beauty of LinkedIn Answers: There are a lot of Pay It Forward networkers out there willing to lend a helping hand and answer a question. On top of that, LinkedIn gives those whose answers are chosen as the "best" an *Expertise Star*, a designation that remains with them on their profile. These Expertise Stars can even be searched for via the Experts Database in the LinkedIn Answers application. This gives many people an incentive to try to show off their expertise, and is another way you could strengthen your own LinkedIn Brand.

I will go through the mechanics of Answers in the following sections, but, if you have yet to ask a Question, before reading forward, go ahead and experiment. I think you'll be pleasantly surprised with both the quality and quantity of responses. If you are an expert in something, which we all are, why not donate some time each week to answering a few questions and helping people? LinkedIn gives us the tools for Windmill Networking. It is up to us to utilize them.

LinkedIn Answers and Your Trusted Network of Advisors

Have you ever wondered what other professionals think about a certain subject? Looked for a solution to a business problem but didn't know who to ask? Been in a fight with someone over whose opinion is right? Can't decide which piece of equipment for your home or for your office you should select?

Instead of wasting time googling information or spending time on the phone, you now have 24x7 access to this information through "LinkedIn Answers." Yes, it is that awesome. The beauty of LinkedIn Answers is, regardless of the size of your network, your question will be accessible to all 40+ million members of LinkedIn. You will also be able to access the database of 2 million questions asked and answered by the same huge network!

LinkedIn Answers is not going to be able to answer every single question you might have. After all, the questions and answers are being asked and answered by professionals. **If you think of LinkedIn Answers as a virtual Trusted Network of Advisors, you are beginning to understand the value of its existence.**

I used to be a skeptic myself, but, one day I became a believer: My wife and I were debating over whether we really needed anti-virus software or not, and if we did, which brand would be the best. "Why don't you ask a few of your friends?" she asked me. Not many of my friends had this sort of expertise. I'll do something better than that, I thought: I'll ask The Network (picture that Verizon guy with his support group behind him).

A little more than twenty-four hours after I posed the question, I received 69 answers from professionals, many who worked in the Information Technology field. The answers varied; everyone seemed truly sincere in wanting to help me solve my problem. I was honestly overwhelmed; it was then I began to recognize the potential for LinkedIn Answers to supplement my own Trusted Network of Advisors.

Since then I have posed questions on other occasions. Questions like: "What resources are available to help me publish this book?" For instance, I have helped my brother find advice on buying new or used IT equipment, along with which vendor he should use. I have also asked if anyone has heard of websites I wasn't familiar with to find out what potential value they offered.

I hope these examples illustrate the value that "LinkedIn Answers" can and should provide for you. It took me a while to get used to the concept of publicly posing these sorts of questions on LinkedIn; however, considering the high quality and often passionate responses I have received, I am definitely hooked—and I am sure you will be as well. **Answers may be the best kept and most valuable secret on LinkedIn.** Consider the potential value there can be when solving business problems through gathering advice here.

There's more to LinkedIn Answers than just asking your own questions. There is also the other side of the equation: the answers, and specifically those who answer them. Yes, there is the searchable database of all of the Answers. In many cases you need not even have to ask a question. By answering a question, you are not only showing off your expertise to 40 million people; you are also creating a new relationship with someone else on LinkedIn. You are now truly becoming part of the LinkedIn *community* of professionals once you start contributing in this way. You are also participating in Windmill Networking when you start contributing to the success of others.

Finding Information

Now that you recognize LinkedIn Answers as an immense database of information by and for professionals, how do you go about finding relevant information?

The "Answers" tab is located in a prominent position on the top of your LinkedIn page, on the top navigation bar, slightly to the right of the LinkedIn official logo. By selecting this tab, you will be taken to a busy looking screen with five different tabs. If you just want to take Answers for a test drive, take a look at the Browse window on the right-hand side. You will see that LinkedIn has conveniently categorized all of the answers into 20+ categories.

As Answers is for professionals, you will see the categories smartly organized by either industry or professional-specific subject matter. For instance, "Administration" as well as "Law and Legal" have their own categories, but there are also categories labeled "Personal Finance" and "Using LinkedIn."

Pressing any of these categories will give you a snapshot of open questions from your network in that category. Be forewarned: Not all of the questions are professional in manner. Some people advertise themselves or their companies or want you to join their Groups. Others are very open-ended "What do you think of President Obama?" type questions. If you sift through the many questions you should find quite a few diamonds in the rough. Your mileage will obviously vary depending on the category.

So how are things categorized? The author of the question can choose up to two categories in which he or she can post a question. That's right, this is an open community; therefore, neither LinkedIn nor some sort of engine is doing the categorizing. That means if someone is trying to reach out to a certain professional group, his or her question could be completely irrelevant to that category.

You will also notice the "Open" and "Closed" terminology. When you ask a question, it becomes "Open." It will become "Closed" automatically in seven days, unless you manually decide to close it beforehand. If you are not looking to answer a question but are searching for an answer, it should not make a difference to you whether the question you are viewing is open or closed.

The final important thing to point out on this page is the “Experts” column. Whenever a question is closed, the questioner can decide whether or not one of the answers was a “Best” answer. Those who receive “Best” answers in a particular category receive an expert “Star” for that category and are thus listed here. The idea here is if you look at the answers on their profile, you are able to glean information without going through the entire Answers section. Alternatively, you can consider contacting them directly for specific advice. After all, if they are experts AND are openly lending their expertise to the LinkedIn Answers forum, chances are they would more than likely enjoy hearing from you. I know I would!

I hope you now have a feel for how Answers works. But if you really want to find specific information, you need to navigate using the “Advanced Answers Search” tab. This is where you can enter keywords and then further filter out your answers by selecting a category and their corresponding subcategories. Unfortunately, at the time of this writing, Answers apparently did not support multiple category selection through the control key on my Chrome browser, but I hope they will add this functionality soon.

After entering your keywords and choosing your category, tens or hundreds of answers may appear. Depending on the subject, you may have to search through not-so-relevant questions, but I hope you can see the potential here. If you don’t find the answer you are looking for, ask a question!

Asking a Question

If you skipped the previous section entitled "Finding Information," please go back! If everyone, before asking a question, did an advanced search to see whether or not their question was previously answered, it would potentially provide you with quicker advice, it would also help improve the overall quality of the Answers database by avoiding repetition. Please try to make this a habit before asking a question. As I mentioned earlier, the quality of Answers will only be as good as the content we create (or don't recreate!).

So now you are ready to ask your first question. What to ask? It really depends on what your objective is in asking the question. From my LinkedIn experience, I believe people ask questions for the following reasons:

- They want an answer to a question or solution to a problem they are facing
- They are trying to gain more subject matter expertise in a particular field for their professional objective
- They are using the question to potentially show off their expertise or connect with more people who have similar interests
- They are advertising something (Group, Event, website, product, etc.)

I will not go into the benefits of the above approaches, as I will cover them in later chapters of this book. However, it is important to understand that Answers can be leveraged as part of your overall LinkedIn strategy, not just to satisfy your curiosity.

Asking a question on Answers is easy. Navigate over to the "Ask a Question" tab, enter a question in the top tab, and add further details in the "Add Details section." Choose your category or optional second category and then press the "Ask Question" button. Done! Whenever someone answers the question, you will get an email with the answer message. Sit back and watch the answers unfold!

In order to get the most optimum answers to your question, I recommend you do the following before pressing the "Ask a Question" button:

- Do NOT select the "Only share this question with connections I select." This defeats the whole purpose of Windmill Networking, and prevents you from being able to question the 40 million professionals on LinkedIn! If you want to ask your own network something, send out an email or call them!

- Always add relevant details to your question. Remember, you are asking for time from other professionals to stop what they are doing and answer your question, so the more details you provide, the better. These details illustrate your seriousness in asking the question. Details also pinpoint the information you are looking for, resulting in higher quality answers.

- If it is relevant, try to choose two different categories in which you post your question. You will only see the option show up after you choose one category, but you might as well get the biggest bang for your buck if you are going to invest the time and energy to ask.

- Unless your question IS location-specific, do NOT select the "My question is based around a specific location" option. I have never selected it, but doing so may make your question visible to only a subset of the LinkedIn community.

- You will also notice three other options at the bottom before submitting your question. I have never selected any of these options, but my understanding is, if you want to fill a position, advertise a service, or want to announce that you are looking for a job, you should not be asking a question! There are other areas of LinkedIn that are tailored to these objectives; the Answers section is not an appropriate place to do so.

Once you start receiving answers, if you are satisfied with what you have received, please don't wait for the automatic close. Instead, go ahead and manually close your answer to save other's time. You will then be given the option to choose "Good" answers, and then a "Best" answer from the "Good" answers. Go ahead and reward those who took the time to give you a thoughtful and excellent answer.

Answering a Question

Answering your first question may seem intimidating. I highly recommend you take a deep breath and contribute your expertise to the LinkedIn community.

The Answers database is a true orphan of the Web 2.0 world, as it is often neglected. This section of LinkedIn is only as good as our contributions.

Why answer questions? To me, answering questions is one of the fundamentals of networking and communicating with others. I assume if you are on LinkedIn AND you bought this book, you are interested in expanding your network.

It all comes down to the Pay It Forward concept of Windmill Networking. You may want someone's help for a particular purpose, and vice-versa. Answering someone's question utilizing your own expertise is one of the nicest things you can do to help jumpstart a relationship with another professional.

The fact that you answer the question in your own domain of expertise means there may be advantages in getting to know the person who asked the question—or even the other people who answered the question. These are truly open and virtual forums for you to network with your peers. The question is merely the vehicle in which to do so and is a great example of how you can leverage LinkedIn for the purpose of Windmill Networking.

As previously mentioned, answering the question gives you a chance to show off your expertise. LinkedIn gives you the option to actually display all of your questions and answers right on your LinkedIn Profile, so your expertise will be seen by all if you choose to do so. I recommend displaying these questions and answers, as they help enrich your LinkedIn Brand.

Answering a question is as easy as finding one. If you are looking to answer a particular type of question to jumpstart your networking and/or show off your expertise on LinkedIn, you can either go to the "Answer Questions" tab and browse open questions by category, or go back to the "Advanced Answers

Search" tab and then choose the "Questions Only" under the keyword match. You can then choose the option to show only unanswered questions if you want to be the first person to answer them. Remember, you cannot answer closed questions, so be sure to look only for the open ones.

Once you select a question there will be an "Answer" button you can press. You can then enter your answer in the text box. You will be reminded here that your answer will be seen by all LinkedIn users, so be sure to do a spell check as well as a sanity check before you send it. If there is a website that further supports your answer, enter the URL below. I never check "Select an Expert," as you are trying to show *your* expertise; however, if there is someone in your Windmill Network that you want to show respect for, this is a great way to do so. You can also write a personal note, which is recommended if you really want to connect with this person and get more background on them and/or their question.

That's it! Press "Submit," and your Answer, along with your Profile Headline, will appear under the Question.

You can see how simply answering a question not only shows off your expertise, but also gives you exposure. Anyone who visits this question will see your Profile Headline. You are essentially advertising yourself here as well. Your answer is now part of your LinkedIn Brand.

One recommendation to follow: When answering questions is to always read the previous answers to make sure I am actually building upon what was previously said and adding some value. It is annoying if you are saying something that is identical to someone who previously answered. This will actually work against what people think of you. If someone already answered the question the same way that you would, don't answer it. Perhaps refer to someone's previous answer and give further information from a slightly different angle. Referencing previous people's expertise who have answered and adding your own additional expertise is a truly classy way to contribute to the Answers forum.

Remember, above all, answering questions is about adding value, NOT about advertising yourself.

Becoming an Answers Expert

As you start answering questions and contributing to the LinkedIn community, in time some of your answers will be chosen as the best ones. When your answer is chosen as the best one, you are not necessarily notified unless the person who asked you the question informs you. If you want to keep track of your best answer tally, and you have chosen to display your answers on your profile, select "View My Profile" from the left-hand navigation bar. A "(Your Name) Q&A" section appears on the right-hand side of your profile underneath the logos of the Groups you are a member of. This is exactly how your expertise will look to others who view your profile.

If any of your answers are marked as best answers, it should display a big green box with a white star, and inside this box will be a listing of all of these answers. Considering LinkedIn is a site for professionals, and seeing that it is also a site where can people be found, being labeled as an expert in a particular field definitely makes your profile gain respect from the community.

Some people will take an active approach to answering questions. Based on my experience, if you really want to become an expert in a particular field, I recommend answering questions, as doing so is always a learning experience when you teach others. If you want to aggressively build up your expertise, I recommend doing the following:

- Your Home Page gives you the option to add modules containing the latest questions that have been asked in a particular category. Adding these modules to your Home Page on LinkedIn gives you the opportunity to check out the latest questions whenever you refresh the page. On the right-hand side of your Home Page you should see a "Who's viewed my profile" text box. If you keep scrolling down, you may already find a LinkedIn Answers box that has been added to your Home Page. You can edit this to the category of your choosing, or keep going down to the bottom where you should see a + sign with the wording "Add an application." This gives you the opportunity to add additional

Answers category modules to your Home Page. I currently have six categories showing on my Home Page, so even if you check this page only once or twice a day, it will give you a chance to efficiently monitor questions you may want to answer. If you want to receive the new question information in real-time, you can subscribe to an RSS feed of each category in Answers by browsing that category from the "Answers Home" tab. Then look for the orange RSS symbol on the right-hand side of the page under the heading "Subscribe to new questions in:"

- Once you start answering questions for a particular category, you will notice there are a few other people who are also answering the same questions. If you can somehow "beat them to the punch" and answer the question before they do, it will put them on the defensive; they may feel the urge to come up with something that does not sound like what you have written. If it is a subjective question, this is another story, but for many objective questions this could set you apart from the competition in your quest for expertise. **As I mentioned before, if others have already answered the question in a way that you wanted to, either don't answer or differentiate yourself by adding value to the conversation.**

- Depending on the category, you may notice the same questions come up and you are often repeating yourself. Create a Microsoft Word document and keep your answers ready. But always try to customize them for the particular situation. You want to come across as real and genuine and not as a "copy-and-paste answerer."

Best of luck to you on your quest for expertise! Remember to check back on the Answers Home Page and browse the experts' rankings for a particular category to see how you rank!

A Note on LinkedIn Answers Etiquette

As you begin to further realize the value of asking questions and providing answers on LinkedIn, it is a good time to think about the proper etiquette for participating in the Answers forum. Now I am no Mr. Proper, but there are a few things I have noticed that I would like to share with everyone. I may have alluded to some of these in previous sections of this chapter, but I think it is important enough to warrant its own section. Let's recap the proper etiquette to follow when asking and answering questions.

When asking a question:

- **Make sure you completely enter your question.** There have been many "partial" questions that have been cut-off mid-way or that just look incomplete. Before pressing the send button, take another look at it and make sure it makes sense!

- **Choose the most appropriate category.** When you enter a question, you need to choose at least one (with an option to choose two) category in which you want to broadcast your question. Don't choose a category that is totally irrelevant to your question (you'd be surprised as to how many people do this). On your Home Page, you have the option of "subscribing" to Answers categories where these questions are broadcast; the "experts" diligently look at questions in their category on a daily basis. If you want to earn their trust and receive intelligent answers, make sure you categorize appropriately.

- **Send out thank you messages to each person who diligently answers your question.** I realize this is difficult when you receive a lot of answers—I am not perfect in this respect either—but I believe taking the time to write these thank you messages is a worthwhile goal that pays dividends in the long-run.

- **Rate your answers.** Many people answer questions so they can get a "Best Answer" rating and acquire expertise "stars" in that category. If you ask a question, be sure after your answer is closed that you rate the answers by first picking good answers (if applicable) and then picking a best answer from those good answers (again, if applicable). It will make the person who asked this question very, very happy. As I mentioned earlier, LinkedIn will automatically close your answer in seven days, but you will still need to manually choose a best answer.

When answering a question:

- **Be real.** Be genuine. Be deep. Don't just provide a few word answer. Everyone can see your answer, and your answer can also be found on your profile. Every single answer becomes a part of your LinkedIn Brand. Answer questions in a way you would want to represent yourself to the world. Be thoughtful and add supplemental evidence. Providing a meaningful answer will make you stand out and help you connect with new people. I have made some solid new connections through the Answers section.

- **Look at the other answers before you answer something.** If you don't have any value to add, don't answer. Even if you want to say the same thing, at least put a different spin on it or add more detail than the person before you did.

There is a tremendous amount of value in LinkedIn Answers. If everyone followed the above etiquette, the value to all involved would substantially increase over time.

What Happened to My Question?

I don't enjoy getting into controversial discussions about LinkedIn; however, because the Answers is an open forum, it has its advantages and disadvantages. Up until now I have only discussed the advantages. Before concluding this collection of chapters on Answers, it is necessary to look at the potential negative aspects.

I have seen some truly unprofessional questions posted within this professional forum. Any average day will present some pretty bizarre questions. Just today I saw someone ask, "How much does a passport cost you?" in the "Utilizing LinkedIn" category! You may not mind answering questions that make no sense; you may not mind looking at the multitude of questions that are not questions, but are merely advertisements. But regardless of how you feel about this, it is a shame that LinkedIn does not have someone monitoring the Answers section to filter out some of these "irrelevant" questions.

Actually, we can all volunteer our time to monitor the Answers. For any question that is asked, if you go to its respective answer page, there is an option to "Flag" the question. When you press the "Flag this question" button, you get to choose why you are flagging this question from all of the valid reasons why some of these questions *should* be flagged:

- Duplicate post
- Job-seeking message
- Recruitment message
- An advertisement
- Inappropriate comment
- Connection-building spam

- Misrepresentation
- Others (including a text box for details)

We should all be on the lookout for absurd questions and flag them, as this is essentially reporting to LinkedIn. LinkedIn's policy seems to be that because this is user generated content, it will be user monitored as well. Unfortunately, with the increasing amounts of truly inappropriate content and spam rearing its ugly head, you have to start wondering whether or not this is a valid policy. When will LinkedIn start policing the Answers board to protect its value?

On the other hand, what happens when the users themselves abuse the system of flagging questions that probably should not be flagged? What happens when they begin flagging valid questions because they either dislike the person posing the question or are simply having a bad day? Couldn't happen on LinkedIn? Think again.

I have never had one of my questions flagged, but a good friend of mine has. I actually answered his question; I checked back an hour later to see the question had been removed. Apparently on my friend's screen there was a message saying the question had been flagged by others because it was seen, among other things, as containing "inappropriate content." Do you know what the question was concerning? It was actually asking for people to read my LinkedIn blog post and comment on my post entitled "I Have Lots of Connections...What Do I Do With Them?" I did not ask him to do this; he was simply interested in hearing LinkedIn users' opinions on the subject. Is this really "inappropriate content?" You will have to be the final judge of that, but the implications make me feel *very* uncomfortable.

Upon further research on the subject (although I could not personally confirm this) apparently the baseball rule of "three strikes and you're out" governs how questions are removed on LinkedIn. In other words, three flags and your question is removed. Imagine, 3 out of 40 million professionals can get your question removed from LinkedIn. My friend actually contacted LinkedIn Customer Service to ask for further explanation as to why it was considered "inappropriate content" and never received a response.

I only bring this issue up because I think there is a serious fault in the system. Either raise the number of flags needed to remove a question; monitor people who inappropriately flag questions, or set up an internal or external board of people who make the final decision of whether or not to remove the questions. Although I am sure questions are not flagged as inappropriate very often, it leaves a bitter taste in the mouth of those who ask genuinely appropriate questions.

Upon conducting more detailed research on the "Using LinkedIn" section of Answers, I uncovered further restrictions. For example, I discovered there appears to be limitations as to both the number of questions you can *ask* and answer in a certain time period. LinkedIn always seems to be in a state of flux, but if you are interested in keeping up on these topics, please check into the "Using LinkedIn" category of Answers. This is the area that will keep you the most up-to-date.

Is There Business to be Found in Answers?

If you have never asked a question on Answers before, the potential to find business here may seem ludicrous. It's like saying someone will look at Yahoo Answers to find hidden purchase orders. But let's look at the demographic and psyche of those asking the questions on LinkedIn. The people asking questions:

1) Fall into a professional demographic
2) Have, on average, a six—figure income[2]
3) Are usually asking a question because they are looking for advice they can't find in their own physical network

Everyone asking a question, along with those answering, are all *Windmill Networkers;* they are reaching out and receiving and/or providing help to a virtual network.

I mentioned in an earlier chapter there is business to be found on the Discussions Boards. Why would Answers be any different? The Group Discussions Boards are based around a particular community you trust; something you ask there may be geared towards a certain demographic or skill set you are confident exists in that Group. For instance, when I was looking for an editor, instead of putting a question on Answers, I went to the Alumni Group of my college, as I felt the people responding to my question there would be at least of a standard that met my expectations.

So what is asked on Answers that wouldn't be asked on a Group Discussions Board? Let's look at a personal example. I needed to better understand my options for self-publishing. I was not a member of any Group that communicated with the people who may possess this knowledge. The people who look at Answers, though, come from every demographic that is on LinkedIn. I knew if I asked a question and made sure it appeared on the Answer board in an appropriate category, I would get the best answer—and I did get the best answer. There were companies selling me their wares, and I ended up using a company recommended by others. The publisher of this book, as well as the company I plan to use to issue the press release announcing this book, were both "found" through recommendations on LinkedIn Answers—and they will get real money from me.

If you are in sales and/or business development, you need to be looking regularly at the Answers boards for the particular category in which you have something to sell. Not every question will provide business leads, but as more people join LinkedIn, I hope they will begin to see Answers as part of their virtual Network of Trusted Advisors—in a Windmill Networking sense. There will be more professionals with very specific questions who will be looking for Answers that may lead to new business for you.

You can monitor Answers from the "Application" modules on the right-hand side of your Home Page, though it is better to make a habit of monitoring the Answers for your particular category or categories on a daily basis. You can do so via the real-time RSS feed. Otherwise, you could be missing out on potential business.

Chapter 8

Chapter 8Applications

- What are Applications?
- Reading List by Amazon
- Google Presentation & SlideShare Presentations
- WordPress & Blog Link
- Box.net Files & Huddle Workspaces
- My Travel by Tripit
- Events
- Company Buzz
- Polls

What are Applications?

LinkedIn released the Applications functionality, after much anticipation, in October of 2008. That's right, Applications have not even been around for a year as I write this book—and it shows. Their adoption rate, as indicated by the number of my connections who display Applications on their profile, has been mixed as best. Let me explain some potential reasons why in more detail to give you some background.

Applications continue to be a misunderstood value-add to your LinkedIn Profile. It's a shame they are under utilized. As you read my next sections detailing the various Applications, you will see there is tremendous value that has something for everyone, regardless of your LinkedIn Objective.

The user interface in accessing Applications is a little tricky, so let me do my best to first of all give you a glimpse of what Applications are available:

- You can go to the Applications page by accessing it on your left-hand navigation bar and selecting "Applications" in bold.

- Applications can also be displayed individually. You can then add them by selecting the appropriate Applications after pressing the "Add an Application" button at the bottom of the right-hand navigation bar.

- The "Events" application can only be found by selecting "Add an Application."

When browsing through these Applications, you will notice a lot of 3rd party application names (Google, WordPress) along with Applications developed by LinkedIn. The common thread: these are all optional and additional modules that were created using the LinkedIn API (see "API" in the Glossary if you are unfamiliar with this term). **Applications allow professionals to communicate, collaborate, and share information to make them more effective and competitive as LinkedIn advertises**. I urge you to continue reading this entire chapter, find Applications that are relevant to you, and take them for a test drive. There is a potential treasure trove of information and value in utilizing Applications to achieve your LinkedIn Objective.

As noted above, the original intention of these Applications was undoubtedly to help professionals become more effective. I think you will find that LinkedIn has done an excellent job of doing this within a professional framework. Some people may have thought LinkedIn was trying to emulate the way Facebook has implemented an Open API [An API that is publicly available for anyone to create an application and fully access core functionality and profiles] and the ability to extend your profile with a multitude of applications. It is clear that the applications LinkedIn has developed with their partners are purely for professional use, not for entertainment.

From a creative perspective, Applications give you the freedom to customize your profile and extend your LinkedIn Brand from a number of different angles. The profile format is the same for every member; before Applications, the only way to add "color" to your LinkedIn Brand was either through your choice of words, Recommendations, or LinkedIn Groups memberships. By simply installing an Application, your profile will literally be displayed in a different light. Thus, utilizing Applications is one way to customize and display your brand online.

Although some people may want to try to install *all* of the Applications for a test run, it is clear that not every Application is for every professional. Some of the Applications overlap in terms of functionality.

If you don't use Applications correctly, their presence on your profile could actually dilute your brand image and work against you.

For instance, I was using the "My Travel" application for about two months. It would show my network when I was traveling and where I was going. Though an interesting tool, this information did not really align with my LinkedIn Objective, so I deleted the application. I think it took people away from the "meat" of my profile. You will have to install an application and then click "View My Profile" to see if the appearance looks professional enough to you. Remember: These "Applications" will be displayed right after your summary and right before your work experience, so they occupy prime real estate on your Profile.

I used to think that all of these Applications would automatically appear on my Profile; this may be the biggest misunderstanding of Applications. Yes, Applications will show up on your profile by default. But you have the option to control what shows up on your profile and what shows up on your Home Page, for your eyes only. You may see a lot of profiles that have been "diluted" by putting too many or potentially inappropriate Applications on their Profile, but don't be discouraged. You can install Applications, and *choose* not to have them displayed on your Profile. If you are ever in doubt, choosing Applications from the left-hand navigation and then selecting your particular installed Application will give you the ability to customize this through two checkbox settings on the right-hand side: "Display on my profile" and "Display on my LinkedIn homepage."

WindMill WISDOM

What capabilities does Applications have? Below is a snapshot of each Application, as well the types of people who may be interested in installing them:

- **Like to Read Books? → Reading List by Amazon**
- **Travel Often? → My Travel**
- **On or Interested in Twitter? → Company Buzz**
- **Do You Have a Blog? → WordPress or Blog Link**
- **Do You Want to Share a PowerPoint or Other File with the World? → SlideShare Presentations, Google Presentation, Box.net or Huddle Workspaces**
- **Have an Event to Advertise? → Events**
- **Interested in Market Research? → Polls**

This is really only a shorthand list to give you some ideas of which Applications may interest you. I encourage you to read on about each and every Application, as some of the value they can provide is multi-faceted. For instance, even if you aren't interested in Twitter, if you are in Marketing, you may be interested to find out what "Buzz Words" are being associated on Twitter with your company, which can be found in the "Company Buzz" application. This is just one example of the potential value each Application offers for multiple demographics with varying objectives.

The value of many of the Applications only begins with LinkedIn. Many of these Applications are mash-ups with established websites. For instance, by installing SlideShare, you could be making your presentation not only accessible to all LinkedIn members, but also to everyone in the SlideShare community on their website. **Thus, when using Applications, you are potentially Windmill Networking over multiple social networks!**

Reading List by Amazon

If you enjoy reading books, you are in for a treat with this Amazon application. I originally installed it, believing it would be cool to let people in my network, or people who read my profile, know what I was reading. I thought that depending on my choice of books, it could actually add to the value of my LinkedIn Brand. It was only when I recently accessed the application from my right-hand navigation bar, for the first time in a long time, did I see this application as an alternative to searching through Amazon.com for a new book to buy or read. After reading this chapter, you will see how it provides unique functionalities to add to both your Windmill Networking and your LinkedIn Branding.

First of all, let's begin with what happens after you install the application. Assuming you enter a book you are either reading or plan to read, these books, their cover photos, and your comments will appear in your profile, together with a link to their respective pages on Amazon. You first have a text box in which you search for a book title. The navigation is clumsy, as you will only have a few book covers and titles to view at a time; the more targeted your search is in terms of appropriate keywords, the less headache you will have. Once you find the appropriate book, you can indicate that you either want to read it, are reading it, or have read it. If you have read it, there is an option to add a "I recommend this book" thumbs up logo that will appear above your comment. Finally, you have a huge text box in which you can comment on the book as you so desire, as long as it fits within 5,000 characters.

Since I believe only the most recent two books you read will be displayed on your profile, you can see how you can utilize this to help extend your LinkedIn Brand. If you are in sales and consistently display the latest cutting edge books on sales and sales management, commenting on them as you read them, wouldn't this add to your brand?

After you've created your initial book review, let's navigate back to the "Reading List by Amazon" link on the left-hand navigation bar. In addition to your own entries under the "Your Reading List" you will notice there are tabs for “Network Updates,” “Industry Updates,” and “All Recent Updates.” The purpose of these tabs is to connect similar-minded LinkedIn members, as well as provide a way for members to view what the entire LinkedIn Network is reading. The one thing to note is that the “Industry” is chosen for you based on the default industry of your current company, NOT the industry you chose for your profile.

Trying to find potential books to read as recommended by your network or industry is not as easy as it sounds, probably because you can only navigate through five books at a time. Nevertheless, LinkedIn has given you the opportunity to “follow” other people and to easily navigate to what is on their reading list. The option to “watch” someone’s list is displayed next to each book you find as you navigate the tabs here, but if you find a profile on LinkedIn that has this application installed, you can also “watch” that person by viewing all of the books they have read.

The cool thing about “watching” someone’s book reading list on LinkedIn is that this information will start populating in the right-hand side of your “Your Reading List” tab in a module entitled “Who’s Watching Who?” It will not only show the people who you are watching, but also who is watching you! Don’t be surprised if someone has started watching you, as you will not be notified once this happens. I hadn’t looked at this screen after installing the application a few months ago and noticed I already had 5 followers. Your mileage might vary.

The fun continues in that not only can you see the other people following the same person you are following, you can see which people the person you are following is following. I hope you get the idea that through watching other people that you find with similar interests, you can get pretty personalized recommendations as to what books you may be interested in reading.

But wait, there’s more! If there is a particular book you are interested in, by selecting it, you can see which LinkedIn members are reading that book; if they have a comment, you can also see what they are saying about it! This is like a mini-Amazon recommendation done by a professional demographic that may even serve as better advice than what Amazon.com can offer. Each person reviewing the book has a link to their profile together with their name. As a point of reference, the average Amazon recommendation and number of reviews, together with a link to the Amazon site, does appear with each book.

Here is another way of finding people with similar book interests: Simply search for a book you have read and see who has reviewed it. If you like the review, it may make sense to follow that person for future references. But take note: This only works for books you find on a screen that displays what either you or someone else has read. If you search for a new book to recommend and then choose that book, you will be led back to the Amazon page, instead of who on LinkedIn has read it. This is unfortunate if you are looking for LinkedIn reviews of a book that neither you nor anyone in your watch list has read. The only reasonable option in this case is to add the book to your Reading List as a book you plan to read in the future by selecting it.

Unfortunately, if you are looking for reviews of more obscure books or those that the LinkedIn professional demographic might shun, you might not find many reviews. For instance, a book like *What Color is My Parachute?* had more than 200 reviews. On the other hand, I was the first one to review a book my cousin, Dylan Schaffer, wrote called *Life, Death & Bialys: A Father/Son Baking Story*—despite the fact that this book has 17 Amazon customer reviews.

Whether or not you read books, you can see how utilizing this Application can add to your LinkedIn Brand. It could also help your Windmill Networking objective by allowing you to connect with people that have similar book interests. If you do like reading books, this Application will definitely add a lot of value to your reading experience!

Google Presentation & SlideShare Presentations

Google Presentation & SlideShare Presentations are two different ways for professionals to introduce themselves as well as their work. The idea is that you upload a presentation and then let the whole world see it.

Why you would want to display a presentation on your profile depends on your LinkedIn Objective, and may also be related to your LinkedIn Brand. What you display here helps paint a picture of who you are. You want to be careful. However, there are several intelligent ways to use these applications:

- To display your company's standard presentation and increase your brand recognition (especially if you are in sales and marketing)
- To showcase your recent talk at an industry show or seminar
- To display your portfolio, especially if you are in a field where pictures hold more value than words
- To introduce yourself in a unique way, especially if you are on the job hunt
- To share a "heavy" presentation that is inconvenient to email to several people
- To promote your LinkedIn Brand in a creative way

Creating a Presentation

Utilizing these applications is simple enough. Let's start with an overview of Google Presentation. You simply upload a PowerPoint presentation or create a new presentation online using the templates as part of the Google Docs application. If you use Google Mail or already have a Google Docs account, you can understand the benefits of choosing Google Presentation over SlideShare

Applications. You can easily access your Google Docs page from within the LinkedIn Application, which will open a new browser tab pointing at Google.

Creating a new presentation online with Google Presentation is easy; however, upon saving it, it didn't synch up automatically in the LinkedIn Application when I used it. I had to literally press the "Google Presentations" button in the left-navigation bar again in order to see the newly created application show up within LinkedIn. I hope you will not have this same problem.

After selecting "Share this presentation with my connections," Google Presentations will create an Inbox message that reminds your connections to visit your profile to see the new presentation you have posted. Furthermore, when uploading to your profile, there is an option to broadcast the fact that you are adding a new presentation to your profile by checking the box that says "Send network update."

SlideShare Presentations: The Choice for Windmill Networking

For all that Google Presentation has going for it, I rarely see it on someone's LinkedIn profile. For those showing off presentations, SlideShare Presentations seems to be the most popular choice. Let's take a look at why this may be the case. One major restriction I found with Google Presentation is that you can display only *one* presentation on your profile at a time. SlideShare Presentations gives you the ability to display up to *four* presentations. But there is much more to the story than just this simple fact.

I believe the original concept behind Google Presentations, which was obviously available before it was made a LinkedIn Application, was about replacing Microsoft PowerPoint and creating online applications that can be created and accessed anywhere for free. SlideShare Presentations goes beyond simply creating presentations and revolves around sharing them with anyone, anywhere. You can literally share your presentations with the world or you can keep them private. With thousands of presentations on its site, SlideShare Presentations, as its name suggests, is apparently the world's largest community for sharing presentations. **In other words, it is the LinkedIn within the world of presentations—the place for you to find presentations, as well as have your presentations be found.** Because the SlideShare site includes the following features, it can be seen as a social networking site akin to

LinkedIn. Windmill Networking can be applied to SlideShare Presentations in order to:

- Connect with other professionals with interesting content
- Join groups of professionals related to an interesting subject
- Advertise or look for events
- Participate and vote in contests

I have heard many Windmill Networking success stories from LinkedIn users after displaying SlideShare Presentations on their LinkedIn profile. Their LinkedIn profiles were then displayed on the SlideShare site; people they had never met were choosing the presentation as a "favorite" or offering this person paid work as a result.

The potential is definitely there to leverage SlideShare Presentations as part of your LinkedIn Objective; utilizing SlideShare in conjunction with LinkedIn is certainly a productive step on your personal path of Windmill Networking.

Since SlideShare was designed to be a social network in itself, what you create and put in your LinkedIn Profile can also easily be added as a module to your blog or website, as well as shared on social bookmarking sites. If you are already using SlideShare, you understand the value. If not, LinkedIn does you a great service by introducing this great social network to you, which you can now leverage inside as well as outside of LinkedIn. You can now increase your Windmill Networking power by virtually connecting to a different demographic on the SlideShare website that may not already be on LinkedIn! Furthermore, there is a similar plug-in for Facebook, so you now have the option to synch up your LinkedIn Brand with the 200 million Facebook users around the world.

The Mechanics of SlideShare Presentations

After adding the SlideShare Presentations application, you will need to either synch your present account or create a new username & password, which you can do within the LinkedIn Application. Once you are in, you cannot create a presentation; instead, you will be immediately asked to upload one. Whereas Google Presentation is presentation-centric, SlideShare Presentations gives you the ability to create presentations from a number of file types and presentation file varieties, including Word documents, Excel spreadsheets, and even PDF files.

Moreover, because SlideShare Presentations is a *social* networking application, after refreshing the application, you will immediately see the Network Activity of all of your connections who either posted new presentations, commented on a presentation, or even "favorited" a presentation. To gain a better understanding of what your network is doing and the value of these social features, you can find the major functionality in the "Your Slidespace" tab. By selecting "Your Connections," you can not only see your presentations and those you marked as favorites, you can also see all of your connections' presentations displayed in chronological order, the most recent being first. Furthermore, you can also see how many views and comments they have. I found more than 1,500 presentations total through my connections, meaning there is approximately 1 presentation online for every 10 LinkedIn connections I have. Google Presentation completely lacks this social accessibility.

You can also choose "Your Application Settings" from the "Your Slidespace" menu to get an idea of additional functionality and social aspects of this application that Google Presentation simply lacks. Not only can you now post up to four presentations for display on your profile, but you can also decide how many thumbnails for your multiple presentations can be displayed on your website. You can also display one with the full player on screen like Google Presentation. Furthermore, every time you "favorite," comment, or upload a presentation in SlideShare Presentations, it can be broadcast out to the Home Page of all of your connections. You have the option to receive email notifications every time someone comments or "favorites" your presentation. Phew! That's one functionality-packed application!

But, wait, there's more! By pressing the "Explore" tab in the SlideShare Presentations application you can see all of the presentations from all LinkedIn users! You can filter your search by either "Most Viewed" or "Latest!" What amazes me the most is when viewing a presentation, everything is done from *within* LinkedIn. The display of the presentation gives you the ability to do most, if not all of what you can do on the SlideShare website from within LinkedIn, including the ability to post the presentation to a number of social networks, post a comment, share the file by email, download it, favorite it, and tweet it! If that is not enough, related presentations are displayed, so you may find similar presentations that interest you. By clicking on the username, a new window will open, displaying that person's LinkedIn profile. What more can you want?!?

By giving you the ability to go beyond your network, SlideShare allows you to do some serious presentation-centric Windmill Networking.

When you upload your presentation to SlideShare Presentations, whether done via LinkedIn or via the SlideShare website, it can be made available for everyone to see. By going to the SlideShare website, you can now do some serious Windmill Networking. The other important difference with Google Presentation, in addition to this "social" aspect, is that SlideShare allows you to add audio to your slideshow and create a "Slidecast." This is truly a unique feature that can add a multimedia facet to your LinkedIn profile.

One thing I didn't like about SlideShare Presentations (in addition to the fact that it didn't seem to work well with Google Chrome but worked seamlessly with Internet Explorer) is that after uploading a presentation, it took a minute for a *blank* presentation file to be converted into the SlideShare format. With Google Presentation, I was able to instantaneously see my work on my LinkedIn profile; depending on the size of your file, there may be a minute or more delay on SlideShare.

Embedding Video into Your LinkedIn Profile

I often describe LinkedIn as being a very static site with no dynamic or multimedia features. Yes, Slidecast is one multimedia feature, but

both SlideShare Presentations and Google Presentation are invaluable in that each application gives you the ability to add video to your LinkedIn profile!

Google Presentation allows you to easily insert a video from YouTube into a presentation by selecting "Insert" and then "Video". You then have to search YouTube and find the video you want to embed into your LinkedIn Profile by using a keyword. Furthermore, once you "paste" the YouTube video onto the screen, you will have to manually maximize the screen to make the most of the space provided.

With SlideShare Presentations, the process is even easier. After uploading and editing the presentation, you will see an option to "Insert YouTube Videos." Not only can you insert up to 5 videos, you also have the option to decide their order. Whereas Google Presentation prompts you to search YouTube with a keyword, SlideShare allows you to directly enter the YouTube URL into the screen to easily embed it into your presentation. There is no need to play around with the dimensions of the video screen size like you do with Google Presentation. I can confidently say that SlideShare is quite elegant in the way it works, making Google Presentation seem too simplistic in its approach.

From a viewer perspective, anyone who sees a video from either player on your LinkedIn Profile will see the same size screen. Furthermore, each application gives you the ability to easily see the video in full-screen mode. On Google Presentation, simply hit the rectangular button on the right-hand side of the row below where the video appears. When viewing a SlideShare presentation on a profile, simply hit the "full" button at the bottom right-hand corner of the SlideShare player.

SlideShare Presentations further differentiates itself from Google Presentation through its sharing functionality. On the left-hand side of the presentation viewer there is a "share" button next to an image of an email, which leads you to your Inbox. Anyone who views your presentation on your profile can now easily notify others in their network to visit your presentation. The interesting thing about this is that a Tiny URL is automatically created inside the email which leads that person to view the presentation in the comfort of their own Home Page without having to install the SlideShare Presentations application. They also don't have to visit the profile where the presentation is displayed! This is passive Windmill Networking at its viral best! Google Presentation completely lacks this functionality. **Upon reviewing all of the above-mentioned benefits, you can see why I feel that SlideShare Presentations is a better and more feature-rich way of sharing videos than Google Presentation.**

As with everything else you do online, the video you display in your profile will be inherently connected to your LinkedIn Brand. Showing videos of funny commercials may be appropriate for Facebook, but definitely not for LinkedIn. Unfortunately, it also opens up the door to post potentially offensive videos on LinkedIn. Let's hope this does not happen.

Getting back to the Application comparison: what happens when you have the module installed for each Application to show up on your Home Page? Is there a difference there as well? Once again, I feel SlideShare Presentations outperforms Google Presentation in this capability. Google Presentation allows you to edit, change, or view the video in your profile. The SlideShare Presentations module not only give you the ability to manage your presentations like Google does by providing a link to jump directly to Your Application Settings; it also displays the latest presentation uploaded from your connections. You also have the ability to jump to view "Your Favorites" as well as "Your Connections." Being able to jump directly to "Your Slidespace" from this module is another convenient add-on that SlideShare Presentations offers.

If there is only one Application you decide to try from all of LinkedIn's Applications, my recommendation is you take SlideShare Presentations for a spin. Remember not to show any funny YouTube video or inappropriate comments on your profile, as the presentations or videos that you display will become an integral part of your LinkedIn Brand.

WordPress & Blog Link

Do you have your own blog? If you do, I am assuming it is a natural extension of your LinkedIn Brand and you would like more people to see it. LinkedIn allows you to easily display your latest blog entries on your profile. There are no gimmicks here, and the applications work as advertised.

If you don't already have a blog, you can install the WordPress application; instead of putting in your blog URL and password, it will show a link to allow you to register for a free blog at WordPress. Blogging is easy and free. If you have subject matter expertise to share or have ever been interested in blogging, there is no easier or better way to get started, as what you write will now be displayed on your LinkedIn Profile. Explaining the benefits of blogging would require a totally separate book, but I highly recommend the exercise for whatever brand or even passion you have that you would like to advertise. Blogging is also another excellent passive way of Windmill Networking and attracting similar-minded people to communicate with you.

Since I was originally blogging using the WordPress platform, it was quite serendipitous when LinkedIn announced an application that fully supported this. I installed the application, entered the URL and password, and voila! Links to my latest three blog entries, together with a few lines of text, were now appearing on my profile, together with the other applications displayed below my Summary. These links were all being displayed below the title of my blog using the WordPress branded color and text. Pretty sharp looking.

Once you install WordPress, it will automatically synch up with your blog. There are times when I've gone to my profile and have realized that for some reason the link is "broken"; I then need to re-sign in to WordPress to synch it up again. If you are going to your LinkedIn Home Page often, you may want to make sure this is not happening to you. This may also be a "bug" that has been fixed since then.

LinkedIn has also added more functionality to this application, which you can edit according to your needs. When you create a blog entry, you can attach "tags" to them. Let's say you blog about a variety of things and you don't want to display all of them on your LinkedIn profile. You can choose to only display those things that are tagged "linkedin" to display. If you blog on a variety of topics, or there are some things that are inconsistent with the image you want to display on LinkedIn, you now have full control over what content is displayed.

But what if your blog is not using the WordPress platform? After all there is TypePad, Blogger (run by Google), LiveJournal, and so on. That is where the Blog Link application comes in. This application will display *any* blog regardless on which platform it was created and/or hosted. If you did not create your blog on WordPress, this is the only choice you have to display your blog in your LinkedIn profile. But even if you use WordPress, it may make sense for you to use this application. The reason is that Blog Link provides one additional piece of functionality: The ability to see blogs you deem important from around your network right there on your LinkedIn Home Page.

Unfortunately, although it has been out for almost a year as I write this book, it looks like there are still some fundamental issues which prevent me from recommending that you utilize Blog Link. It may display more than you want it to, it does not pick up blogs from my network, and the appearance is not nearly as visually appealing as the WordPress application.

Let's start with how you tell Blog Link to display what information. After you install the application, it will automatically search for those in your network who have their own blogs. It does this by searching the three websites that each of your connections has included in their profile. After conducting that search, it will ask you to add your websites and blogs to your profile. Once you press that link, any website that is a "blog" will now be displayed as part of the Blog Link module.

But here's the catch. In my profile, I use one website entry for my blog, and another to lead people to my Twitter homepage. Blog Link picked up both my blog as well as my Twitter feed, and thus my three latest tweets as well as my three blog entries were being shown on my profile! There are no settings to turn one on and the other off, and even though my blog website is listed above my Twitter URL in my profile, my tweets are appearing above my blog entries! Needless to say, I don't want to display all of my tweets here (I have the Status

Bar to do that), so I can't use this application to just show my blog unless I delete the URL leading to my Twitter homepage. As Twitter becomes more popular, I can see how this will seriously prevent many people from using this application.

What about the killer functionality Blog Link has that WordPress doesn't: The ability to display blogs from my network. Isn't that one up on WordPress? Well, yes, but only if it works, and in my case it didn't. Despite the fact that I have over 17,000 connections, it told me it could not find any websites or blogs for my contacts! When searching through my network, it did say that it might take a little time if I have lots of connections, but not to find any proves this application is simply not scalable. I know from my LinkedIn connections that the functionality works for some. Even if it may work for you now, as your connections grow, you may encounter the same problem.

Finally, the visual appeal of Blog Link pales in comparison to WordPress. With WordPress, you get a nice gray band with your blog title in white letters and the cool WordPress "W" logo on the right-hand side of the text bar. The colored band breaks up the monotony of your LinkedIn Profile and makes your blog really stand out in a visually appealing way. The title for each blog entry is several font sizes larger than the synopsis text below it, and is even in a blue color to make it stand out from the grayish text.

For Blog Link, on the other hand, there is no colored band separating its content from the rest of your profile, with the exception of a very small BlogLink logo. There was no enlarged title for my Twitter feeds; instead, it just displayed "Twitter / nealschaffer" in the same color and size of the text below it. The blog entries, on the other hand, did have a large title in blue for each posting, together with the summary text in a smaller and different text color. But the title for my blog was repeated above the title for each of my posts. It just looks incredibly unprofessional for a site like LinkedIn. Yes, the information is displayed, doing the minimum that is advertised, but it really does not compare to WordPress.

I wondered why LinkedIn would have two separate blogging Applications. Although I feel WordPress is the best choice here, with support for Blog Link, LinkedIn becomes a truly open platform able to display any blog—even Twitter. On the face of things, LinkedIn can do a lot to enhance the visual appeal, customizability, and functionality of Blog Link. But until that happens, you may not want to even experiment with Blog Link unless you do not use WordPress for your blog or you do not have Twitter as one of your three websites in your profile. If you are new to blogging and want to give it shot, WordPress is hands-down the right way to go here.

Box.net Files & Huddle Workspaces

If LinkedIn has a uniquely professional demographic, wouldn't it be great to have an application where professionals can collaborate when co-editing spreadsheets, documents, and presentations? I suppose there is a need for this in the professional world, but wouldn't companies want their employees to do this through the protection of their own corporate Intranet—not on a 3rd party site like LinkedIn? If this is the case, then, who would be the ultimate user of this service? Is there a role for such an application in Windmill Networking?

Before trying Huddle Workspaces, I was very skeptical as to how an average user could potentially utilize these sorts of applications. The Application Preview for Huddle Workspaces, which can be seen by selecting "Applications" from the left-hand navigation bar and then "Huddle Workspaces," contains a link at the bottom titled "Learn how other people are using Huddle Workspaces." Selecting this gives you an idea of typical user case scenarios. The categories of people listed here are Group Leaders, Recruiters (to speak with Employers), Employers (to speak with Recruiters), and Board Members. So are these applications only for Management types and Recruiters? Well, if you have ever used an FTP service to "send" files or have gone back-and-forth on file-related feedback emails that has made you crazy, keep reading, as there is definitely some value here.

Box.net Files and Huddle Workspaces are two types of applications LinkedIn supports providing the above-mentioned functionalities. I have lumped these applications together in that they both allow you to easily manage and share content online. The "connection" with LinkedIn is that it enables people who are connected (i.e. 1st degree connections) to collaborate, share, and access files securely and easily. Both services provide you with 1GB of free storage to use at your own discretion. I will now focus on the differences between the applications to help you find the one that meets your needs.

Functionality Comparison

When you install either Box.net Files or Huddle Workspaces, there is one distinct difference to be aware of: Although both of these services have their own Internet portals through which they exist and service their customers (www.box.net, www.huddle.net), only Box.net Files requires you to create a username and password, after which they send you a separate welcome email. I prefer the approach of Huddle Workspaces, which does not have this requirement. If you wanted to use this service outside of LinkedIn you would have already become a member on each of their respective websites in the first place, right?

After both applications are launched, their differences become even more noticeable. Box.net Files has immediately created a folder for you, and any file you upload to this folder will be displayed in your profile if you selected this option when you originally installed the application. This is extremely convenient if there is a file (portfolio, resume, etc.) you want to share with *everyone*. The ability to easily store your files in folders make it very easy to use and understand.

Box.net Files can be described as being very file-centric. For every file you initially upload you have many options, including, but not limited to:

- Sending the file to your connections utilizing a message composed from Inbox, which sends them a link that will lead them to your file
- Getting a Web link for you to communicate to your connections in other ways
- Sending via Gmail
- Downloading
- Editing with Zoho (which opens up a separate browser window in the www.box.net site, utilizing the online suite of applications from Zoho)

Huddle Workspaces, on the other hand, creates a private workspace open to only those who you provide access to, as opposed to the public folder default that Box.net provides. There are no folders. In addition, the only common options here you have with Box.net is the ability to download and edit the file (as with Box.net, it will open a new browser window to enable you to edit the document). That's right, there are no options here that send the file out; instead, the expectation is you will invite contacts into your private workspace and allow them to access the information there. Unfortunately, every time I pressed the "Invite Contacts" button it came back with an error message saying I must select at least one contact to invite. If this isn't a classic catch 22 I don't know what is. On the other hand, Huddle Workspaces gives you the option to create a new file online, which Box.net does not support.

Where does collaboration fit in to all of this you ask? On Box.net, you have the option to invite connections to access a particular folder with certain permissions, such as viewing-only. And that's it. While Huddle Workplaces has this functionality, it also adds discussion boards where you can post comments—a collaborative whiteboard if you will. Apparently both sites offer additional functionality on their websites, but as far as I could see, this is the majority of the main functionality you can access within LinkedIn.

When comparing the two applications, you should also note the restrictions. Since Box.net Files is file-centric as the name implies, it is also apparently file-agnostic and can handle, from a sending aspect, almost any file type. I could not find any information on their website to dispute this. On the editing side, because Zoho supports PowerPoint, the ability to edit files is there from the main Microsoft Office applications of Word, Excel and PowerPoint. Huddle Workspaces, unfortunately, only supports Word and Excel.

The difference in the way these two LinkedIn Applications interact with your browser should also be noted. I admit I am a Google Chrome user, but only Huddle Workspaces has caused me problems. I had no problem using Box.net, and even when the Zoho editor came up it simply opened up a new tab. Huddle Workspaces, on the other hand, did not allow me to edit a document until I used it on Internet Explorer, and I had to turn my pop-up blocker off in order to allow the editor to run. Why can't Huddle Workspaces operate as easily as Box.net Files does?

I think you can see if you have a need for this type of application, Box.net Files seems to be the easiest and most feature-rich and least restrictive of the two Applications.

Why Use These Applications?

But what is the potential value in utilizing these applications? Well, you do get 1GB of storage you can use privately, or you can share documents with others in your LinkedIn network. If there is a file (or, in the case of Huddle Workspaces a document or spreadsheet) that you want to collaborate on with someone else in your LinkedIn network, or if you want to have access to a particular file from within LinkedIn, there is value in using this application. In addition, in the case of Huddle Workspaces, there are discussion whiteboards where people in a group can leave and edit each other's comments.

If you are a professional and are in constant communication with someone else or a group of people regarding a document, a spreadsheet or the exchange of ideas, using Huddle Workspaces is much more efficient than exchanging loads of emails. If you want to send the same files to a bunch of people, you can simplify the process by using Box.net Files as your personal FTP, allowing them to freely download it from your profile.

Both LinkedIn Applications synch up directly with the official website services. If there is serious editing you want to do, it makes sense to do this either on your native Microsoft application or on each service 's website—*then* make it accessible to your LinkedIn network. Which really brings up a bigger question: Is there a need to access these services within LinkedIn? I find LinkedIn to sometimes be a bit slow and sometimes I need to refresh a page a few times in order to see content. Does it make sense to have this application installed and then force people to come to your profile to view it when you could be collaborating *outside* of LinkedIn? If you use LinkedIn everyday, but not Huddle Workspaces or Box.net Files, it makes sense to have one of these applications. If you need a collaboration environment like what Huddle Workspaces provides, you need to ask yourself what the value is of having this installed *within* LinkedIn.

Although I see the potential value in utilizing Box.net Files or Huddle Workspaces within LinkedIn for some demographics—primarily those who want to openly share files—the final verdict is unclear regarding the value of using these applications within LinkedIn versus directly on their websites. You will have to experiment to determine not only which application best fits your needs, but also which style (website access vs. LinkedIn access) is best for you. As for how using these applications fits into your LinkedIn Brand and Windmill Networking, you will have to be the judge of that. It comes down to whether you want to control how people view your document in SlideShare Presentations or give them the ability to freely download a document in Huddle Workspaces or Box.net.

My Travel by TripIt

I already mentioned I tried to use My Travel before and deleted it soon thereafter. Being a constant world traveler because of my career in international sales, it sounded like a cool way to let people know where I am. I was not aware at the time, but My Travel is a separate service that already exists and I needed to sign up for it in order to use this application.

My Travel is referred to as being a "business travel dashboard." The idea is to be able to see where other people in your network are to connect with them when either of you are out of town. My Travel has the potential to foster more face-to-face meetings to supplement your virtual Windmill Networking; however, as you will see, it is only as good as the information you and your connections supply.

After you install the application, you will need to sign up for the service if you are not already using My Travel. It is a pretty painless process, but the importance is in being able to add potential connections who are already on My Travel, whether it be via the web, mobile, or LinkedIn. You can invite people through Settings, and you have the option to invite people through your Internet email address book, LinkedIn Connections, or by directly entering email addresses.

To give you an idea of how many people on LinkedIn are actually using My Travel, I used my LinkedIn account to look for connections who were already on. When I did this I had about 13,500 direct connections. It only found 55 people, well below my expectations. Now, if you have close contacts that always travel to similar locations like you do, it makes sense to have a micro-network of people on My Travel. Even if you don't travel but you have good friends that do travel, if they have this installed and you do as well, you can hook up when they are in town by planning well in advance.

So you invite people to connect on My Travel and then they accept. What happens next? You can add your own itinerary for them to see while sharing your travel plans by email. The key function is being able to see who is close to you right now. There are also "Travel Stats" to see who, out of all of your LinkedIn connections, has been to the most cities and countries. If you are someone who brags about how many lifetime miles you have flown on a certain airline, you may get a kick out of this and start religiously entering all of your trips to come out in "first place." If you are someone who must travel for business often while being away from your family, you probably don't want to end up being in first place here.

There is more functionality within the MyTravel section that you can access by selecting "Settings," which will bring you to the My Travel site by opening a new browser window. I am sure LinkedIn had good intentions in creating this application, and it may have value for some of you; however, until it becomes more popular, its value to you may be very limited.

That is the big problem with My Travel: It is one of those services that has to be used by everyone to have any value. There are lots of examples in this Web 2.0 world of ours of services that are great ideas, but never "cross the chasm" because they are not adopted by the masses. LinkedIn works very well in the United States because so many people are on it, but in countries like Japan or Korea, where local social networking sites are much more popular, its presence is minimal. If you want to do social networking via a website in these countries, you will need to use the local alternatives that have a much greater market share, thought they only target a local audience.

Look at My Travel: not even a half of one percent of my connections have it installed! This is a pretty disappointing outcome for an application that has been around for five months at the time of my writing this. This number will probably go up over the next few months as more people join and become active users of LinkedIn, but until then, unless you see the application appearing in the Profiles of those you really want to closely keep in touch with, you may not want to waste your time with My Travel.

It is also important to note the potential privacy and security issue with using this application. Do you really want to advertise to the whole world that you are several thousand miles away from home and will be out of town for the next several days? It raises potential security issues, and recently the first potential "Twitter Robbery" was reported in the mass media.[3] You may want to read this article before installing My Travel.

On a final note, LinkedIn has recently been pushing this application with a blog post containing an interview with one of the co-founders of TripIt.[4] The message seems to be "meet up with your LinkedIn connections during your next business trip." Since I don't use My Travel, I suggest you create a LinkedIn Event and then send out an email blast to everyone you know in that geographic area asking to meet up. You will have a better chance of meeting up because not everyone is on My Travel, and you may actually have a chance to meet people outside of your network who spot that one of their common friends has RSVPed to your event. **The objective of My Travel is very much aligned with that of Windmill Networking**, but there are better methods of implementing it than using this application at this time. This may very well change in the future as My Travel picks up traction, so make sure you give it a test spin if you are at all interested in it.

Events

The official line on this "Application" is a little confusing. The idea is if every professional lists all of the events they are either attending or organizing, it will help not only advertise our own events and the fact that we are going; it also gives us the ability to reach out to our virtual networks or even removed networks (i.e. 2nd and 3rd degree connections) for in-person **Windmill Networking**. This can take the form of meeting business prospects as well as meeting up with our old acquaintances. The concept is certainly a great one.

Let's clarify a few things about this Event "application." You will notice that "Events" does not show up on the Applications menu on the left-hand navigation bar. So is Events an application? Well, the other option to add an Application is on the bottom of the right-hand column of your Home Page. The "Application" menu here includes non-applications like Jobs and Answers, but this is where you can add Events. Since it leads you to a page similar to other Applications in that it gives you the option of choosing whether or not to display the Events on your Home Page and/or your Profile, I think it is fair to consider Events an Application.

I have always been skeptical about this Events application. When LinkedIn implemented their new Home Page sometime ago, I originally felt this module was a default eyesore that appeared every time I logged on to LinkedIn and viewed my Home Page. It never displayed any event that made any sense to me, either by subject nature or by locale. Once I deleted it, I never reinstalled it until recently. Upon reinstalling, it displayed three events located in faraway places, one being overseas! Can't LinkedIn simply link your zip code and industry and display three upcoming events here that may make sense to join?

It is safe to assume you should be able to find events recommended to you based on the industry in your profile as well as your job function, but it just isn't happening in this module. If you do plan to install this application, I do not recommend displaying the module on your Home Page until things improve.

Looking at Events as something to display on your Home Page, however, is only one piece of the pie. You also have the option to see the popular events that people in your industry are attending, as well as events your connections are attending. You can search the Events database for potential events you would be interested in, you can create your own event, and you can manage all of the events you have created or planned to attend. Let's take a look at these options one at a time to see what value there may be in installing this application.

Searching for Events

Upon clicking on Events on the left-hand navigation bar in the Applications section, you will be sent to the main Events page, you will see a chronological list of the most popular events in the industry in which your current company is listed, and you will also be able to browse events which your connections may be attending. Unfortunately, because I have a large network, I was unable to see any events my connections would be attending. **Assuming this works as advertised, it is a killer functionality which can enhance your ability to Windmill Network in person.**

The "Find Events" tab is where the primary search functionality for the Events database can be found. The search capability was actually a pleasant surprise. You have the ability to search by keyword, date, location, and event types. I think one common usage of this search would be to see what events are happening within the next month near you. Although the metropolitan area that is listed in my profile (in my case "Greater Los Angeles Area") is listed as a default location I could use in my search, I wanted to see if it could pinpoint Events closer to where I live. Much to my surprise, after entering my zip code, I was introduced to 324 events that are happening in the next three months. Quite impressive! Not to say that all of them interest me, but as with My Travel, the more people that register their events here, the more value it will have for everyone. Simply through the sheer number of events, if you are looking to do some face-to-face Windmill Networking and don't know where to look, you are bound to find something of interest here. More than 20% of the Events I found in my area were networking or meet-up events. The only issue is it will take you a long time to look through the events: They are not displayed in chronological order and there are only 10 events per screen to navigate through.

RSVP

Once you find an event that you may want to attend, you can see all of the other users who have already RSVPed. This is a great "networking" feature which truly makes LinkedIn feel like a snug community, especially if more and more people utilize this application to advertise their events and actually RSVP to the events they plan to attend. LinkedIn has made it easy to RSVP to events by pressing the "Attending" or even "Interested" buttons which appear when you focus on a particular Event's text bar. There is also an option to share the event with others if you want to invite one of your friends or colleagues to attend with you.

Entering Your Own Event

When entering your own event, there are many options thrown at you in addition to the standard date, time, location, and organizer. You can add a website to promote your organization or the event, 300 characters of text that will be seen by the public should they browse your Event, Keywords to make your Event searchable, as well as categories for your Event such as Event Type, Industries, and titles of who should attend. I probably don't need to go overboard here, but if you plan to put on an event you want people to find, the more relevant and searchable information you enter, the better.

After entering your event, not only will it be displayed on your profile for everyone to see; LinkedIn also sends an update to your network to announce the event. Free advertising...even cooler! You can also share this event with others through an Inbox message that LinkedIn will automatically generate for you with a description of your event. There is always the option to advertise the event on LinkedIn using their own Direct Ads service. In fact, after installing Events, LinkedIn displayed that not only do you have the option of advertising through Direct Ads, but "Premium Events" and "Premium Events Plus" paid services will be available soon to allow companies to not only do highly targeted advertising, but also to create communities around your events and manage recurring ones for the future. It is almost as if LinkedIn is trying to replicate the type of service that a site like Evite has here. They could well be successful because of the sheer number of professional events that exist and the millions of people worldwide who attend.

The most intriguing and potentially valuable part of Events is what happens AFTER you create and advertise your own event. People will RSVP for it, and then YOUR event will show up on THEIR profile page! You can see how viral it can become if you can get a few people to RSVP. I cannot think of any other application which gives you the ability to get free advertising space on other people's profiles as the Events application does. Furthermore, in my experience, I feel the people who RSVP for your event through the Events application have a better chance of attending because 1) they can confirm the other people that will be attending and 2) they made the conscious choice to attend knowing their RSVP would be displayed on their profile.

If you host events on occasion, the Events application certainly has value:

1. It will spread the word to all of your network connections
2. It will be searchable within an open database that may result in more attendees
3. It gives you the ability to manage the RSVP count, which can always be a logistical challenge
4. It has the ability to virally advertise on other people's profiles
5. It is free

Even if you don't host your own events, assuming your main contacts are here on LinkedIn and you are targeting a professional demographic, you need no longer use Evite or Meetup.com. The ability to find events that may interest you, look at who else may be attending an event to pre-plan meetings, or even being able to pinpoint and track someone down at an event are all strong reasons why you should be utilizing LinkedIn Events as an integral part of your Windmill Networking strategy.

Company Buzz

Are you on Twitter? If you are it will be easy to understand Company Buzz, but I will first assume you are not. So let's introduce Twitter before getting into the Company Buzz application and how it can be applied to Windmill Networking.

Twitter is a micro-blogging platform. It has received increased attention in the social media industry through its adoption by professionals and enterprises. The term "micro-blogging" is used because you are limited to 140 characters in what you post. But the ability to shorten URLs through services like TinyURL and BudURL give you the ability to post a short comment and link to a website to provide more information. Because a lot of intelligent professionals are commenting on many things going on in the world, Twitter is an important companion to LinkedIn in terms of both obtaining subject matter expertise as well as branding yourself. If you are serious about Windmill Networking, Twitter should also be part of your daily social media activities. As Twitter will be subject for a future book, I will stop here, but if you are interested please follow me at twitter.com/nealschaffer for more real-time advice on Twitter AND LinkedIn.

Because Twitter has an Open API there are tens if not hundreds of applications that Twitter has spawned that you can use for specific purposes. It's like having a special application to rank your connections, manage your invitations—the things that LinkedIn doesn't do but you would like it to. Twitter fosters a very creative community of people developing applications that further enhance both its value and its reach.

Company Buzz

LinkedIn has developed its own application using the Twitter API, branding it towards its demographic of professionals by calling it Company Buzz. It is essentially a targeted keyword search application for Twitter. Twitter also provides the same capability, but even if you are a power Twitter user, installing Company Buzz will have some benefits for you. If you are looking to gain subject matter expertise through Windmill Networking to supplement what LinkedIn offers, Company Buzz is a "must" application to install and utilize.

Installing this application will not display anything on your profile when others view it. This is purely information for your eyes only. A feed from the topic of your choice will be displayed on the right-hand side of your Home Page; to access all of the functionality, you need to select it from under Applications in the left-hand navigation bar. To get you started, LinkedIn has taken all of the companies and schools in your Experience and Education sections and populated them in a Manage bar. By pressing on one of these you will see the most recent Twitter "Buzz" or tweets where these subjects are mentioned. This functionality is also available on Twitter, but the Company Buzz user interface is quite sleek and makes it easy to switch from topic to topic. Do you want to search for another topic? Easy! Just enter it in the Add a Topic text bar!

What else does Company Buzz deliver?

It gives you a list of 5 "Buzz Words" that it must have calculated using its own algorithm of what popular terms are associated with one of your topics. For instance, for the topic "LinkedIn" the five buzz words that appeared were *group, twitter, join, profile*, and *great*. I am sure LinkedIn is happy to know that "great" is a keyword often associated with its service! If you work in Marketing, you definitely want to be checking on the "buzz" to see what people are saying about your company!

As enterprises realize the value in utilizing social media to communicate with their customers, monitoring Company Buzz can be a valuable thing for your company to do.

In addition to this information, Company Buzz also provides statistical data in a graph format of how many times the Topic was mentioned in Twitter each day for the last week. If you want to promote your social media image for yourself or for your company, and if you believe that the more coverage of your name/company the better, this is an important statistic to follow over time. "LinkedIn" was displayed on Twitter between 771 and 1,664 times over the past week when I wrote this. Entering my own name displayed how many tweets and times I had been mentioned over the same period. Very cool!

Finally, you can directly access the author of each tweet by selecting their name, after which a new window in your Browser will be launched directing you to that person's profile on Twitter. You can then post a reply, follow, or send a message if you are mutually following. If you regularly search on Twitter to follow people based on a keyword, you can now do this within LinkedIn and get the associated buzzwords and statistical data. **This is definitely a well-constructed and valuable application for those who understand the value of Twitter.**

But like everything else in LinkedIn, there are some things you should be aware of. First of all, there is an ability to "share" a tweet that displays. The idea of being able to immediately forward an interesting link you found on Company Buzz to someone in your LinkedIn contact list is excellent. However, after you select "share" and an Inbox message is created, the link for Twitter is extremely long. If LinkedIn had done what SlideShare Presentations or others do by automatically creating a TinyURL to shorten the URL, it would make it a lot easier to send to others. The TinyURL is both easy to cut and paste to include in a message as well as your Status Bar or even your blog. It is a shame that portability of valuable tweets was not given more thought.

The other problem is that sometimes it will take time for the Buzz Words, and even longer for the Trends graph, to appear. With a popular topic like "LinkedIn" the data appeared immediately, but for my own name the process took more time. I don't see why this has to take so much time, as it only adds to my impression of LinkedIn as being a slow program. I checked back a few hours after installing and I finally got my Buzz Words (linkedin, twitter, link, blog, social) but still haven't gotten my graph.

If you are not on Twitter, Company Buzz is a great stepping-stone introduction to Twitter. If you are on Twitter, especially if you are in Marketing, Company Buzz has appeal and should be another sticky application to keep you coming back to LinkedIn.

Polls

LinkedIn Polls are an interesting way of gathering information for anything you may want to investigate. There are other ways to utilize a virtual network to gather intelligence aligned with your Windmill Networking strategy, such as asking a question in Answers or posting a message on a Group Discussions Board. But for a simple "which of the above do you agree with" type of multiple-choice question, LinkedIn Polls is a pretty direct and sometimes fun way to ask something. LinkedIn positions the Polls application as a market research tool for companies to gather information about the professional demographic that is LinkedIn, so it may not be intended for the casual user. There are also restrictions that you should be aware of if you plan to use it for free.

You mean it costs money to use the Polls application? Not exactly. After you load the application by going to the Applications page on the left-hand navigation bar, it makes it clear that while Polls is free to gather responses from your direct connections, there is a $50 minimum of cumulative pay-per-response if you plan to send out a poll for a targeted demographic. In fact, after creating your first poll, you will realize that the default or first option you have is to pay money for it. Because it is a targeted way of gathering information from a specific demographic, LinkedIn has implemented an ingenious way of monetizing their network through creating this application and offering this sort of service. Bravo!

I am assuming you are interested in creating a "free" version of Polls, so first let's see how this works.

Why use Polls in the first place?

I find Polls are very similar to Answers in that you are trying to gather responses from everyone on a particular subject. You are limited to a 5-answer question, but you can understand and analyze the potential for different demographics to give you different answers. For instance, you could ask "Which Anti-Virus Software Do You Most Recommend" and have a bake-off between the leading 5 companies, seeing what the results are industry by industry. If you did the same with Answers, you will only get text answers. Although they will be from anyone who answers them (including the option of sending out the question to 200 people in your network), you may only get answers from those people that troll the Answers boards—instead of the broader demographic that might take a few seconds to answer a simple poll.

To be honest with you, I did not see the benefit of the Polls application until I had a reason to use it. That reason was conducting research for this book. I created a poll to get an idea of the following: To see which applications people see the most value in, and which applications people use the most. The Question text box gives you 75 characters to play with, and then 30 characters for each answer. You have the option to allow the application to randomly display the answer ordering as well as the option to display the Polls in the Poll Directory, which means anyone looking at the Polls can see them. It also notes that your 1st degree connections are notified as a Network Update, not an email, that you created this poll. Not too many people may be looking at your Network Update, so it is questionable as to how many people will actually see the poll. You are given a URL for your poll, which you can advertise in your blog, via Twitter, or any social networking tool you use to spread the word.

Polls is still a relatively new application, so my gut feeling is you may get fewer responses than if you asked the same thing in Answers. The reason—there is no clear way to navigate to the Polls main screen! If you have installed the application it will appear in the Applications section of your left-hand navigation bar. But if you haven't installed it, you may be able to spot it occasionally as a Direct Ad in the top right-hand portion of your Home Page. Perhaps someone in your network created a poll and it shows up as part of your Network Updates. But where oh where is the main link for Polls you ask? At the very bottom of the page in the "Tools" section. No wonder a lot of people aren't contributing to answering Polls!

If you haven't installed the application and find the "Polls" link via any of the methods I described above, it will send you to the main Polls page labeled "Poll Directory." From here you can browse and answer other Polls that exist. You can only see three Polls at a time and they are divided into two sections: recently created polls and polls from your network. There are no categories that separate the Polls so you can navigate them like you do in Answers. Who would think of utilizing this service then?

Compared to Answers, the results of the poll will give you the opportunity to see how people voted by Job Title, Company Size, Gender and Age. If you are in business, this sort of market research information is very valuable, which is why LinkedIn has a paid option for this. Since LinkedIn will prominently display this poll as a "Direct Ad" in the top right hand corner if you are in the demographic that is being targeted, the idea is not for you to create a poll and find people—but for the poll to find you! If you do not have criteria that require a demographic analysis or a simple 5-choice answer, you may be better off asking a question in the Answers section.

So who was Polls really created for?

Polls was clearly designed for businesses that want to collect market data. The business model for Polls is a pure pay-per-response model which is similar to a pay-per-click web advertising model. LinkedIn Polls gives you the option to target up to two of the following categories: Company Size, Job Function, Industry, Seniority, Gender, Age, and Geography. Depending on the category, the price is $.50 to $1.00 per response. The default is to show the poll to all LinkedIn members, which is $1.00 per response, so it is interesting that LinkedIn is offering discounts for better-targeted polls. It seems they may not want to spam their customers with potentially uninteresting polls. FYI: The two most expensive targeted categories are Company Size and Seniority. In other words, for a targeted response from a custom poll, the price isn't too bad if your company has the budget.

The coolest thing about this Polls application: If you proceed to create a poll for money and put in sample data, the screen where you decide which audience to target will actually show you how many LinkedIn members there are! If you choose "Show poll to all LinkedIn Members," this number will appear in the upper right-hand corner under the "Your Selected Audience" heading. If you ever wanted to know the exact membership numbers and don't want to wait for LinkedIn's next press release, this is the place to look for the information. As I am writing this on March 31, by the way, the number is 37,837,955; when I edited this on July 15, the number was 43,479,359! It will be interesting to see how this number changes over time, so subscribe to the Polls application and check it out!

If you are wondering about the potential for gathering information on paid polls, I studied some polls I had answered after seeing their ad in the Direct Ad part of my Home Page. One particular poll I responded to had more than 27,000 responses in three months! **So, with the proper advertising and the right wording to attract people's participation, LinkedIn Polls can reach an incredibly large audience.** For the poll that I created for free, I had less than 50 people respond in the same time period. You don't get the same interaction you get in Answers because you can't see the names of people who answer unless they also post a comment. For this reason alone, Answers is a more preferable method for Windmill Networking, but LinkedIn Polls offers precious value to enterprises who have the budget to advertise on it.

Chapter 9

Chapter 9 Jobs & Companies

- Finding Jobs
- Posting Jobs
- Researching Companies
- Finding Service Providers
- Profile Names for Businesses
- Setting Up Your Company Profile

Finding Jobs

The scope of this book is really about understanding, leveraging, and maximizing LinkedIn through utilizing Windmill Networking. Some Research shows that most jobs are found through personal networks, and Windmill Networking *can* help you find your next job. In fact, my editor found her job through Windmill Networking while editing this book![5] Needless to say, any introduction to LinkedIn could not be complete without taking a look at the "Jobs" tab that is so prominently displayed in the top navigation bar.

Pressing the "Jobs" tab will lead you to the Jobs page, but the real value here is in the "Advanced Job Search" tab. If you are or have been looking for a job, you are probably quite used to using websites to search for a job. **LinkedIn supplies their own engine to search for jobs, in competition with Career Builder, Monster, and HotJobs, among others.** Because LinkedIn is lesser known for a jobs database than the other Big Three previously mentioned websites, you will find fewer jobs here. But in the same way, you may also have less competition. In my personal experience, I found many jobs on LinkedIn that did not exist elsewhere, so that in itself is a good enough reason to give LinkedIn's job section a look.

Before talking about the positive points and tips for looking for a job on the Jobs page, let me start with the big negative here: there is no email alert service provided like the other sites have, and you can't save your searches. You will have to manually revisit the page, re-input all of your search query data, and do a search on a regular basis if you want to effectively use this section. To partially offset this negative, one of the criteria for searching for jobs is "Date Posted;" you can sort search results by "Date Posted," so if you get into a weekly habit of doing this, you simply ask LinkedIn to display jobs that were posted within one week. Problem solved.

The benefits of using LinkedIn Jobs, other than finding unique jobs that may not exist elsewhere, are:

- **LinkedIn is clear in displaying which jobs are exclusive to LinkedIn.** These are the hot jobs that may have fewer applicants than the others. I think there are many job sites out there that aren't clear enough on this, so kudos to LinkedIn for making this clear.

- **You can see the name of the recruiter as well as your relationship to them in each job posting.** This makes it easy for you to directly contact the recruiter or hiring manager if you are connected, or to utilize Introductions or networking to communicate with them if you are not directly connected. This is extremely unique in that most websites do not list the recruiter, nor do they give you a complete infrastructure through which you can contact them!

- **When you click through each job posting, it is extremely easy to upload your resume and write a cover letter.** Cover letters and resumes are not saved, so you will have to do this for each job you apply to. I personally prefer this approach and feel more in control than other websites that try to automate too much of the process. Furthermore, since your entire LinkedIn Profile is already online, your LinkedIn Brand will also be communicated to the recruiter, in addition to all of the wonderful Recommendations you have already received. *No other website offers you a chance to include a branded profile and recommendations submission in addition to your resume.*

- There are many postings that prefer referrals through networks, but **LinkedIn makes it easy for you to receive a referral.** What this means is they want you to go through the formal Introduction process to reach out to the recruiter before applying, and by doing so you will be visible. If you have been Windmill Networking, I hope when you press the "Request Referral" button, which leads you to the Introduction functionality, you will be able to choose from many people to refer you to the recruiter.

- **For every job posting, you can also see similar jobs that other people who viewed the same job saw.** Every search engine has their own algorithm, so there are always jobs that may interest you that just didn't appear in the search results. This gives you additional job postings that may interest you, and once again is a feature that is not necessarily included on every website for job seekers. You can find "People who viewed this job also viewed" at the bottom of each job posting, directly below "Similar jobs," which could provide additional useful information.

- **You can easily forward any job posting to others in your network.** You don't need to know their email address; simply input their name. There is even a "Not interested in this job?" feature that is in beta that will pre-populate a job posting forwarding email to people that LinkedIn feels, through their own algorithm, may be interested in the job. While the verdict is still out on how well LinkedIn pre-populates this, the ability to easily forward jobs you may not be interested in makes this feature a great choice for Pay It Forward Windmill Networking.

- **In addition to the LinkedIn Jobs posting, you can also view jobs available elsewhere on the Web through the Simply Hired job posting aggregation listings.** Simply Hired, together with Indeed.com, are two of the leading job posting aggregator services. You can, and should, set up email alerts with both of these services if you are looking for a job (you can delete one of them out if you think it is of lower quality...I personally found Indeed.com to be better). But the ability to click on "The Web" tab and see the search results from Simply Hired without having to re-enter the search query on the Simply Hired website is of much value to the job seeker.

Job seekers can waste a lot of time looking for work on the Internet. Most career coaches will tell you that searching for a job in the 21st century is about staying OFF the Internet. I do believe that Windmill Networking and your LinkedIn Brand will be the most critical part of being successful to indirectly find your next job through networking. If you can create a system of setting up email alerts with Indeed.com and Simply Hired, while supplementing this by doing weekly manual searches on LinkedIn, you don't need to be wasting more than a few minutes a day keeping up on all of the jobs that are posted on the Internet. Considering that my editor found a job on LinkedIn Jobs utilizing this advice while she was editing this book, I think spending a little time surfing LinkedIn for jobs is a productive use of your time.

Posting Jobs

Let me begin this chapter by saying that I am not a recruiter. I have been a hiring manager with previous companies, and I also have an understanding of the mentality of those looking for jobs. So with that in mind, let's look at LinkedIn's system for posting jobs.

We should first look at whether or not there is even a need to pay money to post jobs on LinkedIn. After all, if you are a recruiter and a Windmill Networker, you have probably already connected with people that directly or indirectly fit the bill for the job you want to post. If everyone is Windmill Networking, I hope many people in your network will go out of their way to help you. You can post jobs in your LinkedIn Profile, Status Bar, and Group Boards. You can browse the Answers Boards and the Group Discussions Boards looking for people of expertise for the position you are looking to fill. There are many free ways to do this if you are on a limited budget or if you want to build up a pipeline of talent for future needs.

What is the value of directly posting your job on the Jobs site, then?

- **Time to Market.** Taking the free approach takes time. Posting a job is quick and the results are immediate and passive.

- **Greater Network Reach.** No matter how large your network, you can't reach all of LinkedIn's members—but a job posting can. If you believe that the most valuable talent out there are those who are more passive networkers, this may be the only way to reach these people.

LinkedIn also proposes other ways of finding talent if you select "Hiring Home" after pressing the arrow key on the right-hand side of the "Jobs" tab. Here are the three options:

- **Posting a Job.** At the time I am writing this it will set you back $195 per 30-day posting, although you can pre-pay for packages that can bring this cost down to $145 for 5 job "credits" and $115 for 10 job "credits".

- **Upgrade to Paid "Premium" Service.** Today there are three options, costing $25, $50, or $500 a month. How does this help you find your candidate? You get to send out more Introduction requests & InMails, join and receive OpenLink messages (see the section "To Pay or Not to Pay" in Chapter 14: Putting It All in Perspective for more information on this), have unlimited reach to the LinkedIn database, perform reference searches, get more search results per query, etc. In other words, if you want some more power to enable you to Windmill Network and find your candidate on LinkedIn, $25 or $50 a month may be a small price to pay that will save you a lot of time spent researching your candidates.

- **Utilize LinkedIn Talent Advantage.** This is a complete enterprise software package and no price tag exists on the LinkedIn site, so you know it will not be cheap. According to the LinkedIn screen introducing this service, more than 900 companies are utilizing it, and there seems to be some unique technology above and beyond what even the paid "Premium" subscribers get. If budget is not your concern and you want to use the best tools to help find the ideal candidate in the quickest amount of time, there is no question this should be your choice.

I obviously cannot recommend one approach over the other, as it will depend on your company's situation. But there are advantages of posting a job through the traditional manner on LinkedIn:

- Job seekers are still traditionally using job website search engines to look for jobs, so you will get wide coverage in the excellent professional demographic that is LinkedIn

- You can "advertise" this job for free by distributing it to your network and asking for referrals

- LinkedIn will display the candidates' information with what they label "LinkedInsight." This basically includes relevant profile information and Recommendations, in addition to the standard cover letter and resume, giving you a very insightful snapshot of each candidate.

- If you decide to only list this job on the LinkedIn Job board, it is a win-win, as LinkedIn will display your post as a LinkedIn exclusive; you should then expect to get more attention from the job seeker.

The mechanics of posting a job are pretty straightforward. LinkedIn offers you a lot of very robust options, including: The ability to post in a variety of languages, the option to include relevant company experience (this will not display but will help LinkedIn match candidates to your posting), along with the choice to include how much and to whom you would pay a referral bonus. There is also a tab to easily manage your posts as well as your job credits.

It is clear with the recession of 2009 and the subsequent boom of using social networking sites to look for work that LinkedIn has emerged as the prime engine to source talent. LinkedIn is a vehicle to post a job as well as to network your own way to find talent. It also acts as an enterprise platform to help you quickly pinpoint quality talent. It is no wonder LinkedIn has become THE platform for recruiters; subsequently, it is now attracting the job seekers who want to be found by those looking for talent.

Researching Companies

There is one more tab in the top navigation bar that needs to be covered in order to do LinkedIn justice. This is the ability to research companies.

Why should you research companies?

- **If you are a job seeker, you should be researching companies you may be interested in working for. Create a shortlist of companies you want your network to introduce you to; investigate them in more detail to see if they are the right fit for your experience.**

- **If you are in business, there are many reasons why you want to research companies: to find new customers, partners, distributors, and vendors.**

Because LinkedIn is THE social networking destination for professionals, and since everyone is already including company information on their profiles, Companies is a huge database of information that is slowly beginning to rival the "free" information you can find on Hoovers, the premier location for researching companies. Having used the free Hoovers service, I can vouch that it is actually easier to use the LinkedIn Companies Search because of its ability to select by keywords, location, industry, company size, and by those hiring on LinkedIn. The Companies application also gives users the ability to limit the search to those companies at which you have at least a direct or 2nd degree connection at. This is only the beginning of what makes Companies so powerful. Perhaps the secret behind the power of this database is, in addition to the LinkedIn user-generated data, the Companies database is supplemented with information from the research firm Capital IQ, a division of Standard & Poor's (S&P).[6]

Experiment by entering a random keyword and ignoring the company name matches that LinkedIn recommends. You will probably receive a vast list of companies which includes whether or not you have a 1st or 2nd degree connection at the company, the company headquarters, as well as the number of employees. Up until now, if you were looking for a job in an industry or for a partner or even a competitor of your product, chances are that you either googled a keyword or went to an industry database like Hoovers. LinkedIn Companies allows you to quickly generate a list of keyword-related companies that is more concise than what Google will show (hey, they can only show so many results per page!) and maybe even more comprehensive than an industry database because LinkedIn truly has every industry covered.

If you are a job seeker, the beauty of searching for companies in this LinkedIn database is that companies who post jobs on LinkedIn will appear, with the number of jobs listed in parentheses next to the company name; pressing that link will lead you to the job listing on LinkedIn!

Now let's select any company that appears in the search results. This is where the real value of Companies comes into play:

- **A list of current employees appears.** Anyone in your network will appear here. In other words, you have access to a company database, complete with titles! If you are looking for work, compare your work experience with those that appear here under the similar titles that you would be aiming for. How do you compare?

- **Former employees, new hires, and recent promotions and title changes are displayed.** If you are doing competitive analysis or looking for a passive job candidate, you can imagine how invaluable this information can be. If you are a job seeker, this information may give you an idea as to what type of talent they may be seeking.

- **Previous employer history as well as most connected companies of employees is shown.** Once again, when conducting competitive analysis, looking for talent, or seeing whether or not your career path will be valued (i.e. whether or not you worked at similar companies that current employees previously worked at) this is unique information you really can't find elsewhere.

- **Loads of other information is listed here, including top employee locations, common job titles, top schools that employees graduated from, median age, and gender statistics.** This is in addition to news as well as stock information. Information overload!

There are many possible use scenarios for Companies. I hope after understanding the value, you will see LinkedIn is quickly becoming the premier platform for not just recruiters, but also those doing research on companies for whatever objective they have. If you are in transition, this section will give you a plethora of useful data to use in your analysis of a hiring company. This information will also help you prepare for an interview. Once again, LinkedIn utilizes its user-generated content-laden database to create a very powerful resource. We should be equally taking advantage of this resource for whatever objective we may have.

Finding Service Providers

LinkedIn is not just about finding jobs, talent, or companies. Because of all of the professionals that are registered on LinkedIn, you can make the claim there is a whole other category of people you can label "Service Providers." Service Providers can be anyone from doctors and lawyers to career coaches and consultants. Because of the trustworthy demographic of LinkedIn, wouldn't it be great if a service existed that allowed you to find service providers in your area that were recommended by people you trust on LinkedIn? This seems to be the concept behind LinkedIn's desire to create a Service Provider database.

But where does this exist, you ask? You can find the Service Provider directory by pressing the "Companies" tab in the top navigation bar and then selecting "Service Providers" on the top right-hand side of the Companies page. You can also directly go to the Service Providers page by selecting it from the downward pointing arrow on the right-hand side of where "Companies" appears in the top navigation bar.

Unfortunately, every time I access the Service Providers page I get the same *"We're sorry, but the service provider directory is currently unavailable"* message. The ability to recommend Service Providers is available on this page, and after asking a question on the Answers board, it is clear it is working properly. Perhaps because I have too many connections the functionality may not work as properly as it does for you. I did notify Customer Service but even they still haven't remedied the problem. Bummer.

As more and more people recommend Service Providers in their network, the value here will be akin to that of the Jobs and Companies pages. After all, if you are new to a city or are looking for a new service provider, you are going to ask your network for referrals. If you Windmill Network, you will be asking your Trusted Network of Advisors. The Service Provider directory, if implemented correctly, will go beyond this by automatically generating all of this information for you.

From what I have gleaned, the Service Provider page allows you to search and pinpoint potential providers from a wide variety of industries, including creative artists, consultants, career coaches, financial & legal services, doctors, handymen, child care providers and travel agents! Because people in your LinkedIn network recommend all these people, it is safe to say that they are at least more trustworthy than if you had found them at random from the Yellow Pages. Using Service Providers will definitely save you a lot of time and potential frustration.

Be a good Windmill Networker by Paying It Forward and recommending all of the Service Providers in your LinkedIn Network that meet your expectations. It will mean a lot to them. If you are a Service Provider, don't be shy to ask your former customers in your LinkedIn Network for referrals, in the form of a Service Provider Recommendation.

Profile Names for Businesses

LinkedIn, as you already know, is a social networking platform for professionals. It is no secret there is business to be found on LinkedIn for companies of many sizes and industries. If you are a small business owner, you may be confused as to whether you should use your company name or personal name for your LinkedIn Profile name. Be confused no more, as I always recommend you use your personal name—here's why:

1. **LinkedIn is a network for professionals, not companies**. We're not talking about Hoovers here; instead of being a database of companies, LinkedIn is a database of *people. Professionals* are connecting with each other, finding each other and creating new relationships, answering questions, providing advice, etc. **If your name were a company name, why would I want to connect with you?** What value is there from a social networking perspective of connecting with a business? I realize that, as a business, you want to get some free advertising on LinkedIn, but do this in your profile, not in your name. You will find that people are not necessarily looking for vendors, so an indirect approach (utilizing Q&A and/or Group Discussions Boards with your expertise, etc.) will establish your credibility *much* better than merely sending out advertisements to all of your connections.

2. **The more real and genuine you are, the more people will trust you**. A lot of professionals are still turned off by social networking, and are especially wary of their privacy on social media. If you, with a business name, want to connect with *a person*, they might be suspicious of you. After all, a business name creates a shield and makes you a little invisible. Social networking is all about being transparent and Paying It Forward, so drop the shield.

3. **People buy from people, not companies**. Even companies buy from people, because it is the people inside the company making

> the purchase. If you want to connect with future customers, connect with them from a personal perspective, in which case you'll have a much higher potential of winning business from them. My brother, who owns his own wine label, is an example of someone who created a profile using his name (Larry Schaffer) and not his company name (Tercero wines). As you can see from his profile, he includes enough information on his profile to get you interested in his company without flat-out advertising it. People who want to connect with Larry would naturally want to know more about his wine label, don't you think?

If you are a business owner and you want to register your company name on LinkedIn, instead of using your company name for your LinkedIn Profile name, you can simply register your name in the LinkedIn Company Directory, which I will discuss in the following section. If people are searching for companies with your expertise, you can be found.

On a closing note, if you needed any more reason you should use only your real name for your profile, it is apparently against the LinkedIn User's Agreement to create a profile using a company name. This is because each person is only allowed to have one profile in his or her own name. LinkedIn apparently does remove "fake" profiles. Be forewarned.

Setting Up Your Company Profile

Many small businesses are looking for advice on how to utilize LinkedIn. Offering such targeted advice goes beyond the scope of this book, but there is enough buzz around small companies on how to utilize social media and LinkedIn that I felt this topic should be addressed as part of this book.

Up until now, the preferred way of finding company information was and still is Hoovers. Hoovers provides a huge database of company information, but also adds lots of information and services. Hoovers offers a truly comprehensive treasure chest of data for any company you may want to research. Where does LinkedIn fit in, you ask? Professionals are inputting their personal profiles, including companies they work for, into LinkedIn's huge database. By organizing all of this company information into their own proprietary database, in conjunction with the previously mentioned Capital IQ, LinkedIn is able to give its users a database of information that soon will rival that of Hoovers. In fact, when LinkedIn launched their Companies feature back in March of 2008, they reported more than 160,000 companies had a profile page in the Companies database.[7]

But LinkedIn seems to have its own angle on the company database. In their own words, from their Companies FAQ page on "What are Company Profiles?" "Company Profiles is a research tool that helps users explore and find the right companies to work for and do business with. Company Profiles leverage our unique network data and surfaces the people you need to get business done. They can be used to view job opportunities in your field and better understand the types of roles companies hire for and the latest news on people that have recently joined the company." In other words, where LinkedIn differentiates themselves is by providing targeted people information and job information. If you are researching a company, this is more than likely the reason you are looking at them, right?

So, if you are a small business owner, entering your Company Profile will put your company on the map, making it searchable. As with your personal profile, your company can now be found, so you may start getting some passive marketing power. You will also be given a URL (www.linkedin.com/companies/companyname) and may begin showing up if someone googles your company name. Because it is a free service, every business owner should be adding their Company Profile.

And adding a Company Profile is easy. You simply go to the "Companies" tab at the top of your LinkedIn Home Page and then select "Add a Company." You then need to enter your company name and email address, making sure the email address matches the domain name of your company. In other words, if you are using a Gmail account, I don't think you will be able to add your company to the database here. The other reason why you are asked to enter your email address is that it will check to see if someone else didn't already create that profile.

Once you confirm receipt of the link, you will then be directed to where to enter the Company Profile. Note that the email address you provide will also be added to your personal profile. Although I am not experienced in it, it would not surprise me if you are prompted to update your own personal profile with this company information, if you have not done so already.

The Company Profile will be defined by the Company Name and domain that you first entered. Then you will need to fill out the information in the "Basic Information" section as follows:

- **Description.** This is the main body of text that will describe what your company does, so you should make sure you are branded properly. Because LinkedIn gives users the ability to search for companies using a keyword, make sure this Description is properly search engine optimized.

- **Specialties.** Any keywords that you couldn't enter in your Description can be entered here.

- **Website URL**

- **Industry.** This uses the same database as in your personal profile

- **Type** (privately held, non-profit, etc.)

- **Status** (operating, out of business, etc.)
- **# of Employees** (this is a mandatory item that you must input even if you are the only employee)
- **Year Founded**
- **News Module** (this will bring the Business Week news on your company into your profile)

Next, you will be able to upload your Company Logo, enter Locations, input your Financials (Annual Revenue, Year, Currency), link your company blog (if you have one), and finally enter information for any related companies and what their relationships are. Not all of these are mandatory, and what you enter really depends on how much you want people to know about your company. For the majority of you, in addition to the Basic Information, I only recommend you minimally upload your logo and link your company blog to the page.

The entire process shouldn't take very long, and it will definitely give your small business a bigger presence on LinkedIn. Just be careful to only include the information you feel comfortable with and make your Company Profile searchable by the same keywords as with your personal profile.

I hope to see your company on LinkedIn!

Chapter 10

Chapter 10 Customizing Your LinkedIn Experience

- Controlling Your Email Notifications
- Connections: To Show or Not to Show?
- Display Your Footprint?
- How to Keep a Profile Private
- The Status Update: "What are You Working On Now?"

Controlling Your Email Notifications

As you increase your various Windmill Networking activities, unless you change the default settings in LinkedIn under Account & Settings, you will slowly be bombarded with all sorts of emails from LinkedIn. You can fully control what you can and cannot receive directly. You also have the option to receive 100% of your mail solely through your LinkedIn Inbox, should you wish to do so.

Let me review the options you have with regard to settings as well as what I recommend for optimal Windmill Networking. There are some things that make sense to retrieve after signing in to LinkedIn on an ad hoc basis; however, if you want to provide optimum value to others, there are certain things you may want to directly receive in your email Inbox. This will enable you to follow up immediately.

LinkedIn gives you a choice to receive a real-time email notification ("Individual Email") to the address you used to register, a daily digest, a weekly digest, or no notification at all. Not every option is available for each type of notification. To access this information, please navigate to Account & Settings → Receiving Messages (under Email Notifications).

- InMails, Introductions and OpenLink are important types of communications that I recommend you receive by email. Even with the amount of connections that I have, this does not overload my personal email.

- Invitations can add up very quickly, especially if you follow my guidance when expanding your network to take full advantage of Windmill Networking. At first it is a joy to receive Invitations from others who want YOUR help in building out THEIR virtual networks, but if you feel you are starting to get inundated, do what I've done: Simply choose not to receive an email and choose to check in with LinkedIn on a daily basis. A summary of how many Invitations are waiting for you to act on will now appear in the middle of your Home Page under your Inbox.

- Profile Forwards and Job Notifications are notifications sent to you for a specific purpose from someone in your network. It is important to immediately acknowledge these forms of communication. I recommend you receive these by email so you may take immediate action.

- Questions from Your Connections are received when one of your connections asks a question in the Answers section. They must include your contact information as one of the maximum 200 people to whom they pose the question. As this is usually a very impersonal thing by nature (if my connection had an important question for me I am assuming that he/she would give me a call or send me a separate email), I take a look at these on a daily basis when I check my Invitations. Remember, Answers gives you 7 days to respond to a question; this is another reason why there is no hurry to respond to these.

- Replies/Messages from Connections are things you want to receive immediately, just as you would a regular email.

- I am a Group manager, so there is also an option concerning messages between pending Group applicants and Group managers. If someone is applying to my Group and sends me a message, I want to be able to immediately respond. Once again, I elect to receive these emails to enable quick action.

- Network Updates is a report you can receive in a Weekly Digest; you can also read them directly on your Home Page. At the beginning, when you have a small network, it is convenient to be able to follow what everyone is doing through this Weekly Digest. Once your network gets to a certain size, it is just too much data to follow and may not be worth your time. It is best to start by receiving it, and then try to utilize it. Just be aware that you don't need to receive it if you don't want to.

- Status Activity of discussions is sent to those who would like to follow certain discussions after they have contributed to them on a Group Discussions Board. If you choose to follow a discussion, it makes sense to receive an email when someone responds to it. If you don't want to follow discussions, then you won't want to receive emails here.

- Invitations to join Groups are an option I still receive emails for, but I do receive a lot of untargeted and completely unrelated Group invitation requests. You may want to receive these emails in the beginning and proceed from there. For every Group you join, there is a Group Digest Email you can receive on a daily or weekly basis. If there is a particular Group where you find value in the Discussions and Jobs boards, you may want to receive a daily digest from them. Personally, I have found the weekly digest to be sufficient for the Groups that I belong to. For those Groups that I manage, I choose to receive a daily digest so I can stay on top of them. There will be other Groups that may offer little value via the weekly digest. Every time you receive one of these digests, there is a link at the bottom of the email to customize the setting that will lead you to the Group Settings screen, where you can alter your preferences; once I find there is no more value in receiving a digest, I choose to stop receiving it all together. It is best to start by receiving all digests—then slowly "turn off" those offering little value. Finally, at the very bottom of the page, there is an optional checkbox to receive a maximum once-a-month update from LinkedIn. I think every LinkedIn user should be receiving this. To be honest with you, I don't think I have received more than two or three messages from LinkedIn in the last year, but you never know when they will make an exciting announcement!

Windmill Networking can cause your email Inbox to explode if you are not careful. In order to efficiently provide value to your network and navigate through what is and is not important, make sure to customize these email settings so you can easily sift through information.

Connections: To Show or Not to Show

When you open an account at LinkedIn, the default setting allows your connections to be viewed by anyone. I used to have my connections open, until one day when I was doing some searching in a particular industry for companies to work for, I noticed that all of the salespeople had kept their connections private. To me, this made sense, as they didn't want their competitors to get their hands on their connections. I asked myself if there was any advantage to keeping my own connections open or closed.

The knee-jerk reaction to this is that one's connections should be open if you are an open networker. After all, that's what Windmill Networking is all about, right? Utilizing your contacts to connect people? When you connect with someone, there is a natural tendency to want to browse their connections to see if you have any mutual friends. Another way of looking at it, as a good friend mine of said, "Are you a closed Microsoft type or an open source Linux person?"

On the flipside, you need to ask yourself these important questions: Do I want someone looking through all of my connections to see with whom they can potentially connect? Who would want to look at my connections and for what purpose? Do I want people to see me as a walking Rolodex?

As a Facebook user, I understand the value in searching through your friends' friends for people you may know: scanning a new connection's contacts for someone you might have a lot in common with and then asking your new contact for an introduction is definitely one way to utilize your connections' contacts for efficient Windmill Networking. *But that is Facebook and this is LinkedIn*. LinkedIn, being a site for professionals, is not only for friends but also for business contacts. There is a reason that many of my LinkedIn connections rejected my Facebook invite: Many people reserve Facebook "friend" status for a select few group of friends and family. So the comparison stops there.

The funny thing about it is, if you are looking for someone to connect with when your contact has more than a few hundred connections, it is much faster to use the Advanced Search functionality That way you can pinpoint a person, rather than going through multiple screens of someone's contacts looking for a particular person. The important thing is, if you find someone you need to be introduced to, the person who is connected will appear. That person can then be contacted to facilitate an introduction.

As a Windmill Networker, regardless of whether or not I display my connections, I fulfill an obligation to do my best to connect people when there is proper rationale behind it. I trust that you will as well.

So, if you are in sales or a relationship-centric occupation, I can understand and respect that you keep your connections closed, as I do. If you ever need my help at facilitating an introduction from someone you find on Advanced Search, please let me know and I will do my best to assist you. But if you ask me to open up my connections to you, I will want to know what the purpose is. I have only been asked once and that person accepted my above explanation.

Regardless of what you decide to do, I believe both sides of the story should be respected for whatever they decide to do. This is a question that often appears on Answers, so if you are interested in more opinions, please do an Advanced Answers Search for the latest thoughts surrounding the debate.

On a final note, I was at a local networking meeting where a number of people said this topic was their pet peeve. Many people thought the whole idea of LinkedIn was about finding people to connect with through friends of their 1st degree connections. In other words, Windmill Networking, but only when it is one connection away from their own physical network. Furthermore, many of them looked down on those that closed their connections. In their eyes, the LinkedIn Brand you display when you close your connections communicates a negative, anti-networking message.

Do give some serious thought to this issue, as in the example above. What you do here ultimately may become part of your LinkedIn Brand without you realizing it. If you are not sure as to what your current setting is, you can access it at "Connections Browse" which is part of your "Privacy Settings" in Account & Settings.

Display Your Footprint?

As I mentioned earlier in this book, you have the ability to see a number of people who have recently viewed your profile by selecting the "Who's Viewed My Profile" module in the right-hand section of your page near the top. What this information means is up for debate, as people could be looking at your profile to ascertain whether or not to send you an invitation and nothing more. With a paid subscription, you can see all of the people who have visited your profile, not just the five that appear in this module.

But if you are looking at profiles, do you really want to leave your "footprint" and let others know that *you* have visited *them?* I have heard some in the LinkedIn community refer to this is as a type of **virtual handshake**; if you want to show a hiring manager or recruiter you are interested in a particular subject, then, sure, go for it. But what if you are looking at profiles of your competitors or someone that, for whatever reason, you don't want them to know you were visiting them?

Once again, LinkedIn gives you the capability to customize this setting. By accessing Account & Settings and going to Profile Views, which is under Privacy Settings, you are given three options as to how you "show" yourself when a contact looks at this module:

- Show your name and headline
- Only show anonymous characteristics, like "manager from the real estate industry"
- Don't show that you've viewed their profile at all

The interesting thing is that LinkedIn, for all it is doing to increase user "privacy," has the default setting set to display anonymous characteristics. But for privacy's sake, doesn't it make sense to not show anything? Could it be that perhaps LinkedIn does this to show potential value in upgrading your account so you can the "see" everyone who has visited your profile?

Needless to say, I recommend you don't show your footprint at all. There may be a case for specifically showing your name if you are trying to contact people and want to make a conscious effort to them know you have an interest in them. I see very few people who display their full name, but there may be a case for Windmill Networking in doing such a thing.

How to Keep a Profile Private

I was a little confused when I recently received this question from a former colleague. LinkedIn is really about getting plugged in to a huge database of professionals to facilitate Windmill Networking. Why would you want to be part of this huge network but not want anyone to see your profile or your LinkedIn Brand? I suppose that for some, the ability to find people far outweighs the benefits of being found, so this may shed some light on his request. Or perhaps it was the reception of "spam" mails like Invitations to connect, join this Group, take this poll, etc. that caused my colleague to want to keep his profile private?

Regardless of the reason, there may be some of you who want to know how to keep your profile as private as possible on LinkedIn. Once again, this capability is all located in the details of the Account & Settings page, which you can access in the upper right-hand corner of your Home Page. Let's see what is possible here within your privacy settings, when displaying your profile and minimizing email contact from other LinkedIn members: (I discuss these in order of how they appear on Account & Settings from top to bottom, left to right)

Profile Settings

- You can choose to display your photo to only your connections at "My Profile Photo".
- You have a "Public Profile" option you can turn off; if someone is not a member of LinkedIn and searches for your public profile, it will not be visible.
- You can decide not to show any Recommendations you have received or sent by managing these respectively on the "Recommendations" page.

- You can keep your "Status Update" visible to only your connections via "Status Visibility".

- You can completely shut off your Network Feed in "Member Feed Visibility." Updates regarding actions you perform on LinkedIn will not be visible or broadcasted.

Email Notifications

- In "Contact Settings," you can decide not to receive In Mails, which gives you a bit more privacy. You do not have the option to turn off receiving "Introductions," as this is obviously an integral part of the LinkedIn service.

- In "Receiving Messages" you can tell LinkedIn to not send you emails, giving yourself the freedom to view what you want when you want on the LinkedIn website.

- "Invitation Filtering" allows you to narrow down the invitations you receive to just those email addresses you had previously imported into LinkedIn when you first pressed "Add Connections." You can also choose to only receive invitations from those that know your email address. This will prevent random people from sending you an invitation, assuming you do not list your email address in your profile.

Groups

- "Group Invitation Filtering" allows you to prevent anyone from sending you a Group invitation.

- If you don't want to receive emails from anyone outside of your network, don't join any LinkedIn Groups. Should you join some Groups, make sure under the Settings for each Group that you indicate you don't want to receive Messages from other Group members or Announcements from the Group Manager. You can do this on the "My Groups" page.

Personal Information

- On "Name & Location" you can display the initial of your last name instead of your full name (i.e. Stuart Madison becomes Stuart S.).

Privacy Settings

- There are "Research Surveys" targeting your demographic that may be sent to you, unless you indicate you do not want to receive them.

- "Profile Views" will control what, if any, information about you is displayed in the "Who's Viewed My Profile" module.

- Whenever you make a profile update, a new Recommendation, or a status update, the default setting allows the information to broadcast to your network on their Home Pages. You can turn this off in "Profile and Status Updates."

- LinkedIn is building out a Service Provider Directory. If you are recommended as a Service Provider, you will be listed in that directory. If you want to make sure you are not, please do so in "Service Provider Directory."

- There is a "Partner Advertising" option that allows you to tell LinkedIn NOT to use your private information to present you with targeted information (or advertising) on other sites such as NYTimes.com.

As you can see, there is quite a bit you can do to keep your profile semi-private, as well as to cut down emails that you don't want to receive. **The scary part is that a lot of the default settings I found here are not respectful of your privacy. If privacy is important to you, make sure to look at the above items and confirm that the settings are aligned with your LinkedIn Objective.**

In summary, you can eliminate most, if not all, of the emails you receive from LinkedIn. It is impossible to have a completely private LinkedIn profile. Just remember that you can limit who gets access to your information.

The Status Update: "What Are You Working On Now?"

After you create your static LinkedIn Profile and you begin using LinkedIn more and more, the "What are you working on now?" question will be glaring at you every day on your LinkedIn Home Page. It appears under your Inbox and at the top of your Network Updates section. Anything you enter here, which I will refer to as a "Status Update," will not only get prominently displayed on your profile right underneath your Profile Headline, but it will also be broadcasted as a Network Update on the Home Page of all of your connections (should you have allowed your updates to be sent and your connections are viewing them). What on earth do you enter in this Status Update box?

For those who can remember, this is a fairly new feature on LinkedIn. At the time it was first implemented, everyone thought that LinkedIn was trying to mimic Twitter. Facebook has also had this functionality, with updates appearing on your "Wall." But all three of these social networks have different demographic as well as different things for which people use them. What do you do with your LinkedIn "Status Update?"

If you update your Wall on Facebook, the subject matter may be a little more playful than LinkedIn. You may tweet on Twitter a few times a day, but if you update your status in the same way, only the most recent tweet would be visible on LinkedIn.

That's right, the fundamental difference between LinkedIn vs. Twitter/Facebook is that your "Status Updates" are not archived and cannot be seen past your most recent one.

I should note that, with the recent introduction of the "Activity Tab" on someone' s profile, if they are broadcasting their Member Feed the archived "Status Updates" will appear here. But not everyone is broadcasting their Member Feed to everyone.

Therefore, the first consideration is whatever you put in your "Status Update" should be something "sticky" that can potentially remain on your page for an extended period of time.

LinkedIn is a pretty static website. If you are updating this area several times a day, your network will be blasted with your Status Updates a few times a day and you may stand out in an awkward way. This is not Twitter. For this reason, I recommend you do not update this more than once a day if you can help it. If you have nothing to say, there is no need to randomly update this area, as your most previous comment will remain displayed until it is changed.

As for the subject matter of the "Status Update," it really comes down to what your LinkedIn Objective is and what brand you want to display. My advice: Regardless of the subject matter, always embed your LinkedIn Brand into what you enter here.

Are you trying to show that you are an expert in something? Talk about your latest presentations, exhibitions attended, etc. Looking for a job? I personally wouldn't advertise the fact that I am looking for a job on my Status Update, but use the space to promote your skills and experience in a way that you can't do in your more static LinkedIn Profile. Are you studying something new, trying to obtain a new certificate, networking, or flying somewhere for an interview? These things could definitely add to your brand and add value to boot. If you are a recruiter, sure, if you have one high value hard-to-find candidate that you are looking for, put it in your Status Update. Putting something creative in your Status Update can help you both reach your LinkedIn Objective as well as provide a way of broadcasting something in a timely manner, a manner LinkedIn does not allow in its rigid format.

Everyone will have a different use for Status Updates, but think critically about what you are trying to achieve with LinkedIn and what your LinkedIn Brand is. I am sure that with a little bit of creative thinking, you will be able to create a perfect "Status Update" that is aligned with your LinkedIn Brand.

PART III:

STRATEGIC TIPS TO LEVERAGE THE POWER OF LINKEDIN

It is important to close out this book with strategies specifically related to how to grow your network. If you see the value in Windmill Networking, you can easily understand why a bigger, more diverse network will always be more advantageous in Web 2.0 social networking. We will cover many issues regarding growing your network and spend time looking at the LION movement in more detail. I will also include tips on how to grow your network not just virtually, but physically a s well. I will also introduce more advanced information regarding invitation management. I will close with some important topics to think about as you progress down the road of Windmill Networking to become a LinkedIn "Expert."

Chapter 11

Chapter 11 All You Need to Know...
But Were Afraid to Ask about LIONs

- What is a LION?
- Why I am a LION
- How Do I Become a LION?
- Can I Be a Selective LION?
- Watch Out for Fake LIONs
- What is LinkedIn's Policy on LIONs?

What is a LION?

Before proceeding to the following chapter on how to grow your network, it is important at this juncture to formally introduce you to what a LION is. This is something you may have seen on profiles of other people or invitations that you have received. I believe that LIONs are the most controversial and misunderstood concept within LinkedIn. In fact, the most read post on my blog until recently has been the one where I talked about this subject. While LIONs can be important in growing your network, they make up only one angle of many you can play.

You don't have to be a LION if you want to enlarge your Windmill Network. But it will definitely help accelerate the process.

LION, in the LinkedIn world, stands for **L**inked**I**n **O**pen **N**etworker. I believe the original LinkedIn LION Group (which is now called "LION™ Worn with Pride! [Choose wisely...] < BEWARE OF COUNTERFEITS >") was a community in which members generally agreed to be positively open to receiving and often accepting each other's invitations to connect. This LinkedIn LION Group also runs the LION Yahoo Group as well as the LION Home Page (www.themetanetwork.com), called "THE LIONS' LAIR."

In this way, a "LION" was someone who was originally a member of the above LinkedIn LION Group. With the emergence of other open networking Groups and Group limitations, this should be more closely defined as a movement of open networkers who want to build up their virtual networks for whatever objective they might have in Windmill Networking. I would argue that, in some ways, the LIONs are the true pioneers of Windmill Networking and have taken to its extreme; I confess that being a LION has definitely helped me see the advantage of being a Windmill Networker. But, if you go back to my definition of Windmill Networking, it is not equivalent to merely being a LION: Being a Windmill Networker implies a Pay It Forward attitude and personable approach to social networking based on building out a Trusted Network of

Advisors. Furthermore, Windmill Networking is also about networking with your own LinkedIn Objective, which will help determine who you want to add to your network. In this way, I consider the LIONs to be a movement that is part of the Web 2.0 platform that is LinkedIn. LIONs help accelerate Windmill Networking, but it is only one of the means, not the ultimate goal.

LIONs "often" accept each other's invitations; however, just because someone is a LION does not necessarily mean they will accept your invitation. It does mean they are open to receiving your invitation and *should not* respond with the dreaded IDK. That being said, there is never a guarantee that a LION will not respond with such an IDK (I have received this a few times from people with "LION" in their profile). LIONs will generally be more open to receiving invitations and being contacted, but there is no guarantee that they will not IDK you.

LIONs are basically open to networking with people they have never met before. In this way, they add tremendous value to LinkedIn by bridging networks of closed people and allowing us to be only a few degrees of connection away from each other.

If we all follow the standard rule of LinkedIn and say "I Don't Know" for every invitation that we receive from someone we have never personally known, it would be difficult for closed networks to evolve into the great networking community that LinkedIn is today.

It should be noted there is no authority that governs the LinkedIn LIONs, and thus if a LION (someone who puts LION in their profile on their headline, for instance) responds to an invitation with an "IDK," they are not penalized—you are. I have received an IDK from a "LION" who put the term next to their name on their headline. I even wrote them with the Wikipedia definition of LION and asked them to invite me into their network to cancel out their "mistake," but to no avail.

The interesting thing I have found out about LIONs is that, in my experience, there are more recruiters among these open networkers than any other profession. This makes sense because it is in a headhunter's best interest to Windmill Network to find future potential candidates and/or customers. In this way, LIONs are not a group of outcasts, but are people who understand the practical advantage a large LinkedIn Network provides them.

In conclusion, while it is relatively safe to invite a LION into your network (especially if they are a recruiter in my experience), there is no guarantee you will not receive an IDK as a response. **That is why it is important to review every LION's profile and contact details to confirm whether or not they really do welcome your invitation or not.** The general rule of inviting new people is the same for LIONs as for everyone else: The burden of determining whether they will accept your invitation is on *you*.

For more information about the history of the LION movement and some of its most famous advocates, please see the excellent article written by C.G. Lynch of CIO.com at:

http://www.cio.com/article/470122/LinkedIn_s_Most_Unusual_Members_Meet_The_Super_Connected

Why I am a LION

With all I have written regarding the value behind Windmill Networking, you can understand the value I see in being a LinkedIn Open Networker. I hope you will have a positive opinion of the LION movement as well.

You see, I always hear people bashing LIONs. Some people characterize LIONs as people who "amass connections as if they're Beanie Babies." Others think the intention of open networkers is just to spam you. For all of those who doubt the intention of open networkers, consider this question:

Why are you on LinkedIn?

And, more importantly:

If you are only connecting with people that you know, what is the value of LinkedIn?

Social media and social networking sites are a godsend for the Gen X generation which I represent. Why? Because by the time email and Internet browsing became prevalent, we were already out of college and had potentially lost touch with a huge number of people from our childhood who never had email addresses or cell phones. Social networking sites like Facebook and LinkedIn have given us a chance to revive those relationships, some dormant for 20 years!

If reconnecting with lost colleagues and classmates is the only potential you see in LinkedIn, you are missing the big picture. If you are a professional, the need to "network" with other professionals is more important than ever before. Regardless of the type of position you are in, there is always value in being able to meet with people from the same industry or the same profession. You can even create relationships with others (including recruiters) who may be able to help you out in time of need. **Utilizing LinkedIn is about Digging Your Well Before You're Thirsty, and it is also about classic Windmill Networking.**

That is what open networking is all about, because LIONs like me see extreme value in Windmill Networking.

Open networking is about exploiting the unique virtual networking capability that social networking sites like LinkedIn provide us.

Maybe because I am a Gen Xer and felt like I missed out on something for the last 20 years, but social networking provides opportunities I want to cherish and utilize to the fullest. That is why I openly accept communication from people who may see value in me, because I cannot predict what Pay It Forward thing I can do for them. I also never know what value they may be able to provide to me in the future. I don't send out random invitations, and only target people that are aligned with my LinkedIn Objective.

By proclaiming that I am an open networker and that I am trying to help people I do not know, I have become a "Virtual Networking Altruist" (I hate egotistical phrases like this, but I just couldn't think up a better phrase). Meeting new people. Connecting people. Helping people if I can add value to them. Reaching out to my network when I am in need. Networking in a world of virtual relationships, but always trying to bring those relationships into my physical world.

So. I ask again:

If you are not reaching out and meeting new people on a social networking site like LinkedIn, why are you wasting your time?

How Do I Become a LION?

I hope you are now potentially interested in becoming a LION. So how do you become one, you ask?

Unfortunately, there is no single answer for this, as historically LinkedIn actually discouraged LIONs. At one time, LIONS' LAIR became the default place for LIONs to register, but there is no official LinkedIn sanctioned LION Group on LinkedIn. With that in mind, if you would like to be recognized by others as an open networker (i.e. LION), you can do the following:

- Register on LIONS' LAIR as an open networker.
- Become a member of some of the LION/open networking Groups that I discuss in Chapter 12: Growing Your Network.
- Include the terminology LION somewhere prominent in your profile so you can be found.

In short, a "LION" is merely someone who uses this four-letter phrase as part of her LinkedIn Brand to inform others she is an open networker.

Including the terminology LION in your profile is tricky, as it becomes a SEO (Search Engine Optimization) project for your profile. If you go to the Advanced Search and enter "LION" as a keyword and press enter, you can see which profiles show up on the first page. This will give you an idea of how to effectively portray yourself as a LION to be found by others looking for you.

Obviously, if you brand yourself a LION, it goes without saying you should make sure to follow the golden rule of never responding to an Invitation with an IDK.

Can I Be a Selective LION?

Because anyone can declare himself or herself a LION by displaying the word on their profile, there are many different types of LIONs you will find on LinkedIn. Who you find depends on how they label themselves and their own definition of the LION concept. There are many, like me, who are simply Digging Their Wells Before They're Thirsty and are Windmill Networking. There are many recruiters who are LIONs in order to get better visibility into the profiles of potentially lucrative "passive" candidates. There are also many different levels of open networkers, each with their own rule as to what invitations they will accept.

I believe that a LION can be selective in what invitations they accept so long as they do not respond with an IDK and merely archive invitation requests that they receive but do not wish to accept.

A wise strategy to promote yourself as a LION while you Windmill Network: Selectively accept invitations while actively inviting other open networkers from a specific demographic, in line with your LinkedIn Objective, to join your network.

In fact, if you are not sure whether becoming a LION is right for you, starting off as a selective LION may be a prudent strategy to help you "get your feet wet" and feel more comfortable over time.

I would add two things here:

- You should note in your Contact Settings that although you are a LION, you are especially interested in receiving invitations from those within a specific demographic. You should also explain that for all other invitations, you reserve the right not to accept. At least this way you have a disclaimer, as you should ALWAYS read Contact Settings before inviting someone. Note this may make some open networkers question whether or not you are really "open." I think it is a risk you have to take to be fair to those open networkers who are not in your desired demographic and who may "waste" an invitation on you, should you decide to archive their request.

- I understand that sometimes people want to be selective LIONs, and indeed you can argue that I started off as a selective LION as well. But the beauty of LinkedIn is that you can see and ask for Introductions to 2nd and 3rd degree connections. There may be someone who is not in your desired demographic, but may be connected to many people with whom you want to connect. **That is the power of LinkedIn. That is why I slowly moved to accepting invitations from different industries and geographies when I realized I was missing out on a huge virtual network by archiving these invitations.** I avoided India for a long time, for instance, until I realized there are so many recruiters and candidate sourcers from India that it didn't make sense to exclude them. Shortly thereafter, I was interviewing with an Indian recruiter for a potential job in Japan! This is the beauty of archiving invitations, in that you can always come back to them at a later time and accept them, should you change your mind or LinkedIn Objective. Either way, in light of what I say, I do hope you will rethink how selective you may want to be when accepting invitations if you want to label yourself as a LION.

At the end of the day, a LION is a truly "open" networker. So long as you do not send an IDK, you are really free to do as you wish. I do feel (at a minimum) you should:

1. Make sure you never respond with an IDK.

2. Put your invitation policy in your Contact Settings.

3. Reconsider your selective approach and individually decide whose invitation you want to accept outside of the desired demographic with which you want to connect.

Watch Out for "Fake" LIONs

As a Windmill Networker, when you reach out and begin to connect with people you have not physically met before, there is always a chance that the person just wants to get access to your email address in order to spam you or sell that information for someone else to spam you. With any Web 2.0 social network there is always a danger of this. **I do believe the benefits of Windmill Networking far outweigh the potential negatives.** Once you open up your door, however, it is impossible to keep only the good in and leave the bad out. It is a reality that we all have to live with, and we must remain vigilant by informing LinkedIn when we see people trying to take advantage of this situation.

How do the bad get into the system? There is a trend: These people either indicate they are a "LION" or are joining open networking Groups. Until recently, I had seen many people complain about the existence of fake profiles on LinkedIn. I too had found profiles that seemed fishy in their lack of detail; however, I subscribe to the "innocent until proven guilty" philosophy. I could not cry foul without absolute proof. Nevertheless, I have now seen how fake "LION"s can infiltrate the system. In doing so, they can potentially infiltrate your network, especially if you leave your connections list open for all to see.

Before I get into the explanation, some skeptics may ask why a Windmill Networker would care whether or not a connection is fake. After all, by connecting to that person, you get visibility into who their contacts are. Why should you care since you don't know that person anyway? Well, as I mentioned in my definition of Windmill Networking:

Windmill Networking...is also about being authentic and never forgetting the importance of The Personal Touch... the more you genuinely give, the more you will receive when you really need it.

Being real and genuine is an intrinsic part of Windmill Networking. The idea is that you are not only helping a real connection; when you need help and pull that virtual connection into your physical network, they will be there to help you and potentially *meet* with you. Even real people I connect to don't always help me out, but if the profile is fake to begin with, the chances of future help are nil. Therefore, fake profiles are a threat to all of LinkedIn's users, not just Windmill Networkers.

Because I am a Windmill Networker with lots of connections, I tend to get my fair share of invitations. Recently, I received several invitations from people that I thought were fake. I was able to prove this after I connected with them by looking at their email address. Here is what they had in common:

- Their headline profile had either a "(LION)" or a "(TopLinked.com)" notation.
- Their titles were either recruiters at very large and famous American corporations or owners of their own recruiting firms.
- They all have amassed over 500 connections.
- Although they indicate they are "LIONs," none of them were a member of ANY Group, including TopLinked.com.
- Their email addresses were numbered as in **1@x.y.com, **2@x.y.com, **3@x.y.com (which only became apparent after I connected with them).

So these are fake profiles that 1) pretended they were in large companies and in the recruiting industry to fool you and 2) pretended they were open networkers in their headline profile to attract connections from other open networkers. I have seen others claiming they graduated from top tier colleges.

Why do fake profiles exist on LinkedIn?

Someone who wanted to sell his 1,500-connection email database for $10 once contacted me. Email addresses from legitimate professionals, many who make over six figures annually, are a prized commodity for many companies who want to market their goods to this demographic. These "spammers" are getting smarter in their methods and are becoming more successful, as proven by the previous example of the 500+ connections that fake profiles had already amassed from other unsuspecting LinkedIn users.

Furthermore, whether these people state they worked at some famous company or graduated from top notch universities, here is the commonality: These people can now invite people who worked or went to school with them into their own network, without knowing email addresses. These people can exploit the LinkedIn database through the guise of "open networking" and build a huge database of targeted users from certain universities or enterprises. What they do with this information is anyone's guess.

The minute one of these people with fake profiles reads this book, they will change their strategies and do something else. There is nothing I can do about it. But I hope this is a wake up call to you about the lurking security issue out there. Most notably it shows that anyone can say they are a member of a company and then have the ability to connect with other "colleagues" without knowing their email address. It is in the best interest of each company, if not LinkedIn, to monitor this.

So just because someone shows a "LION" or affiliation with an open networking Group like "TopLinked.com" membership does not mean they are a true open networker. They could be here today; tomorrow, they could be selling your email address to other spammers. **Only connect with authentic people—period.**

So how can you tell if someone is authentic? Well, if you think about it, the only benefit of engaging with social media is if you are real and genuine. I don't trust anyone who isn't. If you are on a site where everyone lists their profile and adds a photo, why would you not want to do the same? What is your reasoning for wanting to connect and interact with people without sharing a little about yourself? There may be reasons, but for many of us on LinkedIn, we are starting to get suspicious of people who don't want to share more details of themselves with the rest of the LinkedIn community. These are the people who I fear the most.

Often, through common sense, you can unearth a lot of fake profiles on your own thanks to the standard format that LinkedIn uses and its search capabilities. Do they have a photo? Any details in their summary or work experience? Recommendations? I think you get the picture of how you can help us spot these fake LinkedIn users before they infiltrate the system.

What is LinkedIn's Policy on LIONs?

First of all, as this book and I are not officially related in any way to LinkedIn, I obviously cannot comment on behalf of LinkedIn. The following only represents my educated guess based on what I have read and experienced.

With all of these LIONs openly accepting invitations, as well as inviting people they potentially don't know on a personal level, you have to wonder what LinkedIn's policy is on the matter. After all, this goes against the entire premise of LinkedIn, as embodied in their User's Agreement, that you only connect with people you know and trust. This is why there is an "I Don't Know" response, should you decide not to accept an invitation from someone that you don't know. In fact, to remind you, the LinkedIn User Agreement specifically states: *"It is intended that Users only connect to other Users who they currently know."* Open networking has been able to flourish because up until now LinkedIn has apparently not strictly enforced the User Agreement, but there is no guarantee that it will remain this way.

In my opinion, I am assuming the problem in LinkedIn's eyes concerning LIONs is their potential to spam people because of the enormous numbers of connections they have. The recent move to prevent LinkedIn Group managers from exporting the email addresses of their Group members was a step towards trying to limit spam. To distance itself from the bad image of LIONs and their relation to spam, the original LION LinkedIn Group has taken the extraordinary step of creating a "LIONs Against SPAM!" LinkedIn Group.

I personally see no connection between an "Open Networker" and someone who spams. The problem, as detailed in the previous section on Fake LIONs, is that some people take on the "LION" brand in order to amass lots of email addresses with the sole intent of spamming people. I don't think this happens often, but even if these people compose less than 1% of the LION population, it is enough spam to be noticeable, and to give LIONs a bad rap.

I was pleasantly surprised when I recently came across a video interview of a LinkedIn Senior Executive discussing his view on LIONs. I believe this is the first public statement that someone from LinkedIn has made on the open networking movement.[8] He commented: (note that I transcribed this myself from a video)

"...generally speaking, we allow people to try to do things that they can as individuals, but it's really important to be based on connections of trust and respect to people you do know. So...if two people are LIONs and those LIONs want to connect, individual freedom, but spamming people who are not so interested we're not very happy with."

So, there you have it. **LinkedIn does seem to allow LIONs to flourish as part of a commitment to individual freedom, but will take a hard line on spamming.** I still think, looking at that video, that LinkedIn unfortunately seems to still equate LIONs with spam. If more LIONs actually start reporting spam to LinkedIn (which is the intent of the new LION Group against spam), LIONs could start being seen as a group of people who want to contribute to the LinkedIn community. If you personally experience any spam from LinkedIn members, please contact LinkedIn.

Before we close this chapter, let's revisit the question with which we began this chapter. Although I believe LinkedIn is officially "neutral" towards open networkers, the trend shows that LinkedIn is clearly starting to place limitations that adversely affect open networking. First the limitation of invitations to 3,000, then Group numbers to 50, and most recently the limitation on the number of connections to 30,000 gives one the sense that LinkedIn is not encouraging open networking.

Despite these regulatory steps, open networking groups and people that identify themselves as "LIONs" continue to grow and thrive in pace with the overall growth of LinkedIn.

I do believe LinkedIn rightfully wants to maintain a community of professionals, full of high quality, trustworthy networks, without users getting spammed. Windmill Networking is also about high quality social networking. I think some people who just wanted to connect with everyone in the early days and spammers may have ruined this for others, but I don't know for sure. LinkedIn wants people to know each other when they connect; that is why they give you an option to send a seemingly innocent "I Don't Know" as a way to turn down a connection. On the other hand, LinkedIn's discouraging others to grow their networks can also be seen as a way to differentiate their paid service from that of a LION. If there can be a value placed on having lots of connections, perhaps LinkedIn would like to reserve this right for its paid customers.

In conclusion, I would say that traditionally LinkedIn has discouraged LIONS, but now seems to take a more neutral stance. If you choose to become a LION, please remember LinkedIn can strictly enforce the LinkedIn User Agreement at any time, should they wish to do so.

Chapter 12

Chapter 12 Growing Your Network

- How Do I Actively Grow My LinkedIn Network?
- How Can I Attract More Invitations?
- My Top Ten LION/Open Networking Groups
- Before Sending the Invitation: My Top Five Tips on What to Look for in a LinkedIn Profile
- One Virtual Networking Strategy: Going Local
- How to Meet and Communicate with People in a Networking Environment

How Do I Actively Grow My LinkedIn Network?

Every time someone invites me to connect with them, I always try to send out a reply thanking them and also asking them to contact me should they ever need any help with LinkedIn. While not everyone asks me a question, by far the question that I get the most is "How can I grow my network on LinkedIn?" Since I, and I hope you, have now become Windmill Networkers, it is absolutely in my best interest to help you grow your network.

As I have grown my network from a few hundred to a few thousand connections over the past several months, I believe I have the expertise to help you effectively grow your network to meet whatever objective you might have.

That being said, there are many ways to achieve this; you will need to decide which methods you use.

First of all, I hope through my discussions about Windmill Networking you will begin to understand why having a large network on LinkedIn is important.

I believe the main purpose for anyone using LinkedIn is TO FIND AND BE FOUND. In order to do this, you need to use the Advanced Search functionality, which will give you the top 100 results based on whatever search terms you entered *from within your network*. Your network is defined as your direct connections (1st degree), your 1st degree connections' connections (2nd degree), and your 2nd degree connections' connections (3rd degree). When you first joined LinkedIn, any search you conducted may not have given you a total of 100 results, but as you grow your network, you will realize why some people pay to get 500 instead of 100 results. A good example is when I was looking for people in the Staffing and Recruiting industry who might be working in my field of specialty (IPTV). I would enter the keyword "IPTV" and select the Staffing and Recruiting industry and voila! 70+ people would appear. I just checked for the first time in a month and the number is now 90. **The larger your network, the more you will find and be found.** Furthermore, your search results will always change as your network grows, so make sure you do regular searches for finding people who are important to you. Don't get frustrated if nothing shows up on your first search.

Now that we know why it is important to grow our network, let's look at some of the common ways we can achieve this. There are two ways to grow our networks: 1) in an active way, utilizing one's own invitations, and 2) in a passive way, hoping that people will find you and invite you to their network. I will cover 1) in this section and 2) in the following section.

1. Invite Co-Workers from Past and Present Companies

This sounds very simple and indeed, it is. LinkedIn offers ways for you to easily find people from your past companies who are LinkedIn members. You can then connect without knowing their email addresses. This is really the reason why most people are on LinkedIn and how LinkedIn began to develop: to find old colleagues. However, you can only find people if your profile is up-to-date. That means the more companies you say you worked for in your profile, the more colleagues you will find. Make sure you complete your profile for every job you have held since you started working for optimum results.

2. Invite Classmates from Present and Past Schools

You will not find nearly as many classmates on here as you will on Classmates.com, or on Facebook for that matter. LinkedIn is really about professionals networking with each other. But you can find old classmates on LinkedIn just as you can find old colleagues. In order to do so, you need to have your profile updated for every school you have attended. About 99% of the profiles I see only go back as far as college. I have added my high school to my profile, but I have only been able to find other classmates by doing a keyword search for my high school name. During and after college I spent time doing foreign language study at colleges in China (including Taiwan) and Japan, and I have added these to my profile. Through this I was recently able to connect with two classmates from a 1988-89 foreign student class in Beijing for the first time! I recommend putting every school you attended since high school in your LinkedIn Profile to maximize the potential benefits.

3. Invite Business and Personal Contacts Using the LinkedIn Functionality of Checking Your Outlook Address Book or Webmail Address Book

This is the way that new people generally get invited in to the LinkedIn network. LinkedIn will conveniently check your address books. It will allow you to see who is on LinkedIn and automatically generate an invitation with one easy push of a button. I caution you here not to just invite anyone and everyone that shows up on these lists. You may have emailed a bunch of companies asking for a quote on some home improvement project, for instance, and these people will show up here. Do you really want to invite the guy whose business you turned down? You could have an Outlook contact of someone who is now working as your competition. Do you want him to be part of your network? You really need to go through the results carefully and only invite those people that 1) are on LinkedIn (they should be displayed in a different color with more information if they are) and 2) you feel will add value to your network. One final note here: I recommend you DO NOT invite anyone who is not currently a member of LinkedIn in light of LinkedIn's limit on the number of invitations you can send out. 3,000 invitations will take you time to burn through, but you will burn through them as you navigate through the members of this 40+ million strong community and build your network. So if there are contacts that are not on LinkedIn that you invite and they never sign up, your invitation will be wasted. Whether the invitation is accepted, ignored, not delivered, etc., it doesn't matter. Your invitation has been used. You will have to remember to diligently withdraw these "wasted" invitations at a later date.

4. Invite LIONs That You Find Through Advanced Searches

LIONs are probably the *least* risky way of adding new connections to your network. Simply putting "LION," "Invites Welcome," "Open Networker" "Accept Invites," "Windmill Networker" etc. as keywords in an Advanced Search will give you a list of plenty of LIONs to contact and invite. One word of caution: I highly recommend you read through each LION's profile to understand their contact settings and their desire to be contacted (or not). There are some people who require you to send a personalized invitation, while others will ask you to open up your contacts to them. Only invite those who truly welcome open invitations.

5. Invite Group Members from Groups That You Belong to

As indicated in the previous chapter on Groups, joining a Group is easy, and once you do, you can search for people within your Group as part of an Advanced Search. You can then see people who may not already be part of your extended network. As for inviting people from within a Group, follow the same guidelines as you apply to LIONs: Check their profile, and, if they say nothing about being an open networker, do not risk one of your invitations. Many LinkedIn users make the mistake early on of inviting someone just because they were members of the same Group. BIG MISTAKE. One IDK later you will realize that, just because you think someone in your Group would welcome an invitation from a fellow Group member, doesn't mean that they agree. Of course, there are Groups devoted to open networkers who, as a rule, are safe to invite. I will discuss some of these Groups in a later section of this chapter.

6. **Invite Other People in Your Network to Connect After Finding Them on Advanced Search**

The value of LinkedIn is that there is no other site for professionals where you can absolutely pinpoint and contact a person in a certain industry with a specific company and title. If you are in sales (or are a recruiter), LinkedIn is like a heaven-sent gift. Keep in mind that you will get kicked out of LinkedIn if you do not respect the wishes of others who do not want to be bothered by invitations. They may report your invitations as spam and yes, this is worse than an IDK! The people who are the most valuable for you to contact are often the most difficult to reach because they do not share any common Groups with you and do not identify themselves as open networkers. Before inviting these people, I suggest you send them an InMail (paid account), or if they have an email address listed somewhere in their profile, first send them an email indicating why you would like to connect with them. Better yet, try for an informal introduction if one of your trusted connections is connected to them. One rule of thumb that I have used: If they have their email address in their profile they are open to being contacted. Just remember to always read their profile and contact settings before attempting to connect.

Windmill Networkers who will accept your invitations are out there...now go and find them!

How Can I Attract More Invitations?

Invitations are a two-way street: they can either be sent by you or received from others. If LinkedIn is about being found as much as it is about finding others, isn't there something you can do to your profile to make it attract more invitations? Absolutely yes!

Below are some methods I recommend you try out as well. Some of them are common sense, but others will ensure you get more invitations from the types of people you want to attract.

1. Completely Fill Out Your Work Profile

This goes hand-in-hand with actively finding people, as LinkedIn is about finding and being found. I recommend including every job you would put on your resume, including early positions you held just after graduating from school. The content is not as important as simply putting the company name and years you worked there in your LinkedIn profile. That is enough to be found.

2. Completely Fill Out Your Education Profile

This follows the exact same concept as completely filling out your work profile. I would put every school attended since (and including) high school in your profile. If you studied overseas during or after college, or you got a Masters, Doctorate, or other degree of higher education, be sure to put those in your profile as well so past classmates can find you.

3. State That You Are a LION in Your Profile

As I mentioned in my previous chapter on LIONs, there is no single way to identify yourself as a LION in your profile. The objective is to be visible: When people search for other LIONs to connect with, in addition to looking for members from specific LION Groups (to be covered in the following section), they will just enter "LION" as a keyword and see who comes up in their network. If you appear in that search, you have included enough information about being a LION in your profile to be found. While this turns out to be an exercise in Search Engine Optimization, the easiest way to do this is to include the term LION as part of your Profile Headline. In doing so, be aware that this becomes part of your LinkedIn Brand, so you need to decide whether or not this aligns with your LinkedIn Objective.

4. **State That You Accept Invitations in Your Profile**

If people read your profile and you indicate in your contact settings, summary, or headline that you accept invitations, it will become easy for you to receive more invitations because open networkers will not be afraid of receiving the dreaded "IDK" from you. There is no fixed way of doing this, so simply do an Advanced Search with "Invite" as the keyword and see how other people do it. Then choose the wording and method that you are comfortable with.

5. **Join Groups for Open Networkers**

By joining Groups for open networkers (I recommend joining a few in the following section), you will become more visible to other open networkers, especially those who are already Group members.

6. **Join Groups Aligned with Your LinkedIn Objective**

As I recommended earlier, I believe every Windmill Networker should actively join as many Groups as they find valuable, even if that means joining the maximum number of 50 Groups. If you are a Windmill Networker and want to be found, I highly recommend searching for Groups and joining those that will help increase your network. This will make you more likely to receive invitations from serious Group members who aren't necessarily open networkers, but may share a common Group interest with you.

7. **Pay to Get Invited**

I will cover this in detail in the section "Invitations on Steroids" in Chapter 13: Advanced Invitation Management.

With the exception of 7, you should not expect to start getting tens or hundreds of invitations a day passively. In my own experience, when I had about 3,000 connections, I noticed I would start getting a regular daily batch of about 10 invitations. So if you are not getting enough invitations passively do not worry—they will come in proportion to how far your network reaches, as well as how often you do the other things I recommend above.

My Top Ten LION/Open Networking Groups

One of the easiest ways to grow your network is to associate yourself with other LIONs and either invite them or welcome their invitations. You can do this by becoming a member of the many Groups that encourage open networking on LinkedIn, subtly letting others know that it is "safe" to invite you.

Joining LinkedIn Groups devoted to open networking is the easiest and most effective way for you to quickly grow your network for Windmill Networking.

I will go over the ten Groups I recommend and have joined, listed by Group members in descending order as of June 2009. Note that I have not been paid to advertise these Groups, nor do I have any special relationships with them or their Group Managers (with the exception of my own Group, of course!).

One thing to note is that LinkedIn has apparently closed down LinkedIn Groups that it feels are competing with them. I know of two Groups that have been disbanded overnight with no advance notice to its members. One of these Groups had over 10,000 members! I actually feel slightly uncomfortable about listing some of these Groups here and potentially exposing them to more publicity than they want. That being said, as old Groups go, new Groups always appear. If you sign up for the mailing lists on my site WindmillNetworking.com, I will do my best to keep you informed of the Groups I recommend Windmill Networkers join.

50,000+ Members

TopLinked.com (Open Networkers)
TopLinked is consistently one of the ten biggest Groups on LinkedIn. They advertise themselves as rightfully being the largest open networking Group on the site. The Group Manager of this site is also running a few other Groups that appear in this chapter, but this particular Group provides value to

Windmill Networking in terms of 1) its website and 2) its "Supporters List" and 3) its "Invite List." TopLinked's website has been the place to find statistics on who the Top 50 most connected LinkedIn users are. This information is especially valuable in that it is no longer as easy to obtain as it used to be due to the new LinkedIn search algorithm. If you really want to build out your network, connecting with all of these people will give you a critical mass that will be helpful when conducting searches. You will see a significant increase in both 2nd and 3rd degree connections. These people are on this list because they believe in the value of open networking and building out large and diverse networks. These networks are also fundamental aspects of Windmill Networking, so it is safe to invite them. There is also a "Supporter's List" of people who are not on the Top 50 but are supporters of TopLinked and should also be "safe" Windmill Networkers to invite. Finally, joining this Group gives you the benefit of receiving a weekly email with a huge list of Group members who are Windmill Networkers and open to receiving your invitation. Personally, I have had great exchanges with TopLinked management, and they have helped resolve IDK issues with other TopLinked members. If there is only one open networking Group you join on LinkedIn, TopLinked would without a doubt receive my vote. www.toplinked.com

15,000+ Members

LION™ Worn with Pride! [Choose wisely...] < BEWARE OF COUNTERFEITS >

This is the original LION Group I referred to in the previous chapter on LIONs. The Group name is a long one, but they want to be sure that you understand that they are the original and leading Group for LIONs on LinkedIn. They urge you not to join other "open networking" Groups that could potentially exploit your membership. If you actually register on their home page, in addition to joining the LinkedIn Group, you can get additional profile information on each member, including the extent to which they are or are not open to receiving new invitations. There are member directories as well as downloadable lists. Note that this Group is rightfully vigilant against those who try to exploit LIONs in order to spam them, so your membership will need to be confirmed before you can gain access to this information. www.themetanetwork.com

OpenNetworker.com

This Group actually used to be called MyLink500.com, but was apparently bought out by the TopLinked.com people as the Group Manager is the same person. More information regarding this site will be detailed in the "Invitations on Steroids" section of the following Chapter 13: Advanced Invitation Management, but they offer a unique networking service through their home page. www.OpenNetworker.com

Leading International Open Networkers (LION)
This Group I would not recommend as highly as the other Groups. Why? Well, first of all, although it is marketed with the "LION" phrase, the name of the Group does not match the original definition of a "LION". Furthermore, I have received an IDK from a member of this Group, and the Group Manager never responded to my request to look into the situation. Just by sheer volume, many open networkers do associate themselves with this Group. Invite at your own risk.

10,000+ Members

Invites Welcome.com (Open Networkers)
This is the biggest Group devoted to people who go beyond the "LION" title and openly state that they openly welcome invitations from anyone. Once again, I have had the experience of receiving an IDK from someone in this Group, and the Group Manager (who also manages TopLinked.com and OpenNetworker.com) actually helped in making sure that justice was served. Highly recommended Group to join and invite people from. www.inviteswelcome.com.

My Top Ten LION/Open Networking Groups

LION500.com (Open Networkers)
This is the newest of the above LION Groups. If I am not mistaken, this was another Group that was originally under different ownership but is now part of the TopLinked/OpenNetworker/InvitesWelcome family. Once again I have positive experiences of the Group Manager intervening when I received an IDK. Highly recommended. www.LION500.com

5,000 Members

Let's Connect (Open Networkers)
This Group and the following Safe Haven Open Network Groups are relatively new Groups that have been spawned within the past year. So far I have had very positive experience with this Group. As the name implies the members here want to connect!

2,000+ Members

Safe Haven Open Network
As mentioned above, another relatively new Group that I have had positive experiences with. As the name implies, this Group is very supportive of protecting the rights of open networkers.

MyLink500.com (Open Networkers)
As mentioned before, MyLink500.com was the original OpenNetworker.com Group. After it changed names, I believe the brand was kept and the Group started over from scratch. As the MyLink500 Group had a very strong brand name upon open networking Groups (they used to have their own open networking member database on their home page which anyone could access), this Group has now emerged as another large one for LIONs to join. For your reference, the same manager that also manages the TopLinked/OpenNetworker/InvitesWelcome/LION500 Groups also manages this Group. www.MyLink500.com

????? Members

Windmill Networking
I will be launching my own LinkedIn Group when I publish this book to connect all of those who believe in Windmill Networking and wish to connect with other Windmill Networkers. This will be a place where members can share their Windmill Networking success stories with everyone. In addition, my So Cal Sushi and The Izakaya Club Groups will also be re-branded "A Windmill Networking Group" after their names, so you can find all of these Groups just by searching for "Windmill Networking" on the LinkedIn Group search. www.windmillnetworking.com

Before Sending the Invitation Before Sending the Invitation: My Top Five Tips on What to Look for in a LinkedIn Profile

We talked earlier about how to navigate through profiles, but I saved this section for you to read *after* you have given some thought as to who you want as a part of your growing network. As someone who has sent thousands of invitations, I can tell you that you want to generate as high of a return on your invitation investment as possible. Not only are invitations a precious resource, but so is your time!

I have written profusely about why you want to avoid the dreaded IDK. In light of what I wrote above, you also want to try to avoid the "Archive" by having your invitation accepted. Even if someone says they are a LION and is a member of the same open networking Group as you are, there obviously is no guarantee they will accept your invitation. With that in mind, **what clues does an average LinkedIn Profile give us so that we can increase the success rate of our invitations?** How do we ensure that we don't send out invitations to potentially fake profiles?

1. **Number of Mutual Connections**—The number of actual connections is a very important sign as to whether or not this person may be open to accepting your invitation. But, for me, the number of *mutual connections* you have connecting the two of you is important, assuming the person you want to invite is a 2nd degree connection. This information is displayed in the "How you're connected to (name)" module in the right-hand section of the profile. If you are a Windmill Networker, it is safe to assume that other people will have already connected with other Windmill Networkers. If you only have a few mutual connections, chances are they are not open networkers because other Windmill Networkers you are connected to have not yet connected with them. I have seen people with 500+ connections and yet only have one or two mutual connections. I absolutely avoid sending out invitations to these people and instead will wait until we have more mutual connections.

2. **LinkedIn Group Involvement**—If this person is a member of a multiple number of the open networking Groups that I recommended in the previous section, it is a very good sign they will also accept your invitation. But what if they are *only* members of open networking Groups? This leads me to believe they are just trying to amass large numbers of connections. On the other hand, if they aren't a member of many LinkedIn Groups to begin with, they may not be investing much time in LinkedIn and may not even be looking at the invitations that come in. I believe the more Windmill Networking someone does, the more LinkedIn Groups they will join. These people understand the intrinsic value that LinkedIn Groups provide when it comes to networking. Use the LinkedIn Groups that are displayed on someone's profile as an indication of the following: Whether or not they are committed to LinkedIn, as well as if they are for "real" or not.

3. **Recommendations**—Speaking of "for real" or not, if someone is on LinkedIn and doesn't have a Recommendation from anyone, I would hesitate to connect with them. Recommendations are not just for people looking for work. They add social media credibility to your LinkedIn Brand. Of the five things I mention here, this may be the one that I put the least emphasis on; however, considering that LinkedIn requires you get recommended by three people in order to get your Profile Completeness to 100%, you want to make sure you invite "real" people who have "real" Recommendations you can read.

4. **Do They Have a "Branded" Profile**—You understand how important your LinkedIn Brand is and why it is important to Dig Your Well Before You're Thirsty. It is also important to promote your LinkedIn Brand, even if it means doing so in a passive way (simply having a thorough LinkedIn Profile). What about the profiles that you are looking at? How much detail do they have? Do they even have a Summary? Do they only list their most current job, without any job details? These people are to be avoided because either 1) they are fake or 2) they clearly don't

see the value in investing more time in LinkedIn. Either way, they probably don't see the value in Windmill Networking with you!

5. **Contact Details**—I can't emphasize this enough: Make sure you look at the profile's Contact Details to ensure they are potentially open to your invitation.

I should also point out that if I had to add a number 6 to this list, it would be to avoid connecting with people who don't display their personal photo on LinkedIn. You literally don't know who you might be inviting!

If you follow these tips, although it will take you some time, you will build up a network of high quality, real people who understand the value of LinkedIn. They will be more open to accepting your invitation and Windmill Networking with you.

One Virtual Networking Strategy: Going Local

One surefire way to expand your LinkedIn Network is through the process of meeting new people and bringing them into your LinkedIn World. If you are curious to experimentally connect with people beyond your physical network, a good and safe bet is to start with people close to home. LinkedIn makes it easy to find people to add to your virtual network who may reside near you. The search functionality includes a location search: By entering your zip code, you can search for people who are literally within 10, 25, 35, 50, 75, or 100 miles of your home, and you can combine this Location field with other fields. For instance, if you want to find someone in your particular industry that lives near you, it is very easy to do so on LinkedIn.

This book talks a lot about Windmill Networking and its benefits, but if you are just starting to branch outside of your physical network, and you are unsure as to whether Windmill Networking is for you or not, why not take the approach of first meeting someone or chatting with them on the phone before connecting with them? Below are a few ways in which you may be able to achieve this:

1) **Join Local Groups**

Do a search on Groups for those in your geography. You should search by city, county, and even state. Join a few and subscribe to receive weekly digests of their Discussions Boards. There are always people who are new to the Group advertising that they want to meet or connect with other people. If you are thinking of posting a similar message, make sure you read any Discussions Board rules. If you decide to go ahead with your posting, go beyond an introduction and ask a question about professional networking associations. You may be surprised by the helpful information you receive. Even if your question doesn't end up being answered, meeting with people who are also interested in Windmill Networking with others may lead to useful advice on local networking groups.

2)**Go to Local Networking Meetings**

There are many LinkedIn Groups (like the two that I manage) that have frequent meetups in person. Once again, check the Discussions Boards, meet people, and connect with them after meeting. This is an ideal situation as LinkedIn should only be a virtual tool in your real face-to-face networking. Two professional associations I recommend because they have monthly meetings nationwide as well as having a LinkedIn presence are Netshare (www.netshare.com) and ExecuNet (www.execunet.com). I have attended meetings for both of these organizations and find them to be an excellent networking resource. The fee for non-members is nominal, and usually there are many local professionals—including executives—you will have a chance to meet. The people who attend are usually open networkers willing to give you introductions to other professionals. I think the key is connecting with actual people in your locale. As you meet them person-by-person, you gain information from them regarding which networking groups work. I have done this where I reside and have found many groups I could not have found just on LinkedIn—or on the Internet for that matter.

3)**Find Alumni Groups**

There are many alumni LinkedIn Groups for former colleagues and classmates. Join these Groups and look for alumni who live in your locale. Because you have a common link, it may be easier to contact these people, and if mutually interested, connect up on LinkedIn.

4)**Invite People that Will Accept Your Invitation**

If you do a search and include keywords like "Invites Welcome," "Accept Invites," "Open Networker," you will find people in your locale that *may* accept your invitation. Never a guarantee, so invite at your own risk. But there are a lot of good people who welcome connecting with others and building face-to-face relationships from an open invitation.

5)**Join an Open Networking Group**

There are many open networking LinkedIn Groups you can join that then allow you to do a local search for other Group members. In addition to the 10 Groups I recommended in the previous section, you can do a search for "Open Networker" or other similar keywords that I mentioned previously on the Group search functionality. Join a few of these Groups, and then make sure you understand their policies on invitations. There are some that openly state they welcome invitations. If you are having trouble finding these Groups, look at some profiles of the people you find on the previous 4) and check out which Groups they have joined. You are bound to find some interesting Groups this way. Then you can search within the Group you have joined in your locale to find local members with whom you can connect.

How to Meet and Communicate with People in a Networking Environment

Advice on attending physical networking meetings actually goes beyond the original scope of this book. It was my editor who first thought it would be a good idea to include this chapter. Like many of you, I also started out on LinkedIn, having never gone to a networking meeting, so maybe my experience can help guide you in your networking journey both on LinkedIn as well as offline.

I am an adamant believer that the best type of Windmill Networking is when you can bring your virtual world into your physical one. I want to go out of my way to encourage you all to attend more physical networking meetings to help build out your networks and connect with people.

Every networking event will truly be a different one, so I can only generalize what you may expect. Every networking meeting I have ever attended seemed to have one, or a combination of, the following components:

- A guest speaker who talks about something that is relevant to the demographic and mission of the Group. Sometimes hearing a motivated guest speaker is as valuable as the networking that results from it!

- Opportunities for you to give your 60-second "elevator speech" and introduce yourself.

- Chance to hear the elevator speeches of many others.

- Meetings can be attended by a few people or as many as several hundred!

Before you attend a meeting, make sure you have enough business cards (if you are in transition, make sure you use a service like vistaprint.com to make a professional looking card) as well as a pen and paper to take notes. I also recommend that you attend professional networking events wearing professional clothing.

Just as your LinkedIn Brand is on display at all times, your physical type of branding will also be on display every time you meet someone in a networking environment.

The most important thing you will need to prepare before networking meetings is your own 60-second or so speech which describes who you are, what your networking objectives are, and how you can help people. Networking is a two-way street, and as a Pay It Forward Windmill Networker, I urge you to talk as much about how you can help people as your own reasons for wanting to meet with others.

How can you potentially help others, you ask? The beauty of Windmill Networking is something that may seem like a trivial skill or experience to you, may be a godsend to someone else. In the scope of networking sessions, if you have a large network or are good at connecting people, broadcast that fact and let people utilize you as a resource.

The other side of the equation is being a good listener and showing genuine interest in what the other person is talking about. Treat others with respect. Anyone who comes to a networking meeting with a one-sided "it's all about me" approach will be avoided and will not win the trust of others. **Remember, give before you receive, and listen before you talk.**

As you hear others talk and mention what their objectives are, make note of it so that you have something to refer to if and when you contact them in the future. If there are areas in which you can help others, let them know after they have finished their speeches and strike up a conversation in order to get to know them better.

If someone says they can help you, great. If not, use the time to help them. Although many people may be attending a networking event, you may end up speaking with and exchanging business cards with a fraction of the attendees. That is OK. If you feel like there was a bond and either of you is helping the other out, I think it is acceptable to send that person an invitation.

The most important benefit of attending Group meetings in person is to be able to make a few connections so you can communicate with them at a later date through a one-to-one meeting. Just as with Windmill Networking, you never know when you meet someone how you could potentially help each other. You will only know if you have a chance to spend some "quality" time together getting to know more about each other.

Even after describing all of this, you may still feel uneasy about attending a physical networking event, like you did when you accepted that first Windmill Networking invitation from someone you had never met. Although I have met many great people through Windmill Networking, the most valuable people I have met are always those who I originally met at a physical networking event; I was then able to build a relationship with them over time through multiple meetings. This is just human nature.

If you've come this far and believe in the power of Windmill Networking, utilizing the same mindset you do in virtual networking in physical face-to-face meetings will provide even more value to you. I sincerely hope that you are willing and able to give it a try.

Chapter 13

<u>Chapter 13 Advanced Invitation Management</u>

- Invitations on Steroids
- The Invitation Tango
- Why Does LinkedIn Limit the Number of Connections You Can Have?

Invitations on Steroids

If you have bought into the fact there is value in having lots of connections through receiving invitations, you can now see why some people would want to pay money in order to be able to receive invitations. In fact, there is a way to receive lots of invitations, so many that I call it **"Invitations on Steroids."** There are many people who want to quickly build out their own virtual network with people who will not respond to your invitation with an IDK (of course, there is never any guarantee here). If you think about it, the growth of this whole phenomenon is the result of LinkedIn's own restrictions placed on its users.

I was on a webinar with a leading social media research company whose presenter discussed how he uses LinkedIn *less* because of all of the invitations he receives from people that he doesn't know. In fact, he called them spam. I will agree there is some spam involved, and that some of these people do want to obtain your email address in order to market something to you. I would also say, based on my experience, that probably less than 1% of those people that connect with me put me on some type of mailing list, and for 75% of those people I can quickly and easily unsubscribe from them. If you use Gmail, the spam filter is good enough to catch any real spam that comes your way. **Despite the fact that I have over 17,000 connections, I continue to get very little spam.** If you are serious about accelerating the reach and depth of your Windmill Networking, you may want to consider one of the services that I am about to introduce.

The LinkedIn Groups TopLinked.com and OpenNetworker.com provide both of these services. The common link between these two Groups is that, in addition to being run by the same Group Manager, they have added additional functionality outside of LinkedIn in the form of a supplementary website.

The general commonality is that if you are a member of each of these Groups, you will receive a weekly email with an "invite list." You will be encouraged to invite these members into your network should you want to "safely" grow your network. Let's take a closer look at each of these two sites and your options.

Note that these sites are always in flux, so I cannot guarantee that prices and/or service options will be the same when you are looking at these sites.

The older of these two sites is TopLinked.com. The original idea behind TopLinked was to list the Top 50 most connected people on LinkedIn, and then to easily allow you to connect to these people, as well as other TopLinked members, by introducing their profiles on the TopLinked home page. This was and still is *the* site to see the Top 50 most connected LinkedIn users. After all, LinkedIn does not show you who has how many connections over 500, and although I can't really verify how TopLinked.com does it, I have never heard anyone doubt the accuracy of the site's content.

TopLinked.com started to monetize their service in 2008 with a "Top Supporters" list. The idea was that those who contributed to ("supported") TopLinked.com would get their name included on a weekly invitation list that would be sent out to all TopLinked.com and thereafter the affiliated InvitesWelcome.com members as well. This is a weekly email that, as I write this book, is currently being sent out to more than 50,000 Group members on a weekly basis. So you can imagine the value in being part of this list.

Shortly thereafter a "Paid Membership" service was added and thus, for a less expensive price, one could add themselves to the weekly list that has become to be known as the "TopLinked.com LinkedIn Invite Me List." From my personal experience, and based on the fact that TopLinked.com is the 10th most popular Group on LinkedIn at the present with more than 50,000 members, I can say with 100% confidence there is no faster way to grow your network than to become a paid member of TopLinked.com.

Finally, with the recent launch of OpenNetworker.com, the only way to get yourself on the Invite Me list is to register here for a paid account; however, this site includes Invite Me lists available for immediate download to other popular social networking sites (Twitter, Facebook, etc.) as well if you become a paid member.

To summarize, if you want the ability to safely send or receive lots of invitations, your options are:

1) Become a free TopLinked.com Group member and receive the weekly Invite list. Safely invite as many people from this list as fit for your LinkedIn Objective. I have never received an IDK from anyone on this list, but I have only sent out invitations to people in particular locations and industries that are aligned with my LinkedIn Objective.

2) Become a paid OpenNetworker.com member and have your name added to the weekly InviteMe list that is sent out to all TopLinked.com Group members. Your membership also allows you to download lists of open networkers from other social networking sites as well.

3) Become a paid Top Supporter of TopLinked.com. By doing so, not only will you be added to the InviteMe list, you will also be added to the Top Supporters list which is found on the TopLinked.com home page for anyone to view. Your name will be added to the same list that includes the Top 50 LinkedIn connectors when someone utilizes the Power Check/Connect feature on the TopLinked.com site.

As a disclaimer to this chapter, I should point out that although I am a Top Supporter of TopLinked.com as well as a member of OpenNetworker.com, I have no relationship with TopLinked.com or OpenNetworker.com and am not receiving any compensation from them by writing this.

What happens if you don't want to pay money to receive additional invitations? Welcome to The Invitation Tango!

The Invitation Tango

If you think about it, because there is a restriction on how many invitations you can send, there is prime value in being able to receive invitations from lots of people. If you are Windmill Networking, you can imagine the potential value for creating a large and extremely diverse network. This is why TopLinked/OpenNetworkers have been able to place a price tag on this service and get lots of people to sign up and pay for it.

To look at it from another perspective, there are other advantages to receiving an invitation rather than sending one: for one thing, there is no fear of receiving an IDK response. Furthermore, there is no research needed to look for high quality potential connections according to your objective. Obviously not everyone you receive an invitation from is going to be closely aligned with your LinkedIn Objective. Still it is hard to gauge each new connection's potential value because you just don't know whom *they* are connected to. This is the very heart of Windmill Networking.

As more Windmill Networkers run out of invitations, they look for ways to somehow nudge people to send them invitations. This is not an easy task, and it has created a lot of creative approaches to the subject, which I call "The Invitation Tango." I am not recommending that you do or don't do any of this, but these are some of the ways I have seen people try to generate invitations sent to them. The subject of any of these emails or discussion posts is that these people are out of invitations but are open networkers and would like to connect:

- Send out an email blast to everyone in the TopLinked/OpenNetworker invite list asking to be invited.

- Send out emails to those you want to connect with by finding contact information on their profile or searching for them in an open networking Group and asking for invitations.

- Post the fact that you are out of invitations and welcome invitations on Group Discussions Boards.

- Send out a Group Announcement (if you are a Group Manager) asking people to connect with you.

In some ways, LinkedIn has created a social phenomenon by limiting invitations. Thus, companies are allowed to monetize their perceived value, while prompting people to do interesting things to receive an invitation.

I will be honest with you when I say that although I have never sent out emails asking for invitations, I have once posted the fact that I am open to receiving invitations on a few Group Discussions Boards. The results were not noticeable. If you are out of invitations, my advice to you is to avoid "the invitation tango" and spend more time Windmill Networking with the connections you do have. Communicate and get to know your LinkedIn connections. It will be time better spent and will help you achieve your LinkedIn Objective faster.

Why Does LinkedIn Limit the Number of Connections You Can Have?

I have already referred to this fact throughout the book, but I wanted to devote a chapter to delve into this fact in more detail. This limit becomes more important as you put the advanced invitation techniques into practice—and propel your connections into the 100s or 1000s.

Just like many of you, I started out on LinkedIn not knowing anything about this restriction, gradually starting my network by connecting with past colleagues and classmates and then expanding my connections to include those with similar interests and open networking ideas. When I first hit the 3,000 invitation limit, I was shocked to discover a definitive number put on the number of invitations someone could send. Of course you don't know about it until after you've sent out your 2,000th invitation. Why the number 3,000? When you have more than 500 connections and they only display "500+" on your profile, I believe LinkedIn is telling you, in essence, that you don't need more than 500 connections. They have been flexible on the invitation limit for those of us who are responsible networkers, so I have not held anything against LinkedIn despite these limitations; I can live with them.

Another restriction was placed on the amount of Groups you can join, but I did not see the problem with limiting the Group numbers to 50. I thought there were more than enough repetitive Groups out there, and indeed I was able to easily reduce my Group membership numbers from 93 to the present 50. In fact, having a limit places more value on each Group membership, and I would not have realized this without the restriction. So this is another restriction that I can live with, although with more than 300,000 Groups to choose from, I am hoping that LinkedIn soon raises this limit.

Despite these restrictions, I have been a happy networker and still believe that LinkedIn is **the** platform for social networking. At least there was no restriction on the amount of connections that you can have

This, however, changed recently, as LinkedIn now places a 30,000 limit on the number of connections you can have.

The first reaction most people have is that 30,000 are more than enough connections to have. After all, how many connections do you need? How many people do you know? If you think about it in the traditional way of networking, pre-MySpace/Facebook time, yes, this is quite a large number and should not be a problem for 99% of LinkedIn users. I myself currently have 17,000 connections so I am still at only 50% of my maximum! In fact, according to the TopLinked.com website, as of June 15, 2009, there are only 14 people with 30,000 or more connections. Could this be that big of a problem?

Well, this is the era of Windmill Networking. It is social networking in the 21st century, propelled by the rapid growth of the Internet and social networking sites like LinkedIn; real relationships *are* developed more and more on a virtual basis. That is, there are more and more people making contact with each other without physically meeting each other and creating relationships. LinkedIn is especially instrumental for making this happen because of its profile-centric approach and inclusion of Recommendations.

Listing who people are connected to gives you a feeling of trust in connecting with and networking with someone without previously knowing them. This is a wonderful thing that could only happen in this day and age.

In this age of virtual networking, then, with the unlimited potential that exists for connecting similar-minded people across the Internet, is it "just" to place a limit on how many people one can connect with? If there are 40 million LinkedIn users, and you are only connected to 30,000 of them, which is a statistically insignificant number, is there a problem with this? What is the issue here?

As I mention to all I know, LinkedIn is my Platform, and I have stuck with it and continue to evangelize it to everyone I know. I am your biggest fan, LinkedIn! I have also dealt with the new restrictions that are placed upon its users because LinkedIn has been able to add value with new applications and functionality. However, limiting of the number of connections, no matter how big or small the number is, is something that should hit home with a lot of us. Windmill Networking, like the concept, should be infinitely reaching in its potential power, just as the wind is. If a limit of 30,000 is imposed on us today, there is nothing to stop LinkedIn from placing further restrictions on that number at any moment. That worries me, and I hope it worries you too. I can only hope that somehow things will change within LinkedIn and that, just as in the past when a new restriction was placed on us, that there will be some new "WOW!" functionality or service that will make us forgive them. In the meantime, beware, and value each connection you make because it could be your last one.

In fact, just as the limitations on the number of Groups that we joined make us value those 50 that we join, someday we may feel that a LinkedIn connection is a similar precious asset.

Windmill Networkers: choose who you invite carefully, ensuring that your motivation to connect always aligns with your LinkedIn Objective. Always remember the real relationships you build with your connections will be much more valuable than a mere status of virtual connection. These relationships will outlast any restriction placed upon you by any website.

Chapter 14

Chapter 14 Putting It All in Perspective

- Who Owns Your LinkedIn Profile?
- I Have All of These Connections: What Do I Do with Them?
- To Pay or Not to Pay?
- Predicting the Future of LinkedIn
- So, You Want to Be a LinkedIn Expert?
- LinkedIn vs. Twitter & Facebook

Who Owns Your LinkedIn Profile?

It is important to always maintain your email addresses registered on LinkedIn to make sure there are no issues when you switch jobs. In doing so, you can ensure you still maintain ownership of your LinkedIn account. But let's move on to a more fundamental issue that should change the way you think about your LinkedIn Profile, as well as any other social media account that you may "own."

In short, your employer may demand ownership of that LinkedIn Profile that you have worked so hard on should you leave your job. At that time, is it theirs or rightfully yours?

The following two stories of LinkedIn Profile ownership are true stories. They unfortunately raise more questions than the few answers I can provide.

Story #1

Imagine that you began a job as a recruiter. Part of your job is to build out your network. After being hired you learn about LinkedIn and sign up using your personal name. You start inviting your network as well as new contacts to connect with you on LinkedIn. You start Windmill Networking. In order to better facilitate your sourcing activities on LinkedIn, your company starts reimbursing you for a paid account.

I think the above is a very likely scenario for a lot of people, not only in the recruiting industry, but in any outward-facing role (such as sales and marketing) as part of a larger organization. If you don't feel the problem about profile ownership brewing, then maybe you need to make sure you don't end up like my networking contact did.

This person decides to leave the company. The company demands ownership of his LinkedIn Profile. That's right, they are not asking for the database of his LinkedIn connections, which is fair game, but for his username and password.

The company wants ownership of this employee's social networking account in its entirety.

I am not a lawyer nor do I have any education in legal affairs, but something tells me 1) the company should have opened a LinkedIn account and provided the employee with a username and password to use (along with a legal agreement that ownership of the account passes on to the company when the employee leaves) and 2) because the company did not do this and merely reimbursed the employee, it does not have the legal right to ask for outright ownership of the account, although they obviously deserve access to the information in the database.

Which should remind you to always make sure to use your personal email address, not your company one, as your primary LinkedIn contact information.

Should you have to suddenly leave your company, you want to make sure your account is completely portable. But this employee did just that, and is still facing a problem. Let's consider a different angle.

Story #2

You are a professional who created your own LinkedIn account, and your company is paying for the Premier service to allow you to send InMails. One day your position is suddenly eliminated, and your employer forces you to hand over your LinkedIn account details; otherwise, they would withhold your severance pay. The employer says that, since they paid for the account, they claim your account as their intellectual property. You don't know if your employer has the legal right to do so, but you've got a mortgage and a family to support. To facilitate receiving your severance pay, you hand over the details of your account to your employer, after which they change the name of the owner.

I think we can all sympathize with this situation, as similar things happens when promised severance pay is not paid without signing on the dotted line on a document that you might not agree with but are "coerced" into signing.

As you can see from these two stories, we are navigating uncharted waters when we talk about social networking. There are no rules established for this.

Professional networks like LinkedIn truly blur the lines between your "professional" network and your "personal" one. Add the fact that there is a paid service available on LinkedIn, and you begin to wonder why we haven't heard about this potential problem before.

So, in these scenarios, whom do you side with, the employer or the ex-employee, and for what reason?

How to Protect Yourself

The point is, if you are in a similar situation, save yourself future headaches:

Create your own personal LinkedIn account, and make sure you separate your private network of connections from your employer's network.

You never know when you may be fighting this same battle when you leave your next job. If you plan to change jobs soon, you may even want to negotiate this into your Job Offer: That you walk away with your LinkedIn account intact. It really is that important to think about before you're faced with this problem.

I wanted to offer additional insight into the topic, with reference to the LinkedIn User Agreement:

First of all, keeping one personal account and one professional account, like you can do with Twitter, is not allowed on LinkedIn according to its User Agreement:

"You represent and warrant that you ... do not have more than one LinkedIn account at any given time..."

Furthermore, it is clear that every account that you and only you own cannot be transferred to anyone else:

"You are prohibited from selling, trading or otherwise transferring your LinkedIn account or any information therein to another party..."

In other words, any employer asking you to turn over your personal LinkedIn Profile is going against the policy of LinkedIn and is also forcing YOU to violate the LinkedIn User Agreement.

If you define "intellectual property" as a contact database that was accumulated as part of your job, I can see the case for providing that data to the company like any other customer database. But we are in a new era—a time when a Corporate Social Media Policy should be negotiated and included in employment agreements going forward.

As social networking, blogging, micro-blogging (Twitter) and the use of social media in general becomes more prevalent in professional society, it is time for all of us to realize that these social networking profiles and list of connections are our individual assets; they are part of our brand, and we should strive to protect them.

I am looking forward to enlightened Human Relations executives picking up on this and creating social media policies that are both respectful to the employee as well as cognizant of this new reality. I am also looking forward to seeing how LinkedIn will deal with this growing problem. Should LinkedIn be saying anything? Will they enact changes in their User Agreement to side with the Employer? Only time will tell...

I Have All of These Connections: What Do I Do With Them?

I was asked the above question by a new connection recently. I believe it is a question that many of you may soon have after doing a lot of Windmill Networking. As you can imagine, there is no simple answer to this question, as it all depends on your LinkedIn Objective. But let's take a closer look as to why you would have lots of connections, how to deal with them, the potential that they have, and finally my simple answer to the above title question.

When we talk about having lots of connections, we need to discuss the never-ending debate of quality of connections vs. the quantity of them. I always get asked, "Do you actually personally know all of the 17,000+ people in your network?" What do you think my answer is? "Of course not." But, an actual physical network compared to a virtual network being built out on LinkedIn through Windmill Networking is like comparing oranges to apples. Yes, I was offended the first time I received an invitation from someone I didn't know. We had a few emails going back and forth as he explained to me why he contacted me and what the potential benefits were for me.

Now that I fully embrace the concept of open networking and the benefits of building out a virtual network through Windmill Networking, I can make the emotional distinction between my own close physical network and the virtual network I am now able to build out through social networking sites like LinkedIn. My close physical network contains people I actually know well and is completely unrelated to connections via social media. My virtual network on LinkedIn is composed of people I may have never met in person; however, I may have the chance to get to know them better should the proper situation arise. Remember,

My LinkedIn Network = My Windmill Network

NOT

My LinkedIn Network = My Physical Network.

Let's look at it from another angle. When you were young, did you ever have a pen pal? You found an ad in a magazine or maybe got introduced to someone through school. I have fond memories of having pen pals from not only within the US, but also far away places like Argentina and Ghana. At the time was I prescreening these people? Of course not! The tools were not in place. But it was a joy to meet new people and learn about new places. Although I didn't realize it at the time, I was already creating a virtual network to satisfy my objective of curiosity and make new friends. Yes, I have been a Windmill Networker since elementary school!

If I had kept in touch with these pen pals until today, seeing that I am in International Business, perhaps we could have helped each other out in some way. So, 1) Just because I wanted to connect (i.e. become pen pals) with these people didn't mean I wanted to sell them something, 2) Creating a virtual network (i.e. exchanging letters with someone you've never met) is an acceptable cultural practice, and 3) As we grow older, there may be ways in which we never imagined where these types of contacts could become relevant in a new light for either or both parties.

How is this relevant to LinkedIn? It is extremely relevant. The only difference with LinkedIn is that you can see the background and Recommendations of said person and decide whether or not you want to connect; you can also see that **the demographic is that of working professionals. As a result, the connection may be more relevant to aiding your career or professional life in the future.**

It all comes down to the concept of "Digging Your Well Before You're Thirsty." Do you believe in this concept or not? If not, I cannot help you in suggesting what you do with your connections. But, since you've bought this book and have read this far, I am assuming you believe in this concept. So allow me to continue.

You may be happily employed today. You may not want to be bothered by recruiters. What happens if your job is suddenly eliminated? Or what about the friend or family member in need who is enlisting your help in finding them a job? I got a job and the position was eliminated 14 weeks later. Think that couldn't happen to you? Think again.

After you find a job, what about the challenge in finding new customers, partners, and service providers? What if you are put in the role where you need to hire someone yourself?

If you move to a new city, how do you go about finding new people to meet? Or finding service providers?

What if, someday, you come up with a great idea and decide to start your own business?

There are many situations we just can't predict in life. Rather than picking up the yellow pages, doesn't it make sense to first contact those in our LinkedIn Network or ask for recommendations from people we trust in our LinkedIn Network? Even if you have never met that person before, LinkedIn gives you the opportunity to mentally vet that person before contacting them, through checking out their profile and Recommendations.

You just never know when someone in your network will prove useful to you. I say this because I have used my LinkedIn connections for all of the above functions within the last several months, without even predicting that I would have! I looked for a job, found a job, looked for potential customers and distributors, hired a service provider who was in my network, lost my job, am looking for a job again, and met new people in my local Southern California area. I am also looking for new service providers.

The beauty is that Windmill Networking has allowed me to do all of this a lot quicker and more effectively than if it did not exist. It is, in essence, my personal and trusted Yellow Pages.

OK. I hope you're a believer now. But how do you manage all of these connections? I think the answer lies in what many consider to be the best article on the subject, "I Am Not a Number!" [9] This article was co-authored by Scott Allen and David Teten, the co-authors of *The Virtual Handshake*. The article goes over the concepts of how to manage connections of what will become your "virtual" network. It points out that just because someone is in your virtual network, it does not necessarily mean they want to be contacted whenever you change a job. They may not want to be solicited either. There is a protocol you need to think about before contacting them. I have tried to echo these sentiments with my own calls for etiquette and advice throughout this book.

Getting back to the question, what do you do with these connections now that you have them? Nothing. Nada. That's right, don't do anything, unless you have a reason to contact them.

If you have a reason to contact them, remember that they are actually people, as Scott Allen reminded us, so use LinkedIn search to break down your connections into the specific demographic that may be interested in what you have to tell them. Then simply customize your message to them.

I'd also like to comment here that just because someone has a lot of connections, it doesn't necessarily mean that they are gathering connections to monetize them. A lot of open networkers with lots of connections have no intent of using their connections for money in the immediate future. Now that could change, as you never know what the future holds, but I would argue that just because you have lots of connections doesn't mean that you can simply monetize them. How would you? Just because you have connections doesn't mean that they are lining up to buy whatever product or service you might have, right? Of course not. If someone does try to monetize their connections and is not careful about how they go about doing it, I am sure that LinkedIn Customer Service will hear about them very quickly and they will not be a LinkedIn user for long! If they are careful and are successful, and provide something that their connections find uniquely valuable, that's living the American Dream, isn't it? More power to them!

Speaking of monetizing, LinkedIn sends out advertisements for its paid service, promoting the fact that you can sell to its 40+ million members. Let's look at the wording of the latest advertisement I received from LinkedIn while writing this book:

"Are you making the most of LinkedIn to drive sales for your company?

A LinkedIn premium account enables you to:

• *find your ideal prospects with access to the full profiles of more than 36 million top professionals*

• *get more search results than your free account allows*

• *directly contact your prospects using InMail™*

• *receive priority customer service and lots more"*

If this is the case, and if you become a paid member, is it now considered OK for you to monetize your connections? If it is OK to directly contact prospects (who you are not even connected to and thus don't know!) using InMail, why can't you also do this through connecting with them directly? Then you can at least research their background. They can then make a decision as to whether or not they want to receive future messages from you.

This is the paradox that LinkedIn faces as it tries to monetize its network. I think all who use LinkedIn and evangelize it would agree that a financially healthy LinkedIn is a great thing for everyone. Let's just hope it moves forward in a way that pleases its members.

Getting back to the subject matter at hand, let me make myself loud and clear: I AM IN NO WAY CONDONING PEOPLE WHO ARE AMASSING CONNECTIONS WITH THE SOLE PURPOSE OF SPAMMING THEM. But there are other reasons why people are connecting with others while amassing their virtual network. It really depends on their objective. **If you don't know what to do with your connections, you need to rethink what your objective is for joining LinkedIn and figure out the answer on your own.**

To Pay or Not to Pay?

Up until now, unless otherwise noted, everything I have been writing about has been using the free account available on LinkedIn. That's right: I have not paid a penny to LinkedIn. In my opinion, you can enjoy utilizing the free platform for the purpose of Windmill Networking. Now this could change at any moment, and should LinkedIn ask us to pay money to continue using their free service, I would. I thought about actually subscribing to the paid service to be able to report back to you, my readers, on the potential value it has, but my fear was that I wouldn't be able to ascertain how much of a certain feature was accessible to free or paid accounts.

Which brings me to the next question: does it make sense to upgrade? Let's first take a look at what it means to "upgrade": (and note that LinkedIn does change these features from time-to-time, so always make sure you check on the latest pricing and features by going to "Accounts and Settings" in the top right-hand side of your Home Page and view the Upgrade options).

- You will have to pay a monthly fee, which at the present is $25 for a "Business Account" and $50 for a "Business Plus Account." You should also know that there is a "Pro Account" for $500 a month available, but for the purposes of this chapter, I will only describe the features available to "Business Account" and "Business Plus" accounts.

- You will have the ability to send InMails (3 per month for Business, 10 per month for Business Plus) and thus be able to directly communicate with someone with whom you are not directly connected. Whether they communicate back to you or not is another story. Free accounts, by the way, do not have any InMails.

- Every time you do a People Search you will get more results, 300 for Business and 500 for Business Plus. The free account default is 100.

- You will be able to save 5 or 7 search alerts while free accounts have 3.

So, is all of this worth it for the price you have to pay? I think it really comes down to your objective, as there is certainly a time-to-market value in:
1) Being able to perform more powerful searches and
2) Sending InMails, which can cut across networks of windmills; they enable you to contact another windmill regardless of your relationship with them.

If you are a recruiter or are in business and you want to utilize these enhanced features, it makes sense to pay. But for the purpose of Windmill Networking, I hope that I have taught you so many different ways of finding and communicating with people while growing your network that you don't need these enhanced features. Would the ability to send InMails and have search results return 500 people like they used to for the free service be nice? Of course, as it would be a time-saver and a general enhancement. But from my perspective, and I believe for the most of you Windmill Networkers, the paid feature is more of a "nice-to-have" than a "must have!"

Why else would someone want to pay for the service? I honestly think for some people it is a status symbol, that they are "professional" or somehow more "serious about networking." It could be considered part of their brand. Many lucky professionals have their companies reimburse the expense. For others, because they get so much out of LinkedIn, they feel the need to somehow pay it back, and for them it provides tremendous value. I could also argue the same thing. I promised myself that I would upgrade as part of my paying it back to LinkedIn in writing this book. But, after serious consideration, it isn't LinkedIn, but the people I have met and networked with through LinkedIn, that I would like to thank the most. As for you, it is really a personal decision that you need to make and should at least consider.

Predicting the Future of LinkedIn

Windmill Networkers have a choice of platforms in which they can invest their time. LinkedIn is only one of these platforms, although I believe it is the platform of choice for professionals who want to find and be found by other professionals. That being said, as we ponder the future of LinkedIn, it is important to understand with the ever-changing landscape of social media and the success and failure of companies to monetize it, there is no guarantee that the LinkedIn of 2010 will look anything like it does in 2009. It may even not be around or be part of someone else's service. After all, in the period of time that I have been working on this book, there have been rumors that Twitter would be bought out not only by Facebook (who has recently been acquiring members from LinkedIn's demographic), but Google (who recently started their own "Google Profile" service) and now Apple! These are all probably rumors, but they do point out that there are no guarantees about the future of LinkedIn. Perhaps, by looking at the trends of the last several months, we can get a view of where LinkedIn may be heading.

Growing Membership Numbers. LinkedIn membership growth has been accelerating to the point that I heard a new person joins LinkedIn every second. Indeed, LinkedIn has recently doubled their membership in record time. As the recession lingers on at the time of my writing, the mass media has been concentrating on LinkedIn and why you should utilize it to help look for a job. As social networking in general becomes more of the norm and less of a fad, I assume LinkedIn membership numbers will continue to grow. LinkedIn has recently been writing many blog posts attracting college graduates to LinkedIn, so if they are successful and can get a good portion of the Facebook demographic to become LinkedIn members, there is no reason why LinkedIn couldn't double their membership numbers again in the next 12 months. This can only work to the benefit of Windmill Networking.

New Features. LinkedIn continues to introduce innovative features. Just in the last year they added Applications; with it comes the ability to network and communicate with 40+ million people in a unique and powerful way. LinkedIn is constantly enhancing its oldest features as well, like adding Subgroups to

LinkedIn Groups. I expect this trend will continue and LinkedIn will keep adding new and exciting features. With that will come more tools that can be used for Windmill Networking.

Sudden Changes. LinkedIn continues to surprise me in the way it enacts sudden changes without prior warning or explanation to its members. I believe and hope that this practice will change, but at the moment it seems to be ingrained in the way they do things. One day I could search and get 500 results, and the next day I am restricted to 100 results. I used to be able to export the email addresses of my Group members, then one day they stopped allowing this. What this means for Windmill Networking is that there will continue to be challenges in effectively using LinkedIn for a platform once you learn how to utilize it. Don't be surprised when something changes, and be creative in trying to achieve the same results in a different way. I have been able to do this and circumvent a majority of the negative outcome of the sudden changes. I should also point out that some of these changes are better, so why not advertise them to their users on the day they release them? I would evangelize them for all they're worth! [Note: The recent introduction of the Subgroups was the first time I can remember getting an email from LinkedIn introducing a new service. I hope it is a sign they will continue doing this in the future.]

Limitations. I believe LinkedIn will continue to increase limitations on its members. There are many reasons why they seem to be doing this: Some are in the name of "privacy," others are because they felt "competition" from its members. There is little doubt that other limitations, like those on search results, are part of their plans to better monetize the service. What about the recent limitation on the number of connections you can have? This means that the size of the network that someone can build has been greatly reduced, which provides more value to their paid customers who apparently have access to the entire network. What about limiting the number of Groups that you can join to 50? Because you can send messages to other Group members, this also limits your ability to reach more people. Limiting the search results is another prime example. I have been told that there are limitations on how many Answers you can give in a day, and recently I noticed that there is a limit as to how many Questions you can ask. These are things that just didn't exist until recently, so be prepared for more changes to come if this is a sign of the future.

More Advertisements and Paid Services. There is no doubt that LinkedIn is sitting on a potential goldmine of future revenue with its database of 40 million professionals. There are many advertisers who want to get in front of this demographic, and through Direct Ads, now have the ability to do so. I expect advertisements that pop up on LinkedIn to only increase, as it is a natural way for LinkedIn to monetize their service. Similarly, be prepared for new "for pay" services as well as new services that were previously free (like the ability to get 500 search results) and now cost money. How LinkedIn balances monetizing their service, while keeping their members happy, is the critical factor in judging their future success. I for one can accept additional advertisements if LinkedIn can continue to add one-of-a-kind functionality to better facilitate Windmill Networking.

Although it may sound like I am complaining, the purpose of this chapter is to provide constructive criticism. I still love LinkedIn, evangelize it, and recommend it to every professional I know as the platform of choice for Windmill Networking. It is important to keep in mind that things still appear to be in a state of flux for LinkedIn as well as every other Web 2.0 social networking platform, so get used to balancing the good (more members & features) with the bad (sudden changes & more limitations).

So, You Want to Be a LinkedIn Expert?

There has been a lot of buzz recently about the explosion of so-called "social media experts." Everyone seems to be branding themselves an "expert" in something, and it leads to the question of just what it all means, especially with regards to the context of what a "LinkedIn Expert" is.

If you read this entire book and execute on every chapter while Windmill Networking, you may soon consider yourself a LinkedIn Expert—and you just might be. But let's first understand that labeling yourself a "LinkedIn Expert" now becomes your LinkedIn Brand. I guess the first question, then, is do you really want to brand yourself in this way?

With the explosion of LinkedIn and its 40 million users, it is no wonder so many people call themselves an "expert." Social media is accelerating the democratization of information as well as expertise. Because differentiating yourself is inherent in branding yourself, a "social media expert" may not be a good brand to have anymore. It is no longer unique.

Remember, there are no barriers to entry here. This is the new Internet revolution. The first revolution, in the 90's, gave us all equal access to the information. Now, with Web 2.0, we are creating and controlling the content. Anyone with an understanding of social media can do this. **And that is the point of Web 2.0—the democratization of the web.**

Some argue that when everyone in the world calls themselves a "social media expert" it starts to lose meaning. This is true. But, you know, there are lots of SEO experts and blog experts—why shouldn't that be the same with regard to social media and LinkedIn? At some point, when being a LinkedIn "expert" really does lose meaning (would you label yourself a Microsoft Office expert today, even though you are an expert in it?), we will stop seeing the branding. I think 2009 has been a year of particularly explosive growth for social media, and thus the amount of "experts" is truly growing. Once people stop paying money for this expertise, the "expert" label will truly start to lose meaning. That hasn't happened yet.

What does this all mean? Before I provide my own definition of a "LinkedIn Expert," let's first see how Wikipedia defines "expert":

An expert is someone widely recognized as a reliable source of technique or skill whose faculty for judging or deciding rightly, justly, or wisely is accorded authority and status by their peers or the public in a specific well distinguished domain."[10]

With that in mind, I propose that a LinkedIn Expert needs to:

- **Be recognized as being a reliable source of information and accorded authority by the public.** Recognition can come in many forms: companies hire you, people buy your books, your blogs are read by lots of people, many people subscribe to your tweets, people want to meet via LinkedIn to gain your expertise. Note, as long as you are "recognized" by others in one form or another, it doesn't matter whether or not you are monetizing this expertise.

- **Provide something unique that is of value beyond the "mechanics" of LinkedIn.** The days of being an expert just because you knew the mechanics of a social media site are long gone. With membership doubling annually on sites like LinkedIn, it is a given that, as an expert, you know the "mechanics" of these sites. But what is your unique contribution to the LinkedIn community?

- **True social media experts are leaders and not followers.** If you are just regurgitating what others are saying, you may have gained expertise, but I would not call you an expert. Assuming you have been recognized as someone with authority and someone who has contributed something unique to our understanding of social media, are you a true leader? In the case of social media, it means sometimes going out on a limb and disagreeing with prevailing opinions on the topic. It means carving your own path, regardless of what others say or what the current trend is.

I find many web posts on social media equating that expertise with some sort of ability to monetize it or the track record of having x number of B2B success stories. I am not saying that you should spend money for consulting from anyone who calls himself an "expert" without looking at their "track record." But the "track record" may be misleading; after all, was it their work, or the original "brand," that made them successful? **As you can imagine, it's hard to measure the ROI of social media.** If you are looking to hire an "expert," it is a business decision like any other that you will need to research and determine whether or not there is value.

What I am saying, in conclusion, is that ***I expect a LinkedIn Expert to be a thought leader and truly enlighten us***. I do hope that many of you will strive to do so and add value to all of us in the LinkedIn community, regardless of whether or not we are Windmill Networkers.

LinkedIn vs. Twitter & Facebook

I may be a typical GenXer in that LinkedIn was the first social network that I joined. How about Facebook and Twitter, you ask? I didn't even venture onto those networks until I began writing this book. MySpace? With reports of its popularity waning and its demographic stuck at a very young age, I decided not to join and instead concentrate my time on The Big Three: LinkedIn, Twitter, and Facebook. If you haven't figured the other platforms out yet, let me take a stab at differentiating between all of these, because it may make sense for you to be on all or none of the above.

There were many social networking sites that I joined after becoming a LinkedIn user because I was getting bombarded with invitations from all sorts of sites (as you Windmill Network I am sure you will soon start experiencing the same thing!). I stopped accepting those invitations and instead filed them away, figuring I could always join those Groups at a later date. You may find my profile on some weird networks, but chances are I've done nothing with them. And I think a lot of people are the same.

Many of my LinkedIn connections have started sending me emails asking me to "follow" them on Twitter, so I thought this was a good time to take a look at what you should be doing differently on each site.

Let's start with LinkedIn. The LinkedIn demographic is composed of 40+ million professionals. But LinkedIn is also very strict on privacy and spamming, and there are many restrictions as to how many connections you can have, Groups you can join, et al. **LinkedIn is not a garden that you can freely roam about and do as you wish; you need to adapt yourself to its environment in order to thrive.**

Twitter, on the other hand, while having what I believe a similar demographic to LinkedIn at this point, still has only about half the members LinkedIn has (I have yet to see the official number). But compared to LinkedIn, with the exception of the limit of adding 1,000 followers per day, Twitter is a place for freethinkers to thrive and for anyone to do as he wishes. That being said, what you can do on Twitter is inherently limited to 140-character tweets. And a profile is limited to 160 characters and a website link.

Regardless of your LinkedIn or professional objective, it makes sense to have a presence on both sites customized for each platform. How to customize?

On LinkedIn you should be emphasizing your own professional brand, establishing credibility, and be primarily using it to socially network with other professionals for whatever your objective might be.

CONNECT ON LINKEDIN. That is the premise of Windmill Networking.

Twitter should be about building out your brand and special subject matter expertise and leading people somewhere else, whether it be to your website or blog or even to your LinkedIn and/or Facebook profile. **GAIN MINDSHARE ON TWITTER.**

If you are wondering, there definitely is a place for Windmill Networking on Twitter as well, and this will be subject for my future blog posts and/or book.

My Facebook experience, on the other hand, has been unlike what I imagined it to be. I recently uploaded my entire (at the time) 12,000+ LinkedIn contact base to Facebook, and, voila! I was already busy adding "Friends," figuring out where my "Wall" was, and receiving and replying to messages from a lot of surprised people! I thought that LinkedIn was the closed site for professionals and that Facebook was the open one without restrictions, but I soon found many of my LinkedIn connections did NOT want to connect with me on Facebook!

Furthermore, I already had contacts who I had met on LinkedIn telling me about the restriction of 5,000 "friends" on Facebook and that I would probably get kicked off after inviting so many people!

Facebook is a social networking platform with 200+ million members that cannot and should not be ignored. I have found it particularly great in tracking down old school friends that I couldn't find on LinkedIn. There are a lot of people finding business and utilizing Windmill Networking on Facebook.

CPSIA information can be obtained
at www.ICGtesting.com
Printed in the USA
LVHW050154250621
691124LV00001B/63

9 781801 569170